Praise for Evolvagility

Michael's book is a game-changer in the Agile leadership space and the greater cause to create leaders everywhere. It challenges conventional "wisdom" and presents genuinely unique concepts, some of which literally took my breath away with their clarity and foresight.

– Lyssa Adkins, Author of Coaching Agile Teams

This book is a tour-de-force, and a must read for agile leaders of all stripes. Read, absorb, change, and truly lead from within.

– Sanjiv Augustine, Founder and CEO, LitheSpeed and Author of Scaling Agile

A go-to source for accelerating individual and collective growth, Evolvagility is a powerhouse of towering human and system development ideas and practical how-to approaches for application. It is developmental medicine for what ails us. It's what we need en route to scale individual capability and collective capacity for future VUCA challenges. On my short-list, Evolvagility is a new favorite to keep at arms-reach.

– Cliff Kayser, President and Founder, XPERIENCE LLC

Evolvagility is a deep exploration into the growth journey of becoming a "sense-and-respond" leader. In my experience, this growth journey is not easy and many times counter-intuitive. I wish I had this book earlier to help me really understand and navigate that journey better. Evolvagility provided me with many powerful insights and practical approaches that will truly support my growth journey.

*– **Ahmed Sidky**, Ph.D., President, International Consortium for Agile (ICAgile) and Chief of Staff, Head of Business Agility, Riot Games*

Although its generally accepted that managers can be developed through education and experience, too many of us still believe that leaders are born not made. Michael helps us understand is that—unlike the overt world of management practice—the world of leadership resides within our hearts and minds and is transacted in the corridors of the relationships that link us together. By opening the door to these interior realms, Michael opens up the door to leadership development for us all.

*– **Charlie Rudd**, Founder of SolutionsIQ*

While many books describe what Agile is, how it should work, and why it is important, Evolvagility is the first book I have ever read that explains how to achieve an Agile organization and culture, through the intentional creation of an environment that speeds up personal development. These techniques and insights are so incredibly valuable, applicable, and effective that I started using them immediately and I constantly have to remind myself I didn't always work this way!

– Esbjörn Hyltefors, *Enterprise Agile Coach, Stockholm*

Evolvagility explores why group cultures do and do not work. Addressing Complexity, Confusion and most of all Fear, Hamman shows us how all humans do and do not make full and accurate sense of their situations, and in many cases how they unknowingly sabotage their best intent. For the leadership needed from all of us, this book presents a framework we can use to understand and sort through organizational opportunities and challenges.

– Howard Bud Phillips, *CIO at Elevate Services*

Evolvagility is for all leaders, with or without the capital "L," who are committed to personal development and to growing a true leadership culture within their organization. The book will help you powerfully up the level of your individual contribution in order to bring about deep and desired change in your organization. The transformation which the book advances—from merely acting and doing to a more complex sensemaking and relating—is both clearly pre-

sented and personally challenging. This book will no doubt have a deep impact on any and all readers!

– **Leonoor Koomen**, *Lead Agile Enterprise Coach at ING and Owner,* <u>*actagile.com*</u>

A lot has been written about the new kind of leadership which is needed for the modern, so-called VUCA world. I haven't seen anyone who has gone deeper and pushed new ideas further than Michael Hamman in his book Evolvagility. A must-read for everyone who wants to broaden their thinking about leadership for the future.

– **Gustav Bergman**, *Editor of Softhouse Lean Magazine*

I expected and was not disappointed by the deep work that Michael has shared in this book. Not only does he capture key transitions that are necessary to solve the complex problems organizations face today, but as a reader you yourself go through a profound awakening, having realization after realization as he shares examples of the mindset shifts leaders need to make.

I highly recommend this book to anyone who cares about their own personal development in business and how they show up to work to get better results for themselves, those around them, and the organization as a whole.

– **Simon Powers**, *Founder of Adventures With Agile*

Michael has skillfully articulated the inner struggle of the 21st century leader who is experiencing the VUCA world through a Predict-and-Plan lens. Along the way, he offers a ground-breaking pathway to help the reader grow their consciousness and expand the quality of their sensing and meaning-making in order to create outcomes that matter.

*– **Sammy Njoroge**, Leadership Circle East Africa Representative and Founder & CEO of Deep Circle Leadership Consultants, Nairobi, Kenya.*

There is no shortage of books on leadership, but very few take a stand for growing it from the inside out. With Evolvagility, Michael guides you through a rich tapestry of understanding about what it means to grow your own complexity of mind in service of cultivating leaders everywhere. He brings theory to life through his own stories of learning, and he provides daily practices that help turn theory into action. Evolvagility will swiftly become a well-worn reference book in my own leadership journey. Helping me identify my leadership edges and set intentions where I want to grow, creating deliberately developmental conversations and relationships that support my own leadership development.

*– **Marsha Acker**, CEO at TeamCatapult*

There is a wealth of knowledge available in the huge number of books about the broad topics of agility. The preponderance of this writing on agility is focused on its operational aspects: there is no shortage of guidance and expertise in process, operating models, and practices, and no shortage of evangelism of the "why" of agile, the values, and the principles. What is most missing is guidance for the path to actually achieving agility—how to actually get there.

Evolvagility focuses on a critical—and probably the most overlooked—aspect of this path: how to develop the mindsets and behaviors needed of the agile leader, at any and every level of the organization. In Evolvagility, Michael has distilled a number of very complex concepts and areas of knowledge—ones normally only accessible to students of organizational development, psychology, complexity, systems thinking, and professional coaching—into a fairly simple, accessible work that anyone involved in transformations towards agility will benefit greatly from.

– George Schlitz, Business Agility and Transformation Consultant, Co-Founder of Big Visible Solutions

Evolvagility is an insightful and energizing read because it integrates and makes sense of many newer approaches to leadership and organization development in a way that enables leaders and organizations to transform themselves – not once, but again and again. It provides great concrete tools for creating conditions where you and others can develop individually and collectively. I like that the tools and concepts - rather than emphasizing just success - focus also on fulfilling vision and purpose as the ultimate goal of a meaningful life as a person or a corporation.

— **Pamela Caraffa**, Ph.D., Organizational Psychologist, Executive Coach, and Former Corporate Vice President, Organization Development, Monsanto

Evolvagility is an evolution in agile thinking, exposing the reader to new concepts like vertical learning and deliberate sensemaking, which can be applied to everyone in most any complex situation. It will resonate strongly not only with enterprise coaches, but with anyone who sees the value in being an effective leader. As Russell Ackoff once said, you don't get to be a great leader by emulating others; Michael Hamman's book demonstrates how to create new mental skills that allow you to take discrete jumps in leadership rather than incremental ones.

— **Jim Elvidge**, Enterprise Agile Coach

With leadership books I want to know fairly quickly I'm going to learn something meaningful, something new, have existing thinking challenged. Evolvagility ticks all these boxes. But more importantly you get to see and learn from the rawness, vulnerability, and experience of the author himself. A book for all leaders and organizations with the ambition to "get there," Michael traces an architecture and presents a map for the journey to the greater capacity for leadership that our world is crying out for.

– Alastair Kidd, *Coach and Facilitator and Founder of Getting There Leadership*

Evolvagility provides an elegant model that encompasses all aspects of change. I am thrilled to use the concepts in helping leaders get a complete picture of their impact. Every change agent, no matter where you are in the organization, needs to read this book.

– Stuart McCalla, *Partner at Evolution Service Corp.*

For the longest time I have been frustrated at my inability to clearly express the nature of a full organizational agility, let alone realize it in practice. It is like mist: we can see it, feel it, but any attempt to grab hold of it leaves just a vague impression of the real thing. Michael's book helps us see through this mist. He provides us with practical ways to create the organizations we have been dreaming of, not by doing more things or creating more structures, but by attending to the internal journey each of us has to undertake in order to become the leaders we have been waiting for. Prepare to find yourself reading into the wee hours of the morning, spellbound by the deep insight and wisdom, and, most of all, with real HOPE for the future.

– Antoinette Coetzee, *Team, Leadership, and Agile coach at Just Plain Agile, South Africa*

Evolvagility is, to my knowledge, the first book to not only point out the biggest blind spot in the Agile community but to also offer a compelling solution to it. This book unravels the mystery of the "mindset" question by shining a light on adult development. It is elegant, complete, highly useful, and full of wisdom. I'm not kidding when I say it has answered questions I've found puzzling since I started out ten years ago. It will keep me busy for ten more years.

*– **Johannes Schartau**, Agile Coach at Holisticon, Germany*

evolvagility

GROWING AN AGILE LEADERSHIP CULTURE FROM THE INSIDE OUT

MICHAEL HAMMAN

Agile Leadership Institute

Published by the Agile Leadership Institute
6550 Fisherman Bay Road
Lopez Island, WA 98261

January 14, 2019

Editor and Advisor: **Lisa Cooney**
Book Designer and Advisor: **Volker Frank**
Book Cover Designer: **Michael Molanphy**
Author photo: **Susanne Hamman**

Reviewers: **Lyssa Adkins, Antoinette Coetzee, Sinead Condon, Katrina Ferguson, Susanne Hamman, Clive Prout, and William Rowden**

Co-founder of the Agile Leadership Institute, Advisor, and Marketing Strategist: **Clive Prout**

To Susanne Hamman, Liv Amrita Kaur—
my wife, partner,
soulmate, and spiritual Other

"*The activity we call 'building' creates the physical order of the world, constantly, unendingly, day after day.... **Our world is dominated by the order we create.***"

-- Christopher Alexander

Contents

Preface

Over the course of my early years in Agile coaching and consulting, particularly as I entered into the enterprise sphere, I became convinced that in order for Agile to work, it had to work at the level of the organization, and for it to work at the level of the organization, middle- to senior-level leaders had to make a dramatic shift in their own leadership.

In recent years my thinking on this has shifted quite dramatically. I suppose it is due in part to my ongoing immersion in the study of human systems and the psychology of human development; perhaps it's just what I've come to see over years of working with organizations. But at some point, something clicked. Organizations are *complex systems*, whose behavior cannot be understood to be influenceable in any kind of *linear* manner. As I continued to dwell in this thought, I started to notice something else: While we are waiting for top-level leaders to "get it"—to become a different kind of leader, a more *agile* leader—many of those very same top-level leaders are waiting for people closer to the ground to become more leaderful themselves: to be more accountable, to take greater responsibility and ownership for their work, and for their impact on others. As Peter Block once said (I can't remember where or when), organizational leaders often go to great lengths to open the doors of empowerment to the people they lead, only to find that no one steps forward.

As I pondered this seeming contradiction, I came to realize that in my focus on coaching and mentoring senior leaders and managers—believing that when *they* get it, all else will fall into place—I myself had fallen into the trap of believing in a notion of leadership as a one-way, linear causality, which happens primarily from the top down. In stepping away from this linear view, however, I began to see the times when people, at all levels and from all walks of life within an organization, exercised their capacity for leadership. From this dawning realization, I started to understand leadership as a *systemic* phenomenon, as a quality of the organization as a whole. I was now seeing the real possibility of leadership as that which arises anywhere and everywhere there is a need—within an organization, within a team, within a partnership of any sort—for someone (or someones) to be willing to take responsibility for what is happening, and to marshal the capacity to lead others, not by what they are *doing*, but by how they are *thinking*, and who they are *being*. I began to see leadership as that which happens in many different ways throughout an organization, manifested through a variety of roles, and on any number of levels of authority.

This book is for anyone who wishes to lead in this manner, regardless of role, title, or position. If you are that person, your company or organization needs you to so lead. This book will help you discover what that means, and equip you with distinctions, ideas, practices, and conditions to help you along the journey toward such a leadership. In this regard, this book is not an "agile" book, per se—it is for anyone who wishes to increase their leadership agility. So, yes, on the one hand, I am speaking to Agile team coaches, enterprise coaches, and organizational managers and leaders whose role is related to the facilitation and the guiding of any kind of Agile adoption effort. But I am also speaking to that township mayor who seeks to bring *agility* to the way in which her town council operates. To that head of a national non-profit who seeks to create an environment in which the mission-focus of his organization's people is channeled through skillful means in communication, collaboration, and leadership—supported by a deep, though still compassionate, complexity of mind. To that committed member of an NGO who wishes to upgrade her and other's capacity to be able to cognitively and emotionally embrace the increasing complexity she finds in the face of global problems in order to meet a demand for thinking and acting in which she currently finds herself feeling "in over her head."

In this book, I regard agility as a way of thinking, as a way of acting, and as a way of *being*. I believe agility can no longer be construed as falling solely under the banner of agile processes and customer development practices. Rather, agility is a capability that individuals and collectives *everywhere* need to be able to embody if we, as a greater society, are to adequately meet the ever-increasing complexity and volatility we face on a daily basis. This book is for anyone who sees agility as the expression of a broad *paradigm shift* in how we think about ourselves in the world, in how we might create impact in an increasingly complex, volatile, and unpredictable world—for anyone whose personal mission is to grow within themselves an agility of *acting*, of *thinking*, and of *being*.

This book is the product of many years of practice—as a consultant, coach, and teacher—and of scholarship—as a long-time student of organizational and human development. Every moment of my practice has been accompanied by investigation in, and study of, any and all research related to the challenges and opportunities in my day-to-day work as a practitioner. Meanwhile, my scholarship and research has always been conditioned by what I experience in the grit and dirt of practice. Beneath all of this, however, lies the deep recognition that all I can possibly do, anything I can influence and have an impact on, will always be a product of who I, myself, am *being*. In this way, I have always held my own capacity to embrace complexity—both within myself and in the world around me—as the single-greatest asset I can possibly have. Not what I know. Not even what I can *do*. But **who I can *be*.** From there arises the skillful means necessary for whatever the world may bring to me.

The source of any impact we might have as leaders will always be a product of our *inner* capacity to face complexity, unpredictability, and volatility with grace and skill. This is the grounding principle of this book. We need leaders—everywhere where people are struggling to make sense of their ever-more complex world—who can lead in the face of and *through* that complexity, in ways that leave both themselves and those around them more able, more capable, and in greater readiness for whatever is next.

Acknowledgements

This book is the product of years of research and practice, and a year of focused devotion to the development (*both* of this book and of me) of what you now have in front of you. None of this would have been possible without the support of many people.

First, I want to thank Clive Prout, my business partner and co-founder of the Agile Leadership Institute (ALI), a foundation for the study and practice of leadership agility as both an individual and an organizational capability. He has furthered and deepened my understanding of what it means to co-lead in ways I never imagined. His challenging and supportive partnership is what made it possible for me to make the necessary leap and dedication needed to get this book started. Many of the ideas in this book, particularly in areas around relationship, have benefited tremendously from our work together in designing and co-leading our workshop, *Evolvagility: Transforming Yourself as an Agile Leader.* Clive is the originator of the term "Evolvagility."

Second, I want to thank and acknowledge Lisa Cooney for her sensitive approach as editor. In some ways Lisa has become my "co-author," challenging me and helping me to think through the myriad issues related to content and organization, and standing for the highest of standards in terms of clarity and consistency. She helped me fine-tune each sentence to bend it closer to deeper meaning and greater clarity, and to make sure that every diagram expresses its intent clearly. But perhaps more than anything, it has been Lisa's love for this book, this project, and this work that has, in so many ways, sustained me through some of the more difficult and challenging phases of the book-writing process.

Third, I want to thank Volker Frank, who not only helped me think through key aspects of the ideas and of their presentation; but, perhaps more substantially, he took charge of book design and layout and of the frustrating, irritating, and thoroughly "un-fun" process of producing both the Kindle and the print versions of the book. Without you, Volker, this book would be poorer in its ideas and less attractive in its rendering.

Fourth, I want to thank my dear friend, Michael Molanphy, a remarkable and remarkably successful graphic designer, for the beautiful book cover. Michael completely "got" what this book was about and has been both patient and inquisitive during the design process.

I want to offer a special thank you to the readers who reviewed earlier drafts: Susanne Hamman, Clive Prout, Lyssa Adkins, Antoinette Coetzee, Katrina Ferguson, William Rowden, and Sinead Condon. Their comments, feedback, and encouragement (especially that!) have been invaluable in helping me think, rethink, and then think again about both the content and presentation of this book. In addition, I want to thank William Strydom and Gary Boruff for their feedback and encouragement, especially in the earlier drafts of the book.

I wish to acknowledge Lyssa Adkins and Michael Spayd. As the "three musketeers" of the Agile Coaching Institute (ACI) from 2013-2017, we created remarkable transformational experiences for hundreds of Agile coaches and managers. It was during those years working so closely with Michael and Lyssa that I grew substantially in my capacity to lead through standing for, and holding space for, the developmental possibility in others.

I want to direct my gratitude to the ALI cohort—Antoinette Coetzee, Jason Knight, Kari McLeod, Lisa Cooney, Phillip Cave, and Clive Prout—who have been instrumental in helping to grow the inner product of ALI and in helping me test and launch the book. But even more, they have been key anchors for me, both emotionally and spiritually, in our weekly conversations throughout this year. You have provided a foundation of love for this work and an environment in which coming out of hibernation, however briefly, could be a source of both great nourishment and personal enrichment.

I want to express my special gratitude to Antoinette Coetzee whose powerful questions and encouragement carried me through some of the more difficult moments in the writing process.

I also want to thank Pat Carrington-House for the conversations that opened the way for me to make the final leap into writing this book in the first place. Thank you for that much-needed—and at times resisted—push.

Thank you to Henry Kimsey-House, whom I wish to acknowledge as a collaborator, and guide, in designing key parts of the *Evolvagility* workshop, many aspects of which have found their way into this book in some way or another. What a delight it was to spend three days with Henry in his home, along with Clive Prout!

Finally, I want to acknowledge my wife, my life partner, my soulmate, Susanne Hamman—Liv Amrita Kaur. You have provided for me the ultimate *holding environment* of challenge, support, and learning tools. You have *inspired* me to move past my self-imposed limitations, *supported* me in taking the time to focus on writing, and provided me with the ultimate *learning tool*: your skill in relationship and communication. Your willingness to be deeply loved, and the generosity of your love for me, teaches me each and every day about how to *be* in relationship, how to *be* present, and ultimately how to truly **love**, and be **loved by**, another human being.

Introduction:
A New Kind of Leadership

Organizations around the globe are struggling to adapt to an increasingly complex and turbulent social, economic, technological, and business environment—whether they be banks, product development companies, or city councils. Many are responding by embracing agility as a way of working—some with a primary orientation around *operational* agility (Agile software development methods such as Scrum and SAFe), others focusing on *customer* development agility (e.g., Lean Startup), while others are embracing a broader *business* agility.

In almost all of these cases, the prevailing notion of agility is concerned primarily with processes and practices, with systems and structures—a form of **outer agility**. But, as seasoned agilists (of whatever stripe) are finding, the biggest challenges with agility revolve not so much around its *outer* aspects—its processes, practices, deliverables, and business outcomes—but around the sensemaking, communication, and relationship intelligence of an organization's people: its *inner* aspects. This is where we find the characteristically *human* problems of resistance, conflict, communication breakdowns, broken promises, people going through the motions with little passion or conviction, deteriorating product quality, managers micro-managing—the world, that is, of mindset and culture—the world of ***inner agility***.

Many organizational leaders and managers take an *objectivist* approach to the growing of inner agility, treating mindset and culture as reified goals to be attained, rather than as holistic qualities to be cultivated. Mindset and culture are viewed as behavioral attributes that exist somewhere out there: in *those* people out there; in *those* behaviors out there; in *those* habits and beliefs out there. From such an objectivist perspective, the tendency is to think about and treat mindset and culture from the **outside in**—as those aspects of organizational reality that we can somehow fix or change from the outside, whether through inculcation, motivational inducement, reasoned argument, or training and mentoring.

Evolvagility takes an alternative perspective—one in which we view mindset and culture not from the *outside in*, but from the **inside out**. From this perspective, we are interested in the *inner* capabilities that determine how people think; how they make sense of complex situations around them; the (often unexamined) beliefs and values they hold, both individually and collectively; people's ability (or inability) to hold perspectives that are different from their own; their ability (or lack thereof) to relate with others in ways that leave those others empowered and enabled. But, even more than this, we want to know how we might help ourselves and others *grow* those capabilities. Again, not from the *outside in*—the world of processes and structures or even behaviors; but rather from the *inside out*—from the world of sensemaking and consciousness, and from there out into the world of relationships and, beyond that, out into the world of organizational environments.

It is from the growing of these inner capabilities—from the level of consciousness outward—that the possibility for a genuine agile leadership, as I will be defining it in this book, emerges. Such a leadership is one that arises wherever people have the urge to take responsibility for their world—whether that be a team or a company—and a willingness to influence others toward a commonly held vision. Such a notion of leadership sees itself as arising from an *inner* capacity for complex sensemaking and consciousness. When coping with the volatile and complex world in which we live and work, each and every one of us— software delivery team members and executive leaders alike—need to have at our fingertips, at any given moment, the capacity to sense, the capacity to respond and—more importantly—the capacity to *make sense* in ways that enable the creation of something *new,* as-yet *un-thought*, and as-yet *undone*, whether it's a new idea, a new tool, a new approach, a new vocabulary, or even a new self-definition.

Only by such an act of *creation*—not just in terms of what *action* we take, but also in terms of how we *think* and how we *make sense*—is it possible to generate outcomes that can have the intended impact on an ever-changing and ever-evolving world. To do this, people need to be able to step beyond their fear of the unknown, of the un-tried, of the un-tested. They need to be willing to question cherished assumptions and to challenge well-established habits of mind. They lead not by telling, not by directing, not even by "going first," or "eating last." They do so by "pointing the way," to use Peter Senge's term.[1]

> When people engage in such a form of creation, they are **already leading**. They are pointing the way, not to a right strategy or goal, but toward a different way of **sensing**, a different way of **responding**, and—most importantly—toward a different way of **making sense**.

I call such a leadership *Sense-and-Respond* leadership[2] to emphasize the highly adaptive nature of leadership to which I am pointing and its inherent grounding in the *sensemaking* dimension by which it is necessarily defined. Just as the term "Sense-and-Respond" evocatively captures the spirit and practice of *outer agility*—emergent software design, adaptive customer development, inspect-and-adapt project delivery, the build-measure-learn cycle of Lean Startup, and so on—so too does it evocatively capture the spirit and practice of *inner agility*, specifically in its holding of leadership as an inherently *sensemaking* capability.

Evolvagility brings together a body of ideas, research, and practices from professional and executive leadership coaching, developmental psychology,

---

[1] Peter Senge, *The Fifth Discipline: The Art and Practice of the Learning Organization* (Doubleday, 2006).

[2] The term "Sense-and-Respond" has a number of sources and references. My first exposure to the term was in Stephan Haeckel's book, *Adaptive Enterprise: Creating and Leading Sense-and-Respond Organizations* (President and Fellows of Harvard College, 1999), which views "Sense-and-Respond" through a management and organizational lens. More recently, the focus that Jeff Gothelf and Josh Seiden give in their book *Sense & Respond: How Successful Organizations Listen to Customers and Create New Products Continuously* (Harvard Business Review Press, 2017) is on adaptive business delivery and the kind of culture that sustains that. But more than anyone else, my adoption of the term was influenced by the work of Dave Snowden. For him "Sense-and-Respond" points to a leadership stance in the face of situations that are inherently complex, referencing a large body of research in complexity science. See David Snowden and Mary Boone, "A Leader's Framework for Decision-making," *Harvard Business Review* (Nov. 2007).

transformational learning, and relationship systems coaching in order to synthesize a *human technology*—a set of tools and practices—for growing agile minds *from the inside out*. This book is for anyone who sees themselves as a leader within a larger organizational setting. By "leader" I mean:

- Anyone willing to take responsibility for their world[3] and able to influence others in creating that world

- Anyone who is guided by a deep inner compass founded upon a profound sense of purpose

- Anyone willing to recognize and evolve beyond the limitations of their current ways of seeing the world, of seeing others, and of seeing themselves

By "anyone" I mean anyone in *any* role, at *any* level of the organization, and within *any* part of the organization. The ideas, distinctions, and practices you will encounter in this book are applicable anywhere people are collectively organizing themselves around common goals and outcomes.

Without a doubt, this book asks a lot of the reader. Reading this book assumes that you are willing to intellectually extend yourself; it assumes you are willing to challenge some (perhaps cherished) assumptions you may be holding; it assumes you are willing to look honestly at yourself; and, mainly, it assumes you are clearly on a path of growth in your leadership and are willing to do some (possibly hard) work to get there.

Main Ideas of the Book

There are five main ideas, or themes, at the heart of *Evolvagility*. These ideas define the theoretical grounding of everything we will cover in this book—in a sense, they are the philosophical **vertebrae** of *Evolvagility*.

---

[3] The phrase "taking responsibility for your world" comes from the definition of leadership in the Coaches Training Institute's (CTI) Co-active Leadership Program. See http://www.coactive.com/leadership/program.

A Paradigm Shift from Predict-and-Plan to Sense-and-Respond

The first idea points to the nature of the mindset shift needed at both the level of organizations and of individuals if we are to grow our capacity to function effectively in the face of the increasing volatility, uncertainty, and complexity of 21st century life. This relatively new and recently accelerating condition can be seen as a threat; but it can also be the source of opportunity for those who are able and willing to *evolve* how they think and how they act.

> In order to fully embrace the challenges and possibilities of 21st century reality, we need to shift from a Predict-and-Plan way of thinking about and acting in the world, to a Sense-and-Respond way.

This is essentially a shift in how people think about their world; it's one that moves us from an assumption of stability, predictability, continuity, and reliability—to an assumption of volatility, uncertainty, change, and ambiguity.

As we make this dramatic shift in our assumptions, we find it increasingly necessary to shift our mode of thinking and action from up-front planning and deciding, and relying on hierarchy, chain of command, and siloed expertise, to planning and deciding as we go, and relying on learning, emergence, and distributed wisdom of the whole to see us through.

I refer to this radically different orientation as *Sense-and-Respond*. As will become increasingly clear as we proceed, *Sense-and-Respond* is not just a different way of doing things; it is a different way of seeing and making sense of the world around us. It is, ultimately, a different way of *being*.

Sense-and-Respond Organizations Require Sense-and-Respond Minds

Evolvagility focuses on how to create conditions that grow the capacity for broad organizational agility—for growing *Sense-and-Respond* organizations. A number of books and other resources teach us how to do this. Many of these resources regard organizational agility from the perspectives of "leaning out" an organization's processes, structures, and processes.[4] Others bring in an agility frame that has a customer-centric focus.[5] Still others focus primarily on organizational culture, and how we might influence and shift the nature of the beliefs and values that underlie organizational performance.[6]

These are critically important perspectives and resources for growing broader organizational agility. Yet, for the most part, these perspectives and approaches reflect a bias and orientation that favors the exterior aspects of *Sense-and-Respond*—what I am calling *outer* agility. This is an orientation that focuses on the objective, observable aspects of organizational agility that include the processes, structures, and systems that determine how people work together. Or, when the approach falls more overtly within the domain of human performance, its orientation is largely *behavioral*, its focus primarily on skill and competence. Or, as is the case with organizational culture, the approach tends to be focused on how to create conditions that affect the collective behavior of people but primarily from the *outside in*.

Regardless of whether the focus is on processes and structures, organizational culture, or customers, one commonality of all such approaches is this:

---

[4] For a representative example of a process, structures, and systems orientation, see James P. Womack and Daniel Jones, *Lean Thinking: Banish Waste and Create Wealth in Your Corporation* (Free Press, 2003). Also see Jeffrey Liker, *The Toyota Way: 14 Management Principles from the World's Greatest Manufacturer* (McGraw-Hill, 2004).

[5] For some examples of resources that reflect a customer-centric focus, see Marty Cagan, *Inspired: How to Create Tech Products Customers Love* (John Wiley & Sons, 2018); Steve Blank, *The Four Steps to the Epiphany* (K & S Ranch, 2013); and Gothelf and Seiden, *Sense & Respond*.

[6] For an example that works in an explicitly Agile context, see Pollyanna Pixton, Paul Gibson, and Niel Nicholaisen, *The Agile Culture: Leading Through Trust and Ownership* (Pearson Education, 2014). For books that don't talk about "agility" per se, but which have direct relevance to the cultural dimension of agility, see William Schneider, *The Reengineering Alternative: A Plan for Making Your Current Culture Work* (Irwin Professional Pub, 1994), and Kim Cameron and Robert Quinn, *Diagnosing and Changing Organizational Culture: Based on the Competing Values Framework* (John Wiley & Sons, 2011).

Unless people "get it,"—unless they are able to truly internalize it within their deepest sensemaking—whatever it is you're trying to make happen won't happen. For instance, unless individuals "get" what it means to create and sustain organizational structures and systems that are inherently flexible and adaptable—and unless individuals can learn to be comfortable with whatever anxiety they experience from the uncertainty and unfamiliarity of the structures and systems they would be helping to create—they will resist. But it usually won't *look* like resistance; it will look like they're "being slow" or "making mistakes" or "merely going through the motions" or "not seeing the bigger picture." You may find yourself scratching your head, wondering things like "How could they not see that?" or "Why do they keep making that same mistake?" In the end their efforts, which, on the face of it, may seem genuine and compliant, will lack authentic commitment, intelligence, and ingenuity.

The same is true whether you focus on processes and structures, culture, or customers: It all depends on the inner capacity of individuals to "get it" and to be able to deal constructively with the anxiety that accompanies any kind of change, particularly change whose nature is to challenge an idea or value that is close to their hearts.

> The ability to grow organizational agility rests ultimately on growing the inner **sense-making** capacity of **individuals**, whether alone or in relationship with others. In order to grow Sense-and-Respond organizations you need to grow Sense-and-Respond **minds**.

What I am talking about here is not individual *behavior*. If we want to "crack the code" on organizational agility, we need to be able to look beyond organizational structures, organizational culture, and human behavior itself. We need to peer into the nature of the *minds* that produce those structures and generate those behaviors. As such, while other authors have written about *Sense-and-Respond* capability from the perspective of processes and structures, of customer development, of strategy and management, of business delivery, and of organizational and team culture—all important and necessary perspectives—here I am talking about *Sense-and-*

Respond from the perspective of the inner *sense-making capacity of individuals*—and of individuals in relationship with others.

As the inner sense-making capacity of individuals, and individuals in relationship with others, grows—and as those individuals alone and in relationship with others come to be able to take responsibility for their world and for the ability to impact others in creating that world—a quality of *Sense-and-Respond* leadership emerges.

I refer to this aspect of agility as *inner* agility. And, it is this capacity for inner agility, and how it might be grown from the *inside out*, that I am calling *Evolvagility*.

Sense-and-Respond Leadership Means Creating That Which Does Not Yet Exist

Here is where *Sense-and-Respond* leadership begins to become fully distinguished, and where this book finds its main footing. Rather than how to bring about the emergence of agility across organizational structures and processes, or even human behavior and culture, the focus of this book is on **what it takes to bring about anything *at all*.**

This brings us to the fourth, and perhaps *key* premise of this book:

> *Sense-and-Respond leadership is the ability, within yourself and in engagement with others,* **to bring about that which does not already exist.**

It is this deep capacity for what Bob Anderson calls *Outcome-Creating* leadership[7]—both in oneself and with others—that is at the heart of what it means to lead in a highly volatile and complex world. In such a world, we rarely know ahead of time what is coming at us; we rarely see the full complexity of what is happening at any given moment; and we oftentimes don't

---

[7] Robert Anderson and William Adams, *Mastering Leadership: An Integrated Framework for Breakthrough Performance and Extraordinary Business Result* (Conscious Leadership, 2016).

know what to make of what is happening. And yet, here we are: We are either moved to, or *called* upon, to lead. Therefore, our reliability as leaders—whether as top-level organization leaders or as a software team member who has taken a stand on something important for the team—comes from our ability to quickly **sense** what is happening—in all of its unpredictability, in all of its complexity, in all of its ambiguity—and to **respond** in ways that leave us and others, in some way, closer to realizing, or becoming more congruently aligned with, our vision in, and for, the world.

Our effectiveness as leaders, regardless of role or title, comes from the deftness with which we are able to navigate this dance of *sense* and *respond*, and from the complexity of mind (both *cognitive* and *affective*) that we are able to bring to bear in the execution of that dance. From such deftness and complexity of mind comes the capacity to *create newly*—from chaos, from uncertainty, from ambiguity—as opposed to adapting, without thought, to what is.

This last point is key to what I mean by *Sense-and-Respond* leadership: If all we're doing is adapting to "what is," the opportunity to introduce anything new to the mix will be limited, and no real *evolution* will happen. It is in our capacity for *creating newly* that it becomes possible to transcend the limitations of the current moment, and to find and leverage the *opportunity* that is latent within it. This is the very essence of *Sense-and-Respond* leadership. It is what *Evolvagility* is all about.

Sense-and-Respond Leadership Arises in Relationship

As a capacity to create that which does not exist, *Sense-and-Respond* leadership, as I am defining it here, is a function of the sensemaking capacity of individuals—it is a product of individual minds. And yet, individual minds don't exist *individually*; they arise within the context of human relationships. The thoughts we have, the feelings we experience, the aspirations we hold—all have a social basis in relationships, and in the feelings, language, and discourse through which those relationships are sustained and leveraged in any number of shared pursuits.

> *Sense-and-Respond leadership is an individual capacity that arises within **relationship**.*

From birth through childhood, how we see others, the world, and ourselves has its basis in our relationships with primary others (mother, father, and later friends, teachers, etc.). This basis in relationships continues into our adult lives when we start to bring work colleagues, close friends, and marriage partners into the mix.

Language is one aspect of this. Throughout all phases of our lives, language remains a key conveyer of the substance of who we are, in relationship. It could be said that, as much as we *use* language to convey our thoughts and feelings, it is also true that our thoughts and feelings are also *determined by* language. The fact that northern-most indigenous peoples have many different variations for the word "snow" demonstrates that language is that which makes important distinctions in the world possible.

But language is not the sole constitutive social basis for who we are as individuals. Relationship *itself* is foundational. The nature of the emotional connections we have with certain others signals deeper and far-subtler psychological exchanges, on the basis of which our own individual sense-making—both cognitive and affective—gets formed. The nature of how we make sense of the world—our thinking and feeling experiences—finds its very *form* in the relationships and relationship systems in which we find ourselves. Indeed, it is in relationships that we *find ourselves* as individuals. This finding ourselves *in relationship* is also what *Evolvagility* is all about.

Sense-and-Respond Leadership is an *Everywhere* Phenomenon

In a complex and ambiguous world, we are *all* called upon to lead at some moment and in some way. The notion of leadership that happens only at the top can't possibly address the needs of the 21st century. Therefore, the term *Sense-and-Respond* leadership applies to *anyone*—regardless of position or role—who holds a vision for their world and who takes responsibility for that world; *anyone* who is able to influence others in positively creating that world; *anyone* who is guided by a deep moral compass; and *anyone* who is willing to recognize and evolve beyond their own inner limitations.

Sense-and-Respond leadership is an "everywhere" phenomenon; it is realized when individuals everywhere, at all levels and in all kinds of roles, take responsibility for their world and are willing to influence others in creating that world. Sense-and-Respond organizations arise when Sense-and-Respond leaders show up **everywhere.**

Given this, we start to see agile leadership as a quality of *leaderfulness*[8]—of "small-l" leadership—that arises anywhere people organize themselves, and influence others, around the creation and realization of shared goals and outcomes.

We still need people who hold positional roles as leaders and managers. However, top-level leaders have the same inner developmental work to do as everyone else. What is different for them is that in their role as organizational leaders, their job is to design organizational environments in which *Sense-and-Respond* leadership can grow and flourish throughout the organization.

Evolvagility is this capacity for an "everywhere" *Sense-and-Respond* leadership.

Defining Evolvagility

Taken together, these ideas point to a new way of understanding and practicing agile leadership and manifesting a deeper *inner agility*. Such a leadership is an *everywhere* phenomenon, in which individuals, throughout all parts of a given organization, show up as "small-l" leaders. Such a leadership entails a willingness to take responsibility for one's world and to recognize, and evolve beyond, the limitations of one's current ways of making sense of one's world. It means being guided by a deep inner compass that is founded upon a profound sense of purpose and a recognition that to lead means to create that which does not yet exist, in oneself and in relationship with others.

---

[8] Joseph Raelin, *Creating Leaderful Organizations: How to Bring Out Leadership in Everyone* (Berrett-Koehler Publishers, 2003).

Bringing these thoughts and considerations together, we can now begin to coalesce around a definition of *Sense-and-Respond* leadership:

> **Sense-and-Respond leadership** is the leaderful capacity of individuals, in relationship with others—and manifested throughout an organization—to **sense acutely**, in the midst of complexity and ambiguity, and to **respond gracefully**, within that same complexity and ambiguity, in ways that **catalyze** the creation of outcomes congruent with our deepest purpose and mission.

The word "catalyze" is key here. What we're talking about is a leadership not so much of *acting* and *doing*, or of *directing* and *telling*, but of **sensemaking** and **relating**. It is a leadership that rests on our ability—whether individually or collectively—to take complex and ambiguous situations that surprise and confuse us, and to make sense of them in ways that help us, and others, navigate that complexity, ambiguity, and confusion. Just as importantly, it is a leadership that rests on our ability to forge relationships and relational activity in which similar sensemaking capacity gets generated collectively.

Such a *Sense-and-Respond* leadership doesn't just *happen*: It is a capability that must be developed and nurtured. It is the body of distinctions and practices by which that development and nurturing happens, which I call *Evolvagility*.

> **Evolvagility** is the activity and practices we engage in, and the philosophical perspective we incorporate into the fabric of our thinking, which grows within us the capacity for Sense-and-Respond leadership.

In this book, we'll explore in depth what *Sense-and-Respond* leadership looks like and what kind of practice one might develop in order to grow oneself as a *Sense-and-Respond* leader. As the book unfolds, you'll see that *Evolvagility* is both a set of *ideas* about leadership and a body of *practices* and *skills* that you can develop to realize those ideas about leadership in terms of real-world impact.

Where We Are Going

Having revealed the primary ideas and premises and having established some basic definitions on which this book is founded, we can now look directly at what specifically we will cover. Several questions form the basis of Evolvagility:

- What is *Sense-and-Respond* leadership? How is it manifested? Why is the notion of *Sense-and-Respond* leadership important in today's organizations? Who is it for?

- What is the nature of the inner constitution of *Sense-and-Respond* leadership? How does it work? How is it different from other types of leadership? What are the key skills required in its practice? What are the key domains of human engagement in which its practice unfolds?

- What is the nature of the way in which *Sense-and-Respond* leadership can be developed and nurtured within an organizational setting? In what ways is that development and nurturement cultivated?

- What are the specific practices and conditions by which we deliberately develop our capacity for *Sense-and-Respond* leadership, at the level of individuals and at the level of relationship systems?

- What is the role of organizational leadership and management in all of this, and of the very nature of management and leadership itself?

To address these questions, this book is organized into six parts.

Part I: *Mapping the Territory of Sense-and-Respond Leadership* provides a view of the nature of *Sense-and-Respond* leadership and of the domains of practice in which it arises and in which it can be deliberately cultivated. Here I introduce the concept of *deliberate sensemaking*, which is an approach to sensemaking that takes our sensemaking itself as an object of discovery and development. We look at the social context in which *deliberate* *sensemaking* necessarily happens and consider the benefits that its practice can yield for individuals, relationships, and organizational systems.

Part II: *The Anatomy of Sensemaking and Action Logic* looks under the hood of human sensemaking to understand what developmental psychologists can tell us about the nature of *meaning-making*—the deeper psychological mechanism that underlies and determines our manner of sensemaking—and the profound impact it has on performance and action. What is the nature of the process by which human beings *make* meaning? How does that meaning-making develop in complexity as we mature? What is the pattern that determines how that development unfolds? Why is such an *inner* development so important for the growth of *Sense-and-Respond* leadership, and for organizational agility more broadly?

Part III: *Deliberately Growing Minds* looks at the precise ecosystemic conditions needed to grow the organizational DNA needed for the emergence of *Sense-and-Respond* leadership—whether at the level of individuals, collectives, or entire organizational enterprises. As we'll see especially in this part, *Sense-and-Respond* capability is not something that can be strategically forced, driven, or otherwise *managed* into existence. Rather, practices and conditions must be *cultivated* that promote, support, and empower its emergence in an ecosystemic manner. What is the design imperative behind the creation of such a deliberately developmental ecosystem? That's what we will discover here.

Part IV: *The Design of a Deliberately Developmental Ecosystem* leverages the ecosystemic approach to fostering development explored in Part III in order to take you through the design of a *deliberately developmental ecosystem*. This part walks through, in detail, the specific practices and conditions needed in an organizational environment to foster the inner development necessary for *Sense-and-Respond* leadership to emerge and fully thrive.

Parts I–IV explain the nature, constitution, and methodology for growing *Sense-and-Respond leadership* as a broadly (and deeply) held organizational capability. By this point, however, we will have said almost nothing about the role of organizational leaders and managers. This doesn't mean that, in a *Sense-and-Respond* environment, the role of manager goes away; in fact, that role is needed more than ever. But the nature of that role changes dramatically. In a traditional Predict-and-Plan world, the focus of the role of manager is on **driving to results** through directing, telling, measuring, and motivating others in what they are to do in order to generate the desired results. In a *Sense-and-Respond* world, the focus of the organizational manager's role is on **tuning organizational conditions** so that they foster and nurture the inner growth necessary for the emergence of *Sense-and-Respond* leadership as an *everywhere* phenomenon.

Part V: *The Role of the Organizational Leader* provides an overview of what that role looks like and teaches you how it is played.

Part VI: *Concluding Thoughts* leaves you with a few parting ideas. *Evolvagility* is not some idea that I, or anyone else, simply dreamed up. Rather, it arises as a response to an impulse not simply to cope with the situations and demands of the current moment in human evolution, but to develop within ourselves the inner and outer mastery needed to move beyond the nature of mind that produced this moment in the first place. In this last part, I want for us to appreciate the call of this moment in history—to recognize that it is now possible to create our world by creating the thoughts with which we define that world, and from that recognition find within ourselves, and within others, the capacity to create the thought that the world wants in its creation. I want for us to see this moment from a place of deep and profound hope—hope in the human capacity to create our world.

PART I

Mapping the Territory of Sense-and-Respond Leadership

In this part, we trace out the territory of ideas and concepts that are at the heart of Evolvagility. We begin by describing, in some detail, the nature of the mindset shift that underlies Sense-and-Respond. This mindset shift is not just a different way of doing things; it constitutes quite literally a different metaphysical stance—a different way of understanding, knowing, and being in the world.

Once we've established the underlying mindset shift, we move on to a deep exploration of Sense-and-Respond as a kind of human systems "operating system." At the heart of this human systems operating system is sensemaking, which points to the depth and complexity with which we are able to make sense of our experience, and our capacity to formulate actions that are congruent with, and can impact, the complex world around us. Along the way, we introduce the notion of an Action Logic, which points to the mental processing that underlies and informs how we make sense of our world.

Finally, we will introduce Deliberate Sensemaking, which refers to a body of practices by which we effectively "open the hood" on our sensemaking processes. The practice of Deliberate Sensemaking allows us to examine the ways in which our sensemaking processes—and the deeper, interior Action Logics that inform them—impact, and potentially limit, our capacity to think and act effectively in relation to that situation.

From Predict-and-Plan to Sense-and-Respond

The mindset shift that is at the heart of *Evolvagility* is the shift from *Predict-and-Plan* to *Sense-and-Respond*. We're not talking here about upgrading operational processes or even broader organizational systems (though these can be an outcome of this mindset shift). Rather, we're talking about a shift in how people think, how they see the world around them, and the kinds of skills and practices they are capable of.

In the following pages, I trace the unfolding of this mindset shift, and, along the way, lay down a set of key metaphors that will orient what follows.

The Nature of 21st Century Life: VUCA

Now well into the 21st century, we are faced with ever-greater degrees of volatility, uncertainty, complexity, accelerating change, and ambiguity. VUCA is a US Army acronym from the early 1990s that names this condition, and which means:

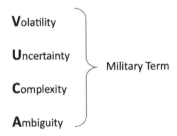

Volatility

Uncertainty   } Military Term

Complexity

Ambiguity

VUCA described the geopolitical world that followed the end of the Cold War, in which the previous period of relative predictability, stability, and certainty gave way to what felt unpredictable, ever-changing, and ever-uncertain.

More recently the term has been adopted in the area of strategic leadership. In this book, the letter "C" has a different meaning:

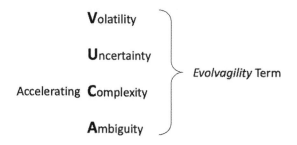

Volatility means that surprising things happen, often in ways we don't like. *Uncertainty* means that we can't rely on things happening the way they did before. *Accelerating change* refers to a sense that the world is not merely changing, but that the *rate* of change is accelerating and that the *nature* of change itself is changing. The element of *accelerating change* is also an aspect of VUCA, especially since it factors in so strongly, and resonates so powerfully, within today's business world. Finally, there's *ambiguity*, which is: "I see something, but I'm not sure what it is; it could be this, but it could also be that." Ambiguity points to the fact that organizational situations and events often occur as *riddles* that, when unsolved (or unnoticed), can trick us into believing our assumptions[9]. One final note: "Complexity" in the context of *Evolvagility* describes more generally the condition to which VUCA refers.

Traditional Management's Response to VUCA: Predict-and-Plan

How do most of us—whether we're a manager or a tester on a software development team—typically respond to VUCA? How do we react when things get wonky, uncertain, unpredictable, puzzling? Usually, we try to exert more control, more structure, more constraints, greater planning. In short, we adopt a Predict-and-Plan approach, the basic assumptions of which are the following:

- The future is predictable

---

[9] I owe the idea of organizational situations as riddles to Karl Weick. Karl Weick, *The Social Psychology of Organizing* (McGraw-Hill, 1979).

- Events and outcomes are by their nature stable, and very little will *substantively* change during the course of a given planning horizon

- We know what the relevant variables of a situation are ahead of time and we believe we can anticipate how to manage changes in those variables

- Cause-and-effect is stable and linear; we can see the effect of a given cause, and we can reliably anticipate the nature of its unfolding

- It is possible to find the "root cause" of our problems, and that once we address the root cause, the problem will be solved

Given the basic assumptions of a Predict-and-Plan mindset, we tend to be inclined to:

- Make elaborate plans ahead of time

- Endeavor to make most of our decisions ahead of time

- Break down large institutional initiatives into smaller pieces that can fall within pre-planned, well-established organization silos

- Create organizational and management systems, processes, and structures that operationalize and enable these assumptions and activities

Predict-and-Plan has a pedigree in the modern organizational context that goes back to Frederick Taylor, some 100 years ago. Within the business environment, the assumptions and actions given by a Predict-and-Plan mindset inform, and are informed by, a wide body of practices and competencies. MBA programs propagate skills and competencies that reflect this mindset, while all manner of certifications (PMP, etc.) further enshrine the kinds of competencies and behaviors we expect in the professional company environment. Resourcing, funding, strategic planning, and project management are all defined in terms of the thinking and operational assumptions of the Predict-and-Plan mindset.

Predict-and-Plan constitutes the very definition of what it means to be an effective business organization and to be an effective organizational player.

The Metaphor of Organization as Machine

Every management paradigm has a way of understanding and modeling the nature of a human organization, and that way of understanding and modeling informs its mode of action. The way Predict-and-Plan views the organization is as a complicated *machine*.

As David Snowden and Mary Boone point out in their HBR article "A Leader's Framework for Decision-making,"[10] a Ferrari is a complicated machine. It is "complicated," and not *simple*, in the sense that it consists of a great number of parts with a great number of interconnections requiring a great deal of expertise to build and maintain. It is "complicated," and not *complex* in that there is a repeatable invariant link between cause and effect; no matter how many times you repeat the same sequence of steps, you will always get the same result. Given the right kind of expertise and equipment, one could repeatedly disassemble a Ferrari engine, reassemble it, and drive it out of the garage the same way, time after time.

Under circumstances that are stable, predictable, certain, and relatively unambiguous, this machine model works well, and most Predict-and-Plan methodologies help us get the job done. However, as we bump more and more into *complexity*, a vicious cycle unfolds:

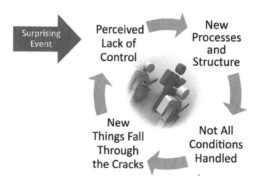

Figure 1: Vicious Cycle

Here's what happens. We're going along fine, and then—perhaps suddenly—a surprising event occurs, and we have the perception of a loss of

---

[10] Snowden and Boone, "A Leader's Framework for Decision-making."

control. In an effort to bring things back under control, we introduce a new process, structure, rule or regulation. But guess what? Not all conditions are met by the controls we've just introduced, because, for the most part, we aren't able to see all of its effects.

So, inevitably, things fall through the cracks, which generates in us, yet again, a feeling of a loss of control. We then renew our efforts to regain control either through the introduction of new processes, structures, and regulations, or through an adjustment of previously introduced processes, structures, and regulations. And on it goes.

When projects fail to satisfy customer stakeholders, the remedy is very often "better, more detailed requirements." When a process is not fulfilling its intended objective, the impulse is to add to it in an effort to fill in the cracks that keep on appearing. When conversations among stakeholders become too uncomfortable, the temptation is to create more processes, more policies, and more procedures in order to regulate those relationships and interactions and to (hopefully) remove the discomfort.

What we fail to see, when we are looking at a VUCA world through a Predict-and-Plan lens, is that we are trying to treat what is essentially a *complex* condition using a methodology that assumes it is *complicated*: we are trying to *manage* something that essentially cannot be managed. In the process, we end up creating a situation of "compounded complication"—more and more processes, more and more structures, and more and more regulations are added, one on top of the other. Over the years and decades, the processes and "best practices" of compounded complication have come to be embodied in the very definition of "effective" organizational management.

21st Century Management's Response to VUCA: Sense-and-Respond

For much of the 20th century, the Predict-and-Plan approach to management seemed to work: it generated many great companies and enterprises, not to mention government institutions that we've come to rely on. Lifetime employment, predictable economic cycles, social stability—all these and many more good things were products of that Predict-and-Plan approach to management.

22

So, while we don't want to abandon Predict-and-Plan altogether, we do want to recognize its "unfitness" in a *VUCA* world. "Unfit" here does not mean "bad." It means not the *right* fit for a given set of conditions.

We suggest that what's needed in the face of VUCA is a radically different approach. A better "fit" for the VUCA world is, we would argue, not Predict-and-Plan, but rather, what Stephan Haeckel coined, back in the 1990s, *Sense-and-Respond.*[11]

Sense-and-Respond rests upon an entirely different set of assumptions than Predict-and-Plan. Under *Sense-and-Respond*, we assume that:

- We *cannot* predict the future

- Things *will* change, often in very unexpected (and sometimes *unwelcome*) ways

- We simply cannot see or anticipate all the relevant variables of a situation ahead of time

- Cause-and-effect may not be easily observable, either because of time (cause and effect may be separated by long periods of time); locality (cause and effect may be separated by large spatial distances); or complexity (cause and effect may be hard to sort out in complex situations, because we cannot see the entirety of a situation)

Given these very different assumptions, people operating within a *Sense-and-Respond* mindset tend to:

- Plan and strategize **as they go** (rather than planning up front)

- Set things up to increase learning, then adjust their thinking, planning, and action based on that learning (double-loop feedback)

- Make decisions quickly, without waiting for all the information, knowing they have ways to quickly recover from mistakes

---

[11] Haeckel, *Adaptive Enterprise.*

- Make things visible and transparent (you can't *respond* to something you can't *sense*, and you can't *sense* something that is not visible)

- Create structures, processes, rules and systems that are highly adaptable and emergent

Sense-and-Respond calls not only for a very different kind of organizational capability in terms of behavior, structures, and culture. It calls for a paradigmatic shift in how we think about the very notion of an organization, and in how we relate to the world.

The Metaphor of Organization as Ecosystem

If the way Predict-and-Plan views the organization is as a complicated *machine*, the way in which *Sense-and-Respond* thinking sees the organization is as a complex *ecosystem*.

To return to Snowden and Boone's metaphor: a tropical rainforest is an example of a *complex* ecosystem. And, unlike a Ferrari engine, which is static, a rainforest is ever-changing; weather is in a state of constant flux, species come and go, populations rise and fall. Meanwhile, small changes in one part of the ecosystem affect changes in other parts, in ways that can be unpredictable. Complex ecosystems are inherently nonlinear: repeat the same sequence of causal steps, and you're likely to get very different results.

Stop and consider what it might be like to try to "manage" a rainforest and you'll begin to understand where this is all going. Social environments, such as business organizations, are, like rainforests, inherently complex. The traditional, Predict-and-Plan management approaches that work in complicated situations only make things worse in the face of VUCA.

Sense-and-Respond thinking reacts differently to surprising events than Predict-and-Plan does:

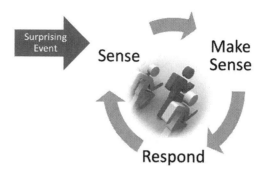

Figure 2: Sense and Respond

When a surprising event occurs, we first **Sense** what is happening. We ask questions such as: What are we seeing? What could we be missing? In what ways might we need to adjust our filters, and our modalities of sensing, so that we can see what we might be missing?

Then, based on what we're Sensing, we proceed to **Make Sense** of what we're Sensing. Here we ask some more questions: What might this be telling us about the organization? About us? About me (as a leader)? What's confusing? What's strange? What's hard to take? What's hard to understand? What *in us* makes it hard to understand? What does this confirm or disconfirm? What seems to be missing?

As we continue to form and make sense of the moment from the perspective of questions like these, we begin to formulate hypotheses on the basis of which we might fashion an experiment or action. At this point, we ask ourselves: What outcome do we want to produce? What experiment *might* we try? What actions *might* we take? What do we expect to find out from our experiment, or what outcome do we want to generate from our action? What new conditions do we want to create? Who do we need to include?

Questions such as these inform an "action" we might take, which constitutes our **Response**: doing something, articulating an idea, giving a direction to others, generating a new design idea, initiating a pivotal conversation, bringing a group of people to think through or strategize something together. Or any number of actions that are informed by an intended outcome or impact in the world around us.

As we *Respond*, we immediately move back into *Sensing*, inasmuch as we are consciously observing the impact of our action.

And the cycle continues.

This cycle happens on any scale of time, from seconds to weeks to months. It forms the methodological center of a number of adaptive process frames, from Scrum (in the Agile space) to Lean Startup (in the customer development space) to Action Learning (at the level of organizations). What differentiates this *Sense—Make Sense—Respond* cycle from that which characterizes a Predict-and-Plan approach is the fact that the *Sensing* phase is not regulated and sidestepped by an automated and regulating sensemaking, as is the case with Predict-and-Plan. With Predict-and-Plan, whatever *Sensing* happens is predetermined by the mechanisms by which that Sensing is governed. For instance, in a traditional project management world whatever we might be Sensing—for instance, we might notice that a given product feature seems to no longer be a match to what the customer really wants—will be subjected to the regulating criteria defined by the project plan, with whatever new information presented by that Sensing being effectively cancelled out. The *Making Sense* part comes to be essentially automated, regulated according to criteria that are prior to and extrinsic to those that might arise in any given moment. By contrast, in a *Sense-and-Respond* world, it becomes possible that the Sensing part will provide new information which could potentially alter our course significantly. Here is where the Making Sense part plays a particularly important role.

In this book, we will not be focusing on *Sense-and-Respond* **operational** or **business** processes. Nor will our focus be, at least not *directly,* on the broader organizational sphere. That's well covered elsewhere. Rather, our focus here is on the layer of capability that lays *within,* or *at the base* of *Sense-and-Respond* operational, business, and broader organizational capability; our focus is on ***human systems capability***.

Figure 3: Sense-and-Respond Capability

From this perspective, we can ask:

What does Sense-and-Respond look like, and how does it work, **inside** individuals, **inside** groups and teams, **inside** organizations, and how can it be cultivated within an organizational setting?

The Sense-And-Respond "Operating System"

A Human Systems Operating System

You can think of *Sense-and-Respond* as a kind of human-systems *operating system* similar to, metaphorically, the one on your iPhone or laptop. The operating system of any device is a piece of software that handles all the low-level operations needed for the applications on your device to run. Without an operating system, none of those apps will run. With the *wrong* operating system, none of them will run.

A computing operating system can be described as having three major components:

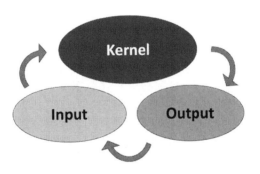

Figure 4a: The Sense-and-Respond Computing Operating System

Information is detected and picked up by the *Input* component and sent over to the *Kernel*, which determines what needs to happen and then, though some kind of directing of traffic, causes an *Output* to be generated (I am simplifying things here).

How the Input and Output parts work, and what they are capable of doing, is determined both by the physical makeup of the device (its "hardware") and by the *Logic* that underlies and determines the traffic-directing activities of the *Kernel.*

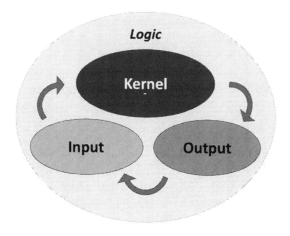

Figure 4b: The Sense-and-Respond Computing Operating System

So how is this like *Sense-and-Respond* within the human systems realm?

If we allow ourselves to paint things in *very* broad strokes (and add the caveat that human system processes are not nearly as linear or mechanistic as is being depicted in this simplified model), we can model the *Sense-and-Respond* **human systems operating system** in a somewhat similar manner:

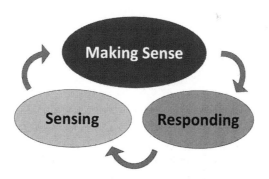

Figure 4c: The Sense-and-Respond Human Systems Operating System

Here, our *Sensing* acts as a kind of human-systems "input" mechanism, while *Responding* behaves similarly as a kind of "output" mechanism (again, I am painting very broad strokes and rendering organically fluid processes in a decidedly mechanistic way). Our *Sensing* takes in what is happening at any given moment, whether "inside" of us—our thoughts, feelings, sensations, moods, etc.—or, "outside" of us—what we can sense through our five senses. *Sensing* also takes in things that fall in those gray areas between "inside" and "outside"; things like intuitions, hunches, high dreams, and so on.

Our Responding constitutes the actions, planning, speaking, communicating—whether alone or with others—in which we engage in the world. Sometimes our responses are intentional: they have a clear goal in mind. At other times, our Responses are the product of an emotional reaction—an automatic, largely involuntary, response to an event that we find, in some way, upsetting (an "event," in this case, can be big, or it can be tiny). At still other times, our Responses are simply the product of thoughtless inattention or lack of intention—a different form of automaticity.

Making Sense is the part of the process where we reflect and think about what we're Sensing. It's where we make comparisons to what's happened before, and where we assess what we might already know. It's where we make hypotheses and draw conclusions about what might be going on, and where, on the basis of the conclusions we've drawn, we hypothesize an action (Response) we might take.

This entire cycle—Sensing, Making Sense, and Responding—is an activity that can happen at the level of the individual (within the consciousness of an individual), a collective (as a shared, collaborative process—a kind of "thinking aloud" together—between and among two or more individuals), and at the organizational level (as an aligned system of collectives, structures and processes).

At the heart of it all is *Making Sense*: it is, in a way, the operating system *kernel* of a *Sense-and-Respond* leadership capability, whether at the level of the individual, groups, or entire organizations. It is the very *fount* of leadership capability. Therefore, we want to linger here for a while and, in the following pages, dive deeply into what it is that is happening when we are *Making Sense*.

Action Logic: Deep Kernel of the
Sense-and-Respond Operating System

As I stated earlier on, our reliability as leaders (whether large-L leaders or small-l leaders) to lead in a VUCA world comes from our capacity to quickly Sense what is happening—in all of its unpredictability, in all of its complexity, in all of its ambiguity—and to Respond in ways that leave us and others, in some way, closer to realizing, or becoming more congruently aligned with, our vision for the world.

At the heart of such a *Sense-and-Respond* leadership is the way in which we are able to Make Sense of what is happening. And, the activity of Making Sense—whether at the individual, group, or organizational level—is always determined by a deeper **Action Logic**—a kind of "grammar" for making sense of our world.[12] Action Logic forms the deep kernel of the *Sense-and-Respond* operating system.

---

[12] "Action Logic" is term that was originally coined by Bill Torbert. For a thorough introduction to Action Logic and its application to organizational leadership and management, see Bill Torbert, Dalmar Fisher, and David Rooke, *Action Inquiry: The Secret of Timely and Transformative Leadership* (Berrett-Koehler Publishers, 2004). For an even more thorough description of the developmental psychology behind the notion of "Action Logic," see Susanne Cook-Greuter, "Nine Levels of Increasing Embrace in Ego Development: A Full-Spectrum Theory of Vertical Growth and Meaning-Making," retrievable on March 26, 2018 at: http://www.cook-greuter.com/Cook-Greuter%209%20levels%20paper%20new%201.1'14%2097p%5B1%5D.pdf

31

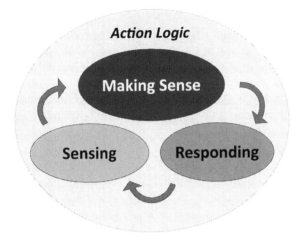

Figure 4d: The Sense-and-Respond Human Systems Operating System

If the activity of Making Sense is concerned with the content of **what we think,** our Action Logic refers to the deep inner logic that determines the **way we think.**

When we delve deeper into the nature of *the way we think*, we might ask ourselves questions such as these:

- What's important to us? What are we committed to?

- What are the beliefs, worldviews, or assumptions that inform our thinking?

- What stories and narratives do we draw on, subliminally, to help us make sense of a given situation?

- What is the nature of the metaphors that frame the ways in which we understand what's going on (Sensing)?

- What's the nature of the thinking that determines how we conceive which actions might be a best fit for a given situation (Responding)?

- In what ways do personal and *shared* histories determine what's possible and what isn't?

The answers to these questions reveal our internal *Action Logic*.

Our *Action Logic* governs the *How* of our thinking and our way of Making Sense at the level of the individual, at the level of relationships and at the level of the organization. At the level of the individual (*individual* Action Logic), it constitutes one's internal *meaning-making* and the way in which that meaning-making determines how we view the world, how we view others, and how we view ourselves.

At the level of relationships (*relational* Action Logic), it constitutes the shared assumptions, beliefs, and psychological interchange that determine the nature of our relationship and the patterns of interaction that characterize how we are *together*.

At the level of organizations (*organizational* Action Logic), it constitutes the more widely shared assumptions, beliefs, and values that determine our community habits, interactions, and feelings of safety (or lack thereof), as well as the organizational structures, roles, and processes in which those assumptions, beliefs, and values come to be embodied. This is where organizational *culture* lives.

Meanwhile, our Action Logic—whether at the level of the individual, relationships, or organization—regulates and constrains both our *Sensing* and our *Responding*. From the perspective of our *Sensing*, our Action Logic determines which aspects or perspectives related to a given situation we pay attention to and which we ignore. It filters out what we might consider "nonsense" while allowing in information that may—or may not—better equip us with the key perspectives we need to be able to take in the full complexity of a given situation. Our Action Logic also constrains (or enhances) our ability to integrate what we're taking in across multiple modalities simultaneously, and the degree to which we can fully trust, and consciously develop, Sensing modalities like intuition.

From the perspective of *Responding*, our Action Logic governs what manner of action (what kind of *Response*) is best fit for the situation. Some actions might seem "crazy" or some might seem "counter-productive" (even though, from the perspective of impact on outcomes, they might be exactly what is called for). Our Action Logic determines what kinds of actions we are more emotionally comfortable taking, and which might be anxiety-provoking, embarrassing, or otherwise *uncomfortable*.

To return to our earlier model of *Sense-and-Respond* seen from the perspective of Human Systems capability, Operational capability, and Business capability—Action Logic comprises the very foundation of it all:

Figure 5: Human Systems Capability within Sense-and-Respond Capability

Action Logic, metaphorically, is the deep kernel operating system that determines the *capability* of any human system. And, by extension, an Action Logic determines the limits—cognitive, emotional, or psychological—of that human system's ability to perform in ways that are congruent with the goals, needs, and aspirations of the organization, of which that human system is an integral part.

Upgrading the Sense-and-Respond Operating System: Introduction to Deliberate Sensemaking

What makes organizational situations challenging often has nothing to do with the situations themselves. Rather, it is that the *complexity* of those situations is beyond the complexity with which we are able to Make Sense of them. Or, more precisely, the complexity of those situations is beyond the complexity of the *Action Logic* that governs how we are Making Sense of them—whether individually or together with others.

When, for instance, organizations have a hard time implementing the operational and business capabilities needed to engage in Lean Startup practices effectively, the source of the difficulty is almost always due to perspectival limitations of the predominant Action Logics being held—within individuals, teams, and entire organizations—and the organizational structures, systems, and practices in which those Action Logics are embodied.

In such cases, there is effectively a *cognitive mismatch*, so to speak, between what the environment calls for, and what the human system is capable of. This cognitive mismatch results in misfires in both our Sensing and Responding—misfires that translate into any number of breakdowns, both big and small, both cultural and structural. This is because we simply can't Sense enough of the bigger, more complex picture, to be able to generate Responses that are the right *fit* for that larger picture, for that greater complexity.

In order to be able to make better sense of what is going on around us, we need to change the way we think; we need to *upgrade* the complexity of the ways in which we Make Sense—which really means that **we need to upgrade the complexity of our Action Logic**—in order to be able to account for the bigger, more complex picture.

This leads us to another key point: **In order to upgrade the complexity of our Action Logic, we need to somehow *make it visible to ourselves*—**if we can't see it, we can't change it. The problem is that, for most of us, living our normal day-to-day lives, the Action Logic from which we are Making Sense is not something we are conscious of, let alone something we consciously reflect on. It is like the air we breathe, or the water a fish swims in; it is not (at least not commonly) a logical frame we know about or pay attention to.

When we are blind to the Action Logic that governs our sensemaking activities, we of course have little, or no, capacity to actually change it, let alone *upgrade* it to a higher level of complexity. And if our current Action Logic is insufficient to the complexity we currently face, this blindness becomes the basis for error-prone and misguided organizational actions and decisions.

> These two things—the need to **upgrade the complexity of our Action Logics,** and the need to **make existing Action Logics visible**—are the *key motivating ideas of this book.*

The primary philosophy and *uber*-practice that this book aims to teach is something I am calling ***Deliberate Sensemaking***. Drawn in part from the work of Robert Kegan and Lisa Lahey,[13] Deliberate Sensemaking is both a way of thinking (a *philosophy*, if you will) and a set of practices which allows us—both individually and collectively—to observe, to reflect upon, and to be able to *shift*, the Action Logic that governs our thinking and discourse. In doing so, it allows us to turn the tables on the way Action Logic usually works: From that which ***does us*** to that which ***we do***. From that which, in its invisible ubiquity, ***defines us***—to that which, in our revealing (for ourselves) of its structure and effect, ***we define***.

Deliberate Sensemaking is a key leadership practice in a *Sense-and-Respond* environment. It points to the capacity for what Bob Anderson and Bill Adams call *Outcome-Creating Leadership*, to which we referred in the Introduction, which is the ability to *bring about that which doesn't already exist*. This capacity for Outcome-Creating Leadership is at the heart of what it means to lead in the face of VUCA. *Deliberate Sensemaking* houses the practices and skills that are key to that.

In the remainder of this book, we will work together (yes, you will do much of the work!) to:

- Uncover the key distinctions that underlie and help us better understand the human technology behind *Deliberate Sensemaking*

- Reveal a suite of practices, conditions, and structures that, in aggregate, serve to operationalize and make real the philosophy and

---

[13] See Robert Kegan and Lisa Lahey, *An Everyone Culture: Becoming a Deliberately Developmental Organization* (Harvard Business School Publishing, 2016). For "deliberate sensemaking," see Robert Kegan and Lisa Lahey, *How the Way We Talk Can Change the Way We Work: Seven Languages for Transformation* (Jossey-Bass, 2001).

practice of Deliberate Sensemaking, and the outcomes that its practice is intended to realize

- Tie it all back to the core injunction of *Sense-and-Respond* leadership, which is (a) that leaders lead not just by what they help others *do*, but in what they help others to *see*, and in who they help others to *be*, and (b) that leadership is an *everywhere* phenomenon, not something that happens only at the top

Toward this end, we will start by examining what the research tells us about the psychological anatomy of Sensemaking and Action Logic. Understanding this anatomy will provide a number of thinking frames you'll need to learn in order to be able to create environments that are intentionally designed to enable us to adaptively adjust our Action Logic and Sensemaking schema in ways that help us flex and flow, cognitively and emotionally, to the ever-volatile, ever-uncertain, ever-changing, and ever-ambiguous situations we face.

This is no-doubt heady and advanced stuff. I know. And, for those of us ready to go there, it is what I think we all recognize as the next crest of the wave in our evolution toward increasingly adaptive and—dare I say—*enlightened* organizational and leadership capability.

PART II

The Anatomy of Sensemaking and Action Logic

In this next part, we look at the anatomy of Sensemaking and Action Logic, starting with the nature of mind itself, and the nature of *inner* growth. We continue by exploring what four decades of research has to say about Action Logic and the psychological mechanism by which our inner *meaning-making* determines its unfolding. Here is where we explore the way in which our individual thoughts, feelings, ideas—and even our own *experience*—are shaped by the meaning-making that constitutes an individual's Action Logic.

From here, we are able to introduce the research on mental evolution, which shows that minds can, and do, evolve and grow in maturity. This notion of the possibility of an *evolving mind*—and the specific Action Logics it moves through—is key to the deeply *creative* nature of *Sense-and-Respond* leadership and is, ultimately, the very source of an organization's *Sense-and-Respond* capacity.

Finally, we discuss the stages of increasing complexity that characterize the evolution of Action Logics possible within a single person's developmental lifetime, noting that it is only with the later stage Action Logics that the capacity for *Sense-and-Respond* leadership begins to emerge.

The Nature of Inner Growth

A fundamental assertion of *Evolvagility* is that our capacity for *Sense-and-Respond* leadership is a function of the complexity of the Action Logics we hold, and our ability to skillfully engage in our world in ways that reflect, and make real, the capabilities that those Action Logics make possible.

In the following pages, we will take a deep dive into the psychology of Sensemaking and Action Logic. It has been my experience that when people come to understand this, light bulbs turn on, and major insights happen—insights that help people grow and deepen both their own Sensemaking capacity as well as that of the people around them. Since this material takes us through a potential field of landmines, in terms of misunderstanding and assumptions about human psychology, I'm going to be fairly deliberate in the steps we take.

Throughout the following we will use the term "inner growth" to refer to the territory of inner, mental life (which includes both cognitive and affective aspects) that determines how we think, how we make sense, and how we see the world, others, and ourselves. It is the inner world of our values and commitments, and of our vision for the world and for what we want. It also points to the internal filters that sift out the unfamiliar, uninteresting, and potentially confusing features of our VUCA world.

In addition to this *filtering* and *defining* aspect, inner growth also points to the territory of our inner capability: our capacity for complex thinking, our ability to truly see others as autonomous beings who hold unique perspectives, our ability to take courageous action, and many others. It is the deep operating system kernel that determines our skills and competencies.

Dimensions of Inner Growth

In this book, when I talk about inner growth, I'm referring to two distinct but interrelated realms of cognitive and psychological growth. Researchers in the field of adult education and development sometimes visualize these growth realms as different *axes*:

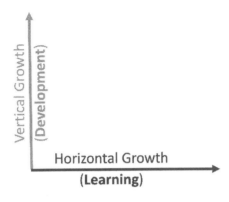

Figure 6: Vertical and Horizontal Growth

The horizontal axis of growth refers to horizontal growth, or learning. When we think of learning, we normally think of it as acquiring new skills or developing competency in some particular area. We learn a new programming language or software tool; we learn how to communicate in a more affirming manner with others; we "learn the ropes" of a particular company, which means we learn the rules of thumb for how to function in an effective manner within that particular environment.

This kind of learning—horizontal learning—expands the range of our *competency*. But note that this competency assumes some level of what we might call maturity—which, in this book, I refer to as "complexity of mind." In order to learn a new programming language, for example, one already has to have developed in oneself an inner, mental capacity for what developmental psychologists call "formal operations," which is essentially the ability to think abstractly. Without this inner capacity of mind, it would be difficult, if not impossible, to learn to program well.

This leads us to the other kind of inner growth: vertical growth, or *development*. Vertical growth focuses on growing the complexity of our way of seeing the world: What we are able to notice, the nature of the meaning we are making from what we are noticing, the range of actions that we can sensibly pursue (and those we can't). Development is key to our inner growth in that it points to growth in the complexity of our meaning-making, and to the degree of environmental complexity that meaning-making is able to integrate and translate into effective action. As the complexity of our inner meaning-making grows, so grows the complexity of the tasks we are able to undertake, and the task domains into which our skillful performance expands—the domain of our Horizontal growth.

Meaning-Making:
The Key to Inner Development

Key to the dimension of Vertical development—and central to our inner growth—is how we make meaning of the world around us, and the degree to which we are able to use our meaning-making is able to integrate and translate the complexity of our world into effective action. In a VUCA world, the *Sense-and-Respond* leader leads not just by telling or directing—or by "going first." Rather, in a VUCA world, *Sense-and-Respond* leaders lead through the depth and complexity of the sensemaking they are able to bring to bear, and the actions they are able to take, in the face of complex situations—and by virtue of the complexity of sensemaking and actions they are able to evoke *in others*.

The term meaning-making comes to us from the field of developmental psychology. It is the way people make sense of their world, how they relate with others, the actions they are able to take, the skills they are able to develop, and the depth of emotional intelligence they are able to bring to bear in any given moment. Understanding the nature of human meaning-making will help us deepen the insight that we are able to bring to our own inner development, and that of the people around us, and will, ultimately, help us get our arms around just what it means to lead through sense-making.

To Be Human is to Make *Meaning*

Human beings are, essentially, meaning-making machines.[14] What do I mean by the term meaning-making, in the context of *Evolvagility*?[15]

---

[14] I first heard the term "meaning-making machine" in a seminar given by Werner Erhard in the 1980s.

[15] The following paragraphs and illustrations are drawn from two landmark books on adult human development and the structure of our meaning-making: Robert Kegan, *The Evolving Self: Problem and Process in Human Development* (President and Fellows of Harvard College, 1982); and Michael Basseches, *Dialectical Thinking and Adult Development* (Ablex Publishing, 1984).

Our experience of the world is always conditioned—and to a considerable degree, *constructed*—by order, categorization, relating, and organizing as imposed by cognition. Without these, our experience would be nothing other than what philosopher William James once called a "blooming, buzzing confusion." Human cognition imposes order and stability on that confusion. It helps us maintain some degree of sameness and continuity amidst the otherwise overwhelming flux of experience.

In this sense, it could be said that experiential reality is not something we find out there in the external world. Rather, it is something we *construct* here within our interior consciousness. To get a sense of this, take a brief moment to look at the following picture.

What do you see?

Most people viewing this picture see either an old woman with a large nose, or young woman with a petit nose. Look again. Can you see both now? Regardless of which one you saw initially, it is usually difficult at first to see the other image.

As it turns out, the picture is an old Gestalt psychology trick. But it does beg the question: Where does the meaning of the picture take shape—on the page, or in your mind? In fact, all that exists on the page are patterns of different colored splotches and lines (or pixels, if you're reading this on a tablet or some other kind of electronic device). The picture itself is simply raw input. The actual meaning we make of what we see is a product of an internal mental process that happens almost entirely unconsciously within the span of mere milliseconds. Our eyes scan the image, while our mind seeks to make sense of it. In the end, whatever sense is made, is made by the mind and does not come from the picture.

The nature of this interior process by which we interpret the visual world around us points to the nature of perception itself and to the fact that much of what we see and experience around us—whether it is an image in a book or something someone says to us in a meeting—is that which gets constructed in our minds. We actually almost never *find* a world—we almost always *construct* it.

Meaning-making is the name which researchers who study this aspect of mental processing give to the underlying mental activity by which the mind constructs the world around it. It is the highly structured cognitive activity by which we, as individuals, integrate what we already know with what we are experiencing at any given moment. Something happens, like a momentary event or interaction with someone, which, for the briefest of moments, surprises us, confuses us, or in some other manner disorients us—or even just captures our attention—and almost immediately the mind adjusts our conscious perception of that moment by adding to it some kind of unconsciously generated meaning that governs how we come to make sense of it. All within the blink of an eye.

This meaning-making activity (an activity of the mind) derives from a deeply internalized set of cognitive "rules," a *schema* that determines how we construct for ourselves a sensible comprehension of situations and events. Similar to a language grammar, this deep structure acts as a kind of mental parsing mechanism that determines the nature of how events in our world map within our minds to a way in which we might come to understand them.

Again, this process occurs over the span of mere milliseconds. It is essentially an automatic cognitive process, happening outside our having any awareness of it. It is a cognitive activity that precedes and completely shapes our thoughts, perceptions, feelings, and ideas.

TWO MEANING-MAKING EXAMPLES

As a simple example of how meaning-making happens, consider an experiment that Jean Piaget conducted with young children. In this experiment, Piaget placed in front of a four-year-old child two identical beakers, each with the same amount of liquid. He then poured the liquid from one of those beakers into a taller, thinner beaker, and asked the child: "Which has more liquid?" Invariably, the four-year-old would tell him that the taller beaker had more liquid.

Piaget then conducted the same experiment with a seven-year-old. Unlike the four-year-old, the seven-year-old was able to see that the two beakers—the wider, shorter one and the thinner, taller one—must hold the same volume of liquid, even though the taller one looked like it held more. The seven-year-old can hold in his or her mind the meaning-making distinction of "durable categories," which tells us that things in the world have persistent qualities, even if it may not always look like it.[1] The four-year-old has not yet developed this meaning-making distinction.

It is important to note that the principle of "durable categories" is not a "thought." Nor is it a "concept." It is not something that one has to remember. Rather, it is a subliminal cognitive organizing principle—an internal mental *schema*—that orients the way we perceive and think about things—whether those things are our own feelings and thoughts, or events and situations in the world around us. Once one "gets" the principle of durable categories (usually at around six or seven years of age)—that is, once one has internalized it into one's inner meaning-making organization—a whole new range of possibilities for action becomes available that previously was not available.

Now, consider another example of how meaning-making might structure a child's actions and behaviors at different ages.[1] In this experiment, Piaget presented one child between the ages of seven and ten with three glasses of differently-colored liquid, which he tells him can be mixed together in a variety of ways to create a variety of colors. He then asked the child to create a mix from the three glasses in order to produce a yellow-colored liquid. The younger child would simply start mixing liquids from the three glasses in a haphazard manner until either he happened to stumble on the right combination, or just give up. Piaget labeled the underlying meaning-making *schema* that informs such an approach "concrete operational," referring to the fact that the child has to actually experiment in a *concrete* way, by manipulating things physically.

A child who has reached early adolescence takes a different approach; she realizes that in order to accomplish any such task, a generalizable experimental principle applies, namely that you have to try all the different combinations, a little bit at a time, until you get the result you're looking for. So, in this experiment, the older child would start by combining a little bit from glass A with a little bit from glass B; then A with C, and then B with C, and so on until she has achieved the sought-after yellow. The generalizable principle at work here is what Piaget termed a "formal operation," in that the child has in her mind a *schema* that formalizes the operation.[1] The older child is able to see the entire operation abstractly, and no longer relies solely on the *concrete*, physical manipulation of objects to carry out the experiment.

To be clear, when we talk about growing and evolving in the way we are doing here, we're not referring to intelligence per se. The seven-year-old who is able to see that the tall and thin beaker holds the same amount of liquid as the short and wide beaker is not necessarily *smarter* than the younger child who can't see that. It's just that the older child has developed a more complex inner meaning-making schema for seeing the world. This equips the older child to be able to deal with a previously unseen level of environmental complexity. Similarly, in the second example, the adolescent who is able to *formalize* the operation of the experiment is not smarter than the younger child who relies on *concrete* actions to conduct the experiment. The older adolescent simply has developed a greater complexity of mind—one that enables her to engage in a more complex world.

Of course, this process of *development*—of moving from less complex to more complex mental *schema*—continues throughout adulthood, with each developmental stage making possible a range of actions and competencies that were not possible previously. This capacity for developmental growth—for growing our *inner* complexity of mind—is essential for growing *Sense-and-Respond* leadership capability.

Meaning-Making and Action Logic

Whether as a child or as an adult, our meaning-making determines not only how we experience the world; it effectively determines the *actions* we are most likely to take in order to create impact in that world. In ordering and conditioning how we experience the world around us—how we understand things, how we feel about things, and even what we are able to actually *perceive*—the structure of our meaning-making effectively defines which actions do or don't *make sense* in a given situation.

In this way, the internal, mental activity of meaning-making is the source of what we've been calling our *Action Logic*. Action Logic brings the deeply psychological activity of meaning-making out into the world of action. In fact, it is William Torbert who coined the term in an effort to bring the concept of meaning-making—and the nuanced theory of adult development it encapsulates—into the world of organizational leadership.[16]

So, how does meaning-making show up in one's Action Logic?

Consider the example of an Agile delivery software team that works in an organization you are leading. This team has, for the third sprint[17] in a row, not delivered what they committed to, and it is causing headaches for business stakeholders. A range of possible actions that you, as team leader, might take comes to mind. That range of actions will be a product of how you are making meaning of the situation—your *Action Logic.*

- One structure, or grammar, that might be determining your internal meaning-making is *a concern for attaining near-term results.* Coming from such a place, you will be inclined to ignore larger or longer-term contextual issues related to how the team is doing overall in order to move to a more-or-less immediate solution of the problem. The resulting Action Logic would likely orient a range of actions that aim to find fast solutions in order to make immediate problems go away as quickly as possible. Under such an Action Logic, it might seem extremely reasonable, for instance, to somehow induce the team to work faster, perhaps even asking them to

---

[16] William Torbert in conversation with Jennifer Garvey-Berger, recorded November 2017. See also:
- Keith Merron, Dalmar Fischer, William Torbert, "Meaning-Making and Management Action," *Group and Organization Studies* 12, no. 3 (1987) (retrievable on March 23 2018 at: http://www.williamrtorbert.com/wp-content/uploads/2012/12/MngMkgMngtAction.pdf).
- David Rooke and William Torbert, "Organizational Transformation as a Function of CEO's Developmental Stage," *Organization Development Journal* 16, no. 1 (1998).
- Torbert, Fisher, and Rooke, *Action Inquiry.*

[17] A "sprint" is a term from the popular Agile practice framework of Scrum that describes a two- to three-week period during which a team works in a highly focused and uninterruptable manner to produce a small increment of potentially shippable work product. When a team plans for a single sprint, they make a commitment to realizing a particular *outcome* in terms of some specific kind of business value.

work some evenings and weekends in order to meet their commitments. After all, the internal logic will be saying, *they're* the ones who made the commitment to those goals and, being well-paid professionals, they need to take responsibility and do whatever it takes to meet their commitments.

- If, by contrast, the meaning-making structure that determines how you make sense of such situations tends to see events as part of a longer-term unfolding in which learning inevitably happens, and in which *team learning is a key longer-term goal*—the Action Logic it generates will orient a range of actions that aim to help the team find *their own* solutions. Under such an Action Logic, you might pose to the team, for instance, a set of intentionally reflective questions for them to ponder, and perhaps learn and grow from. Or you might simply tell them the impact of their pattern of behavior—that not delivering what they commit to is causing problems for product management—and then stand back and let the team work it out.

In this example, it would not be possible for a person holding the first meaning-making grammar (focused on near term results as opposed to the longer-term learning for the team) to frame an Action Logic in which posing reflective questions to the team would make sense. In fact, such a mode of action would, for such an Action Logic, be regarded as *nonsense*. It's not that a person holding such a form of meaning-making would overtly oppose taking a reflective, learning-enhancing approach. It is possible that, if pushed to do so, he or she might really try—but doing so would feel unreasonable and not quite right; it wouldn't quite make sense. Consequently, their approach would be somehow unconvincing, hollow, and ultimately not compelling.

All of this helps us have clearer insight into what might be going on, in people's minds, when they are not doing the things they know they should be doing. For instance, when a developer keeps forgetting to add automated unit tests to new code;[18] when a Product Manager (or for those who are using Scrum, a Product *Owner*) consistently fails to make timely decisions for a delivery team, even though he has been fully empowered and authorized to do so; when a manager keeps reverting back to command-and-control behavior, though she has just completed her class in facilitative management; when an executive leader makes decisions that generate unwanted side-effects that she somehow cannot see.

These are all occasions when the answer may not be more training, incentivizing, motivating, or inspiring. What's going on may have nothing to do with what individuals know, what they know they *should* do, nor even what they know *how* to do. Rather, what is happening is that the meaning-making structure of their Action Logic—that which informs and conditions the very nature of whatever knowing is going on—is simply not capable of generating the range of possible actions most pertinent to the situation.

> In order to increase competence and skillfulness to be able perform and to lead—whether within a delivery team or at the top of an organization—we have little choice: **We will need to grow the complexity of our meaning-making and Action Logic.**

---

[18] "Automated unit tests" refers to an Agile software engineering practice whereby a developer uses a tool to write small tests for small pieces of programming code that can be automatically run by the tool. Automated unit testing is a key Agile engineering practice that helps development teams test the quality and performance of their code automatically, without losing a lot of time having to do so *by hand.*

How Humans Develop

The good news is that minds can and do grow. We see this with our children and we even see it in ourselves and others around us. We just haven't had a way of explaining it because we haven't really had to. But now we have to, if we are to be deliberate and intentional about growing and evolving ourselves and others, as individuals, as organizations and even as societies; if we are to render ourselves better able to deal effectively with the challenges which our 21ˢᵗ century VUCA world confronts us with on a daily basis. We *need* to understand the nature of developmental growth in order to be able to deliberately facilitate that growth, both within ourselves and in others.

An entire branch of psychological research—which is finding more and more application in the field of leadership development—called *stage development theory* provides a wealth of insights and frameworks to help us. The research tells us a lot about the process of developmental growth—what actually happens, mentally (again, referring both to the cognitive and emotional domain of consciousness), as people grow developmentally. Understanding the nature of this process provides a foundation for approaching how we might facilitate developmental growth in ourselves and in others around us.

This research also tells us that as people develop, they move through developmental stages that can be observed and studied. Getting a feel for what each stage looks like, and how the sequence of stages unfolds over the course of a person's adult life, helps us see the range of developmental possibilities available. Perhaps more importantly, however, just reading about what different developmental stages are like can have the effect of *psycho-activating* development within ourselves. This principle will come into play later, when we come to the part of the book that goes into how to catalyze developmental growth in others.

The Process of Developmental Growth

Let's go first to the process of developmental growth from the perspective of developmental psychology.[19]

Recall that *developmental*—or *vertical*—growth is different than *learning*—or *horizontal* growth. Developmental growth occurs when there is some kind of shift in the way in which we make meaning of our day-to-day, moment-by-moment experience. Armed with what stage development theory teaches us, we can now say that that shift can happen when a discrepancy arises between what we expect in our surroundings—whether some pattern of events, situations, or other people's behaviors—and what is actually happening.[20]

In the normal course of events, things happen around us such that we are able to *assimilate* them into an already existing internal meaning-making schema. That is, we adjust our thoughts about the way things are around us in order to fit with our current understanding of them. The infant grabs a pacifier and starts to suck, assimilating it into its current grab-and-suck, meaning-making schema. The analyst comes into work today, as she has on previous days, and begins her workday, assimilating the various tasks of her day into her current meaning-making schema.

An *equilibrium* has been established between what we expect, as determined by our current meaning-making schema, and what actually happens in the environment around us. The skillfulness and competence of our actions are

---

[19] The following pages summarize a rich and extensive body of research on the process by which human beings grow developmentally. Among the major players who have led the way in this research, and whose specific works are cited elsewhere in this book and/or in the bibliography, are: Jean Piaget, Clare Graves, Jane Loevinger, Robert Kegan, Michael Basseches, Don Beck, Susanne Cook-Greuter, William Torbert, Bill Joiner, Paul Marko, John Manners, and Kevin Durkin. This body of work has had a powerful and very deep influence on all that I do in my work in helping people navigate—whether in one-on-one conversations or in larger organizational settings—the process of shifting their minds (whether as a consultant, coach, mentor, or trainer).

[20] The overall flow of the following explanation, and the infant examples given here, are drawn from Basseches, *Dialectical Thinking and Adult Development*.

52

well matched to the demands of our environment. We feel pretty solid in our ability to cope with whatever happens.

At some point, however, something new and unexpected happens—it could be a life-changing event, or it could be a tiny thing someone said in a meeting that triggered us somehow. In our effort to make sense of it—or to make sense of our experience of it—we find that we are less able to easily assimilate some aspect of what's happening into our current meaning-making schema. We find ourselves suddenly rendered unskillful, suddenly incompetent in some new and surprising way. We introduce a rattle to an infant, for instance, which is different than the pacifier she had previously encountered. The analyst comes into work one day and finds out that management has directed her team to shift to this new thing called "Agile" and that she now has a new role title—Product Owner—and that, moreover, the new process of requirements-gathering is being changed into something called "writing user stories," which the whole team will now be helping to create.

At such a moment, we have an experience of cognitive *disequilibrium*. Such an experience often fills us with some form of anxiety, unease, or confusion. The first thing we do is to look for a way to dispel that discomfort. The most common and natural way we do this is to try harder to assimilate the new situation to an already familiar internal schema—to somehow change some aspect of the outer situation to match our expectation. The infant tries to suck a little harder on the rattle in her old, familiar way; or the analyst works harder to fit her new role of Product Owner into the mold of the Analyst role with which she is more familiar, and to find more robust ways to maintain control of the requirements process in the midst of the apparent chaos of collaborative story writing.

At some point, however, our efforts at assimilating our environment to an already familiar internal schema begin to break down. The infant becomes more and more frustrated with the old sucking techniques, or the analyst becomes more and more stressed out in her attempts to protect her familiar role.

Inevitably, there comes a moment when one comes to the realization that the old schema—one's familiar way of thinking and of behaving—simply no longer works. That doing the same thing we did before, or trying harder, is no longer a winning strategy.

Developmental growth happens when, in the face of such a moment of cognitive disorientation, we choose to make some kind of adjustment—perhaps even just a small one—*within ourselves*. In psychological terms, this is referred to as *accommodation*: we change something within ourselves—within the way in which we habitually make meaning of the world around us—in order to accommodate to some (usually persistent) condition in our world. Specifically, we adjust some aspect of our inner meaning-making schema in an effort to acquire a fuller grasp of what's going on, and to gain a greater command of the situation as it is actually occurring. The infant adjusts its inner grab-and-suck schema, perhaps opening its mouth up wider, and placing its hands in a slightly different position on the rattle. Or, the analyst adjusts her inner attachment to her previously defined role when, for instance, she has a first glimmer that in this new working process she no longer has to figure everything out upfront.

Note that such an adjustment is not typically a one-time thing; it usually bears repeated exposure to the disorienting condition. The infant, for instance, doesn't figure out the new coping strategy right away; nor would it be typical for an analyst to suddenly give up her attachment to the more familiar requirements-gathering process in one fell swoop. This is an important point to bear in mind as we begin to think about the idea of creating environments that support growth and development in ourselves and in others—that such an environment needs to provide developmentally orienting (or, rather, *dis*-orienting) conditions that are deliberately structured for persistence over time. You will read much more about this in *Part III: The Deliberate Growing of Minds*.

In the process of better accommodating something within our inner meaning-making structure to a given situation, we find ourselves able to adopt new skills and competencies that are congruent with the new world that the adjustment in our meaning-making now makes possible. The uptick in the complexity and capability of our meaning-making links directly to a new range of skills and competencies that are now within reach. At some point, the infant now finds itself able to consciously "shake" the rattle and, being rewarded by a surprising but pleasurable sound, finds itself wanting to become more skillful—now seeking to practice shaking the rattle in order to leverage this newly won accommodation. Similarly, the analyst, armed with this new way of looking at the possibility of collaboration, finds herself newly able to gain a new level of skillfulness in collaboratively thinking through requirements with others—finding along the way a newly found pleasure in having other people to think things through with, and discovering, perhaps with surprise, the occasional fallibility of her own assumptions about the business they are in.

The Dialectic of Inner Growth

The relationship between vertical development and horizontal learning is key to understanding the nature of inner growth, and we now want to delve a little deeper into this relationship. A developmental shift, in which one accommodates some aspect of one's inner meaning-making schema to a novel situation, makes possible a new kind of skillfulness and competence. In fact, any learning that takes us into a new territory of skillfulness and competence requires some kind of developmental shift. The child cannot endeavor to learn more advanced arithmetic concepts without having developed the meaning-making capacity for durable categories, just as the young adult cannot learn how to write complex software without having embraced the meaning-making capacity for formal operations.

And yet, at the same time, the developmental shift that is required for the growing of a new class of skills and competencies (such as later arithmetic for the young child and complex programming for young adults) is itself advanced through the very acquisition of those new skills. As one grows new skills whose acquisition is made possible by a newly attained developmental shift (whether great or small), the new developmental stance is strengthened and solidified.

So, while the emphasis thus far has been on the primacy of developmental growth in relation to learning, it seems to be the case that inner growth requires learning—or horizontal growth—just as surely as it requires development—or vertical growth.

> Inner growth happens by virtue of a **dialectal play between vertical and horizontal growth**. Just as developmental growth precedes, and is a requirement for, the learning of new skills and competences—horizontal growth—so too does the development of new skills and

*competences contribute to developmental—or vertical—
growth.*

For instance, as a young child learns basic math skills, that learning deepens and sharpens his developmental grounding in the meaning-making structure of *durable categories*. Similarly, as the adolescent or young adult increases her skillfulness in programming, her developmental grounding in the meaning-making capacity for *formal operations* deepens and solidifies.

Let's examine a more complex example of how this dialectic between development (vertical growth) and learning (horizontal growth) relate to each other.

Imagine that you have arrived at a stage in your inner development (a shift along the vertical axis of your inner growth) where you've come to realize that the notion that you can only know yourself through private self-reflection is no longer valid—a significant shift in how one makes meaning in regard to oneself and a developmental milestone which generally occurs some time in adulthood. This realization leads you to conclude that your own, private perspective of yourself cannot take in the full picture of who you are—that in fact such a self-reflective myopia can open you up to a highly distorted view of yourself, severely limiting the effectiveness of your actions, and perverting your impact on others in your organizational environment. From this realization you begin to see that in order to get the full picture of who you are, you will need the perspective of others, specifically how others see you. For this you will need to solicit, and truly take in, other people's feedback.

Previously—from the perspective of a prior meaning-making perspective that determined how you saw yourself—you would have assessed the validity of others' feedback from the standpoint of whether it agreed with your own self-identity. If the feedback agreed with what you already knew about yourself, fine, you would accept it as valid. But if it didn't, then you would, in some way, reject it and even become defensive about it.

Now, as you view feedback through the lens of this newly developed meaning-making perspective, namely, that feedback is an avenue toward the increasing of your self-awareness, you realize that some of the best feedback you'll get is that with which you disagree. Therefore, you reason to yourself, the more feedback, the better.

But now something happens as you begin to solicit feedback from others: You realize, pretty quickly, that the actual doing of it is harder than you anticipated. This is especially true as you start to give others feedback—a practice, you surmise, would of course be welcome by them. In either case—whether receiving or giving feedback—you now start to find yourself in conversations that are more challenging and difficult than you would have ordinarily encountered before. People disagree with your feedback and get upset. Or, you yourself may receive feedback you find surprising and distressful. Either way, you find yourself facing new challenges—both psychological and emotional—that you are not likely to have faced before. This happens because by avoiding feedback in the past—or simply dismissing it altogether as invalid—those particular challenges just simply would not have arisen.

This is a classic example of the **dialectical** nature of inner growth: A new, developmental insight (which happens along the vertical axis of inner growth) prompts a new set of practices and behaviors you might now engage in, and new skills you might grow in yourself (all of which happens along the horizontal axis of inner growth). This quite naturally opens you up to new challenges—challenges that would not have arisen from actions and behaviors prompted by your previous developmental stance. To the degree that your way of responding to those new challenges is skillful, those new challenges become occasions that serve to deepen the developmental insight and to strengthen the developmental ground on which you now stand. Initially shaky and tentative developmental ground becomes more solid and stable as we, in our attempts to deal with the new challenges presented to us, continue to hone our skills and our behaviors.

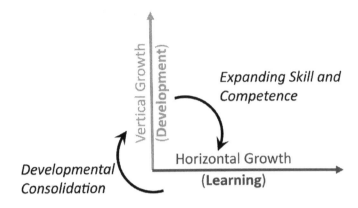

Figure 7: The Dialectical Interplay Between Vertical Growth and Horizontal Growth

This dialectical interplay between development and learning—between the growing of our complexity of meaning-making (developmental consolidation) and the skill and competence we are able to bring to bear in our actions (expanding skillfulness and competence)—is the very essence of inner growth.

Developmental growth and learning go hand-in-hand; inner growth results from both horizontal and vertical growth—and the capacity for inner growth is the foundation of the possibility for organizational transformation.

In *Parts III* and *IV*, where you will learn how to create environments that catalyze inner growth, you will be able to capitalize on this insight. For now, bear it in mind as I move on to describing the meaning-making *stages* individuals move through as they develop and learn.

Developmental Stages

Having delved quite deeply into the ***process*** of inner growth—and the *dialectical* interplay that constitutes its unfolding—we shall now turn to what the research can tell us about the ***stages*** we all move through as we develop over the course of many decades, and even an entire lifetime. Understanding what psychology can tell us about people's stages of developmental growth helps us see more clearly the different ways in which we make meaning of our world, and how the complexity of meaning-making can evolve. Understanding this provides necessary grounding for understanding how we might catalyze inner growth, whether in ourselves or in others, which is the basis of *Evolvagility*.

According to the research on stage development, development happens as individuals move through one particular set of meaning-making character-istics and constructions toward, and through, another, in the adaptive pro-cess by which we accommodate our inner meaning-making schema to an ever-emerging sense of the world around us. The meaning-making con-structions that arise along the way can be observed (and that's what stage development psychologists do: they observe the nature of individuals' psy-chological constructions)[21] to form themselves around distinct stages. Each such stage exhibits particular *structuring* characteristics that determine the complexity of the meaning-making and Action Logics it is able to produce.

Each successive stage carries increasing capacity for complexity, nuance, perspective-taking, and the holding of ever more complex and richer con-textual frames. Those operating primarily from earlier stages tend to hold less such capacity than those operating primarily from later ones. With re-spect to this aspect of stage development theory, researchers often use the terms "early stage," "middle stage," and "late stage" in referring to different tiers along the developmental path. There occurs a kind of bell curve as one traverses the sequence of stages, with a greater percentage of the adult pop-

---

[21] Typically, developmental researchers *observe* and study the nature of individu-als' psychological constructions through highly structured interview processes or through sentence- or task-completion activities. For a detailed account of how the developmental interview works and is structured, see Lisa Lahey, Emily Souvaine, Robert Kegan, Robert Goodman, and Sally Felix, *A Guide to the Subject-Object Interview: Its Administration and Interpretation* (Minds At Work, 2011). For a full account of the developmental sentence completion process, see Le Xuan Hy and Jane Loevinger, *Technical Foundations for Measuring Ego Development: The Wash-ington University Sentence Completion Test* (Lawrence Erlbaum Associates, 1998). For more on the use of task-completion activities as a way to study human devel-opment, see William Torbert, *Managing the Corporate Dream: Restructuring for Long-Term Success* (Irwin Professional Pub, 1987); also Clare Graves, ed. Chris Cowan and Natasha Todorovic, *The Never Ending Quest* (ECLET Publishing, 2005). If you wish to order this book, I suggest you order it directly from http://spiraldynamics.org/resources/books/.

ulation holding middle-stage meaning-making characteristics, while lower percentages hold for earlier and later stages.

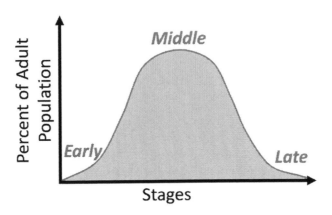

Figure 8: Action Logic Stage Percentages

A key aspect of this—one which we pointed out a moment and ago, to which we will return at several points in the remainder of Evolvagility—is that at any given stage, we consolidate our meaning-making capacity (vertical growth), with respect to that stage, through the growing of new skills and competencies that are informed by the meaning-making capacity we develop as we move toward and into that stage (horizontal growth). It is by this means that, as we pass from one stage to the next, we maintain rather than lose the capabilities given by previous stages. In fact, as we pass from one stage to the next, toward later and later stages, we become increasingly better able to hold—and grow skills and competencies that relate to—the positive capabilities of previous stages, while dropping their liabilities and weaknesses.

A final note on the principle of stage development: as we think about stage development in this way, bear in mind that movement from one stage to the next is a fluid process, with each stage holding gradations as we pass from one to the next. In fact, in most stage development theories, each stage shown comprises several *mini-stages*, in order to reflect this broader fluidity and gradation.[22]

---

[22] In his theory of stage development, Robert Kegan denotes these mini-stages through the use of a numbering scheme. For example, for the stage he calls "Self-Authoring Mind," he uses the number "4." Given this, entry into, through, and away from (moving toward the next stage "5") that stage is denoted by the following sequence of numbers: 4, 4(5), 4/5, 5/4, 5(4). Each mini-stage exhibits specific developmental qualities and characteristics. See Lahey, Souvaine, Kegan, Goodman, and Felix, *A Guide to the Subject-Object Interview: Its Administration and Interpretation*. See also Otto Laske, *Measuring Hidden Dimensions: The Art and Science of Fully Engaging Adults* (Laske and Associates, 2011). Meanwhile, Clare Graves names the mini-stages with respect to a given "value meme" as *First Awakening, Entering, Peak, Exiting* and *Fading Influence*. As with Kegan's numerological nomenclature, each mini-stage exhibits specific developmental qualities. See Don Beck and Chris Cowan, *Spiral Dynamics: Mastering Values, Leadership and Change* (Wiley-Blackwell, 1996).

The Developmental Journey

From the perspective of inner growth, we can begin to think of life as a developmental journey. From this perspective, we shift the narrative that describes that journey, from one defined as a series of events and situations that characterize the *outer* aspects of our life, to one that defines the unfolding of life as a series of stages of developmental perspective—the *inner* aspects of our life—with each stage able to hold greater and greater complexity.

The benefit of taking on such a reorientation for oneself, and of developing a way of seeing the entire course of one's life as a developmental journey, is that it helps us create a relationship with ourselves in which we see ourselves—our inner psychological and emotional selves—as ever-changing; to see, in our own lives, that the very essence of life is that it is ever-evolving, ever-expanding toward greater complexity, greater integration, and greater capacity.

To have such a way of relating to ourselves—and to others—acknowledges the transient nature of any particular meaning-making stance and recognizes that it is entirely possible to move beyond whatever limitations our meaning-making may impose on our capacity for effective action. It recognizes both the possibility and necessity of inner growth in the shaping of ourselves as leaders—whether we are the senior executive of a company or one of the people on our team who has taken a stand for something important to the team. Such an attitude toward our inner growth is the very foundation of deep leadership capability.

In the following pages, I will trace this developmental life journey through the lens of stage development theory.

The Journey Through Action Logic Stages

The particular stage-development theory on which we will trace this journey draws its Action Logic focus primarily from the work of Susanne Cook-

Greuter and William Torbert.[23] In the following pages, we will look at key Action Logic stages as they appear within most organizational settings. But first, I want to offer a couple of technical points as they apply specifically to the Action Logic stage theory of Cook-Greuter and Torbert.

First, the word "logic" in Action Logic is potentially misleading in that it suggests a solely logico-cognitive aspect of consciousness. An Action Logic reflects several aspects of consciousness: the **cognitive** (how we think); the **affective** (how we relate to and experience our feelings and emotions); and the **relational** (how we perceive and understand other people and our relationships with them).

Second, Action Logics are meaning-making structures that exist *within* human systems—whether individuals, collectives, or broader organizations. As such, it is somewhat inaccurate to describe an individual (or a team, or even an organizations) as *being* this or that Action Logic. Rather, people are able to *activate* within themselves, and to operate *from* a given Action Logic— or more accurately *a set* of Action Logics, drawing more from one or another in response to the particular demands of the moment.

Among the set of Action Logics one operates from, and is able to activate within themselves, there is one that forms a *center of gravity*—a developmental grounding where a person (or a group) tends to land developmentally more frequently and more strongly than others. However, this particular grounding is not where a person operates from at all times; it changes based on the situation. For instance, a person might shift to an earlier-stage Action Logic when feeling fearful, anxious, or otherwise stressed. In a similar fashion, one might stretch into later-stage Action Logics in those moments when they find themselves internally stronger and more resourceful

---

[23] See Torbert, Fisher, and Rooke, *Action Inquiry*. See also Cook-Greuter, "Nine Levels of Increasing Embrace in Ego Development." Note that though the stage-development theory that guides the approach taken in this book is grounded in the work of Torbert and Cook-Greuter, it is also strongly informed by the work of Robert Kegan, Bill Joiner, and Stephen Josephs. See Robert Kegan *The Evolving Self* and *In Over Our Heads: The Mental Demands of Modern Life* (Harvard University Press, 1998). See also Bill Joiner and Stephen Josephs, *Leadership Agility: Five Levels of Mastery for Anticipating and Initiating Change* (Jossey-Bass, 2006).

than usual—or when the situation *challenges* one to access those later-stage Action Logics. These movements across multiple Action Logics—whether we are shifting forwards or backwards developmentally—can happen within a mere moment, or over the course of weeks or months, or even years.

Developmental growth over the life span is a process by which we come to be able to activate within ourselves, and to operate from, increasingly later-stage Action Logics. However, to reiterate a point made earlier, as people grow, and as they become better able to incorporate into their sensemaking a more complex Action Logic, they don't "lose" the previously attained Action Logics. Rather, as people become able to activate within themselves, and with each other, new (and more complex) Action Logics, they add to a growing *vocabulary* of Action Logics they can now draw from. As this vocabulary grows, an ever-broader and ever more complex range of capabilities comes online, forming an ever-richer meaning-making foundation on the basis of which individuals (or groups) might now sense and act in the world.

I want to take a moment to emphasize this point. Often we think of a developmental journey as moving linearly through a sequence of stages of increasing complexity, nuance, and differentiation. However, though true, this way of conceptualizing developmental growth is overly linear and deterministic. Developmental growth happens through an increase in developmental *range*—an increase in the number of different Action Logics from which one's meaning-making, at any given moment, can draw. This is where the concept of an Action Logic *vocabulary* has particular bearing: Even though a person's developmental center of gravity might reside at a particular stage, it is possible for them to draw on later-stage Action Logics when the situation or occasion calls for it, just as they are able to draw on earlier-stage Action Logics (when the situation or occasion calls for it). And, in like fashion, groups may also develop the ability to draw from alternate Action Logics at different times or in different contexts.

With this point in mind, the questions become: How capable are we to draw from later stage Action Logics? To what degree do the situations and social structures in which we find ourselves call forth and, in some way, nurture the development of those later-stage Action Logics? This becomes especially salient when later on, in Parts III and IV, we talk about how we can be deliberate about growing and developing ourselves and others.

Bearing in mind the fluid nature of moving between Action Logics, let's move on to the Action Logic stages themselves. In what follows, I will provide a summary of the high-level, and longer term, potential developmental shifts of mind that unfold as a person moves through these Action Logic stages over the course of an adult life-span.

The following pages provide short descriptions of each Action Logic typically found within a professional organizational environment. Not included are earlier Action Logics found exclusively in childhood; nor are later Action Logics shown—ones that are rarely if ever found in modern organizational environments.

Each Action Logic[24] is described in terms of the nature of the meaning-making that underlies that Action Logic and the actions it is able to skillfully take (and *not* take). In addition, the brief meaning-making characterizations for each Action Logic are given in terms of three dimensions referred to above: *cognitive, affective,* and *relational.*

I invite you to read through the following to get a sense of the longitudinal progression of a mind as it evolves over many decades, perhaps even an entire life span, in its capacity to embrace ever-greater complexity.

---

[24] The descriptions of these Action Logic stages are derived from Cook-Greuter, "Nine Levels of Increasing Embrace in Ego Development" and from Torbert, Fisher, and Rooke, *Action Inquiry.* Note that the actual names for these Action Logic stages vary depending on the context of their use. For instance, Cook-Greuter employs different names than does Torbert, since hers is a more overtly psychological research context. Torbert himself has very recently changed the names of some of his later-stage Action Logics—he now refers to what he once called the "Individualist" Action Logic as "Redefining" and, in a similar fashion, his previously-named "Strategist" is now called "Transforming." See William Torbert, "The Pragmatic Impact on Leaders & Organizations of Interventions Based in the Collaborative Developmental Action Inquiry Approach," *Integral Leadership Review* (August-November 2017).

Opportunist Action Logic

Worldview

Traditional

How it Makes Meaning

COGNITIVE: Things are cut and dry, black and white; "Me against the world"; problems are caused by others or by a hostile world.

AFFECTIVE: Confidence in self is fragile; unable to see into its own emotions; highly reactive, emotionally.

RELATIONAL: Others are solely vehicles for its gains; unilateral control; relationships are constituted in terms of power; unaware of and insensitive to others' feelings.

What it Can and Cannot Do

It can:

- Take courageous action
- Cut to the chase in the face of an emergency

It cannot:

- Take responsibility for its impact
- Hold a long-term view
- Organize itself around strategic or even tactical goals
- Work effectively with others

Diplomat Action Logic

Worldview

Traditional and/or Modernist

How it Makes Meaning

COGNITIVE: The world consists of simple categories; "*Us* (no longer *Me*) against the world"; blindly conformist; tendency toward convention and clichés; values only the exterior, concrete world of facts.

AFFECTIVE: Strong need to be accepted and look good; sense of identity tied to important others; intolerant of negative feelings; projects (fake) positivity.

RELATIONAL: Others are the source of its own validation; emotional fusion with others (feeling needy), hence can't see them for who they are independent of itself; nevertheless, highly sensitive to others' feelings (unlike Opportunist).

What it Can and Cannot Do

It can:

- Prove to be very reliable and loyal
- Be tactful and respectful of others' feelings
- Reason logically, though in a limited way

It cannot:

- Think for itself or outside the box
- Give/receive feedback
- Tolerate perspectives different than those of its identified group
- Deliver bad news to others
- See the bigger picture

Expert Action Logic

Worldview

Modernist

How it Makes Meaning

COGNITIVE: The world is complicated, not simple; stability and certainty in its perspective; highly capable of abstract operations; values only that which is objectively measurable; can dig deep but not wide

AFFECTIVE: Strong need to be seen as self-sufficient and exceptional; high moral standards; perfectionist; self- and other-critical; ultra-rational; identifies with its craft or expertise

RELATIONAL: Sees others as genuinely distinct from itself, with distinct needs; nevertheless, others must prove themselves; others are variables in its designs; sees others in terms of character traits but not anything much deeper

What it Can and Cannot Do

It can:

- See different alternatives
- Exercise high degrees of expertise—great subject-matter expert (SME) material
- Think in highly logical and abstract way
- See others as distinct from itself

It cannot:

- See the bigger picture (lost in detail)
- See others as potentially valuable contributors to one's plans
- Deal easily with complexity and paradox

Achiever Action Logic

Worldview

Modernist and/or Postmodernist

How it Makes Meaning

COGNITIVE: Sees that the world is complex; can see the bigger picture, but with a single fixed-point perspective; sees people's aspirations and motivations as important, not just data; values both quantitative and qualitative aspects of reality; looks for root causes, not just surface details

AFFECTIVE: More self-aware and able to see patterns of its emotions; able to deal with a variety of its own emotions; high self-management; values self-knowledge and inner growth

RELATIONAL: Sees others as genuinely distinct from itself, with distinct needs; sees others as needed contributors; able to feel genuine compassion for others; can see others in terms of deep, innate qualities

What it Can and Cannot Do

It can:

- Not only see, but also value, different alternatives
- Let others lead through their expertise
- Enroll and engage a variety of stakeholders in larger, more complex projects, across a variety of time horizons
- Collaborate well with others

It cannot:

- See beyond its own conceptual view
- Integrate the thinking of others into its own thinking
- Unlock itself from its goals; it sticks to its goals no matter what

Individualist Action Logic

Worldview
Post-Modernist

How it Makes Meaning

COGNITIVE: Reality is interpreted, not given; inner thoughts and feelings are now valid aspects of reality; holistically oriented; scrutinizes conventional thinking; distrusts purely rational thinking

AFFECTIVE: Highly engaged in inner growth process; focus on being and feeling; high self-awareness of inner emotional patterns and of body/mind connections; "life is a journey"; it now recognizes the disparate parts that constitute its inner world (something previous Action Logics can't do), but this recognition causes anxiety

RELATIONAL: Looks for and celebrates difference and diversity in others; sees others as ever changing, not fixed; can see the nuances that define how others see the world.

What it Can and Cannot Do

It can:

- Incorporate multiple perspectives in a constructive manner
- Sense-and-Respond to what is going on more readily than previous Action Logics
- Lead from behind; it doesn't have to be in front to lead
- Let go of many of its fixed perspectives

It cannot:

- Stand firm when needed (too concerned with including others)

- Always move away from its fascination for paradox, difference, and the centrality of one's inner process when needed

Strategist Action Logic

Worldview

Post-Modernist

How it Makes Meaning

COGNITIVE: Sees the world around it in terms of the complexity of ever-evolving interrelated systems of processes, contexts, and relationships; deeply connected to sense of purpose, while not being attached to a particular way in which it should be fulfilled; thinking is permeable to the thinking of others, and to other perspectives, more generally

AFFECTIVE: Like Individualist, very engaged in growth process, but less fixated on it; it is able to integrate paradox and ambiguity into its sensemaking; it is also far better able to integrate those disparate parts of itself that cause those at previous Action Logics anxiety or to project unwanted parts of themselves on to other people

RELATIONAL: Sees the differing perspectives of others as essential to its own definition of self; has faith in others' capacity to work out their own inner struggles while willing and able to help them do that

What it Can and Cannot Do

It can:

- Remain calm and grounded in the face of volatility, uncertainty, change, and ambiguity

- Acknowledge and own its own shadow elements, reduce its tendency to project unwanted aspects of self on others
- See the larger system, and help others in seeing it
- Stand firm when needed; less prone to habitually resort to preferred leadership styles

It cannot:

- Easily move away from its principled indignation at the injustices and incongruities it sees in the world around it. This can sometimes leave people with an impression of dogmatism.

From Traditional to Modernist to Postmodernist

If we zoom out from the details of Action Logic stages in the above sequence to take in the longer-term developmental horizon, three fundamental worldviews[25] come into focus: **Traditionalist, Modernist,** and **Postmodernist.**[26] While each of these constitutes a phase along the developmental journey (with each *phase* comprising a sub-sequence of developmental

---

[25] A *worldview* is "the fundamental cognitive orientation of an individual or society encompassing the whole of the individual's or society's knowledge and point of view" (Wikipedia entry for "worldview" retrieved on April 9, 2018 from https://en.wikipedia.org/wiki/World_view.)

[26] It is worth noting, especially for the reader who is aware of Spiral Dynamics and the work of Don Beck, Chris Cowan, and Clare Graves, that there is indeed a rough correspondence between *Traditionalist, Modernist,* and *Postmodernist* worldviews and the *Blue, Orange,* and *Green* value memes as defined in that work. In Part V we will come back to these within the context of organizational leadership and organizational culture. Meanwhile, for more on value memes, see Beck and Cowan, *Spiral Dynamics.* See also Frederic Laloux, *Reinventing Organizations: A Guide to Creating Organizations Inspired by the Next Stage of Human Consciousness* (Nelson Parker, 2014).

stages), we can also look at them as canonic styles of thinking and relating to one's world that are reflected in individuals, but also more broadly in different kinds of *cultures*.

These styles and cultures are easily recognizable—both within ourselves and in the world around us—by anyone. And they figure powerfully in the different ways in which individuals understand and constitute themselves, both in relation to themselves and in relation to the world in which they live. These different ways of thinking can be regarded as schools of thought—specifically as it relates to the nature of organizations, human performance, management, and motivation—that both individuals *and organizations* draw upon as they set about designing the structures, processes, and rules (almost always unconsciously applied and held) by which people define behavior and practices.

If we trace the qualities of each of these worldviews, and of their evolution, not only can we get a feel for the broader developmental arc described by the Action Logic stages. We also get a glimpse, more specifically, into the nature of three different worldviews when it comes to how people—and the organizations they define—understand and define themselves.

The Traditionalist Worldview

The **Traditionalist** worldview holds a conformist view of reality, oriented around the idea that there is a single right way to do things, that there exists a higher authority (boss, religious leader, or political leader) to whom we look for direction, and that stability and order are to be valued above all else. The values its holds are what define us as a group; those who do not hold those values are viewed as fundamentally wrong, and inherently illegitimate.

The healthy and enabling aspect of the Traditionalist worldview is its stabilizing and powerfully socializing force. It is the stabilizing glue that keeps things together and the necessary base predictability that tells us, for instance, that a red light at the current intersection means the same thing as it does at the *next* intersection. It is the basis for much of what we currently rely on in our day-to-day life.

However, as is the case with any worldview, the Traditionalist worldview has its limitations. One of the main limitations of the Traditionalist worldview is its allergy to change, its unwillingness to recognize perspectives different than its own, and its tendency toward fixed and rigid structures (which often manifests through the exercise of bureaucratic mechanisms in larger organizational settings). Any form of innovation is virtually impossible, since innovation means change, and it also means that someone (at least *one* someone) needs to be willing to take a risk and do something differently. This is very hard for a Traditionalist mind.

The Traditionalist worldview encompasses the *Opportunist, Diplomat,* and early *Expert* Action Logics.

The Modernist Worldview

As a mind, or a set of minds, passes from the territory of Traditionalist thinking—defined by *Opportunist, Diplomat* and early *Expert* Action Logics—into later *Expert,* and then into *Achiever* and early *Individualist* Action Logics, it gains a completely new capability that is of critical importance to the functioning of the modern organization, and even to the very existence of modern society as we know it. That capability arises when a mind is able to move beyond the myopic view of "me" and "us" and of the supremacy of higher authority, and to be able to see one's world *objectively,* where rational thought reigns supreme.

This is what the **Modernist** worldview looks like. Viewed historically, the emergence of this quality of mind—which began to emerge during that period in history we often call "The Enlightenment"—brought about the arts and sciences as we now know them, along with myriad technologies and professional distinctions that form the very foundation of both the modern organization, and modern civilization more generally.

At the level of the individual, the emergence of this quality of mind brings with it the capacity for reasoning, for planning, and for working (albeit to a rather limited extent) with others, regardless of whether they think the way we think and value the things that we value. It is the ability to understand the nature of cause-and-effect, and, on the basis of that understanding, make elaborate plans. It is the birthplace of structures and reliable systems. It is also the birthplace of innovation and of specialized knowledge. Without the existence of the Modernist worldview, the modern corporation as we know it would not exist. Nor would the wealth it generates, which makes possible all manner of good things we enjoy today.

Those are the *enabling* aspects of the Modernist worldview. Among its *limitations* is the fact that it cannot see beyond its own view, especially its reliance on rational thinking and specialized knowledge. Only that which can be measured is considered to be real. Consequently, it discounts emotions, intuition, and spiritual insight as unscientific and hence invalid—potentially alienating itself from key sources of information. It's emphasis on expertise and specialization yields highly siloed organizational environments. All of these limiting qualities—and more—make it very difficult for a Modernist mind to deal with the nuances, vagaries, and complexities of a VUCA world.

Moving into a New Territory: The Postmodernist Worldview

As we continue to traverse the path of development toward increasingly complex Action Logics—reflected in late *Individualist* and *Strategist* Action Logics—we move into a very new territory: **Postmodernist**.

As mind reaches into Postmodernist territory, its perspective-taking capacity moves into a new dimension. In order to more clearly distinguish the Postmodernist mind from that which precedes it, we need to point to a key perspective held by the Modernist mind. This view—sometimes referred to as the *representation paradigm*—holds that there is a clear separateness between the interior world of the mind and the exterior world of observable objects and things. Underlying this baseline assumption is an even more fundamental assumption, which is the assumption of reality as essentially preexistent and external to ourselves. Such a separate and self-contained world is composed of permanent, well-defined objects that we can investigate, analyze, and control for our benefit and in alignment with our goals and objectives.[27] These objects have an existence that is completely separate from, and untouched by our own consciousness, by our own way of looking

---

[27] Paraphrased from Cook-Greuter, "Nine Levels of Increasing Embrace in Ego Development," p. 7.

at them. Moreover, the universe in which these objects live is inherently orderly and linearly causal—a kind of gigantic "clockwork."

In short, the Modernist mind—late *Expert, Achiever*, and early *Individualist* Action Logic stages—informs what philosophers of science refer to as the *Newtonian Paradigm*. Based on classical physics, as epitomized by the physicist Isaac Newton, it is a *metaphysical* position—which means that it forms the deep assumptions on which we base our common-sense view of reality—which is ingrained in the institutions that we live by, and into the very psychological fabric that defines how we view, and relate to, our world.

As we move into the realm of the Postmodernist mind, a very different picture of reality takes shape, specifically as it relates to the nature of reality itself. In the Modernist mind, reality is something *given*. In the Postmodernist mind, reality is something *made*. In the Modernist mind, *how* we think and see the world are products of *what* we perceive "in the world." In the Postmodernist mind, this is flipped. Here, *what* we perceive "in the world" is a product of *how* we think and *how* we see the world—with regards to our meaning-making, whether as individuals or as collectives.

As we grow in our development through different Action Logic stages of increasingly complex meaning-making, it is not that we simply gain a different, more complex "picture" of a persistent, unchanging, already-existent world. Rather, different Action Logics—and the worldviews they produce—themselves generate different worlds in the sense that, if for no other reason, the actions I take—inevitably informed by an Action Logic schema—have the capacity to create something that didn't previously exist in the world.[28]

---

[28] This worldview is reflected in emerging sciences that increasingly reflect a view of the world (and of the universe) that is complex and non-linear; a world that is in great part determined by the tools and methods by which we observe it; in which time and space are seen as illusory; in which social contexts determine subjectivity; in which systems *emerge* (and are not *pre-formed*) from the ever-changing and unfolding of the interactions of the agents by which they are constituted. See the bibliography for a (short) list of resources on this broad range of topics.

From Predict-and-Plan to Sense-and-Respond—Revisited

All of this gives a new, perhaps *deeper*, angle on what we mean when we talk about the shift from *Predict-and-Plan* to *Sense-and-Respond*.

> The **Traditionalist** worldview, and the Action Logics in which it is reflected, is the metaphysical mooring on which rests what is often called the "Command-and-Control" mind.
>
> The **Modernist** worldview, and the Action Logics in which it is reflected, is the metaphysical mooring on which rests the Predict-and-Plan mind.
>
> The **Postmodernist** worldview, and the Action Logics in which it is reflected, is the metaphysical mooring on which rests the Sense-and-Respond mind.

The *Postmodernist* mind is able to observe the quality of its own *sensing*, the quality of its own *sensemaking*, and the impact these have on what seems to be happening around it, and to adjust that sensing and thinking accordingly. The depth of this capability depends upon the particular Action Logic stage; later-stage *Postmodernist* Action Logics are better able to do this. The Postmodernist mind is able to see its own meaning-making as an inherent part of the system we need to pay attention to and an inherent part of the system we need to tune and adjust.

This capacity is key to the nature of the inner operating system upgrade called for if we are to grow our capacity for *Sense-and-Respond* leadership. It is the capacity to stand back and *observe* not only *what* we do, but—more importantly—*how* we do it. It is the ability to observe, and then adjust the parameters of how we are seeing the world in order to be able to see the bigger picture, the greater complexity, of the world around us (and *within* us).

It is this capacity that makes possible real *transformation* in a human system. In the way that I am using the term here, *transformation* is the capacity for a system to not just change another system; it is the capacity of a system to change something *in itself*, and in doing so, making possible conditions that allow that other system to change *itself*.

> I assert that it is this capacity for creative and transformative leadership—a shift from a Modernist to a Postmodernist manner of thinking—that is needed if we are to be able to catalyze—both within oneself and in others—our ability to effectively sense and respond in a VUCA world.[29]

The nature of the situations and challenges that arise within a VUCA world requires the *Postmodernist* capacity to hold multiple perspectives. We must learn to let go of our attachment to the "one right way" (e.g., "best practices"), and to recognize the fallibility and the limitations of purely rational thinking. To embrace the broader intelligence gained from the trans-rational and the intuitive is to acknowledge that reality is complex and messy and, therefore, the effort to *solve* reality is not an effective strategy long-term. We must be able to see that the way in which we make meaning of any situation figures prominently in the very constitution of that situation, and realize that reality is as much *made* as it is *found*.

The remainder of this book is designed to help you navigate the shift in mind from the **Modernist** worldview—reflected mainly when activation of the *Expert* and *Achiever* Action Logics predominates, and which constitutes the worldview that informs Predict-and-Plan—to the **Postmodernist**

---

[29] This assertion is borne out by a considerable body of research on the relationship between inner complexity of mind and effectiveness in leadership in an ever-changing world. See Anderson and Adams, *Mastering Leadership*; Joiner and Josephs, *Leadership Agility*; David Rooke, "Organizational transformation requires the presence of leaders who are Strategists and Magicians," *Organizations and People* 4 (1997); and Rooke and Torbert, "Organizational Transformation as a Function of CEO's Developmental Stage." You might also check out the extensive research of Clare Graves, which shows strong correlations between general task effectiveness and developmental stage. This research is documented in Graves, ed. Cowan and Todorovic, *The Never Ending Quest*.

worldview—reflected when activation of the *Individualist* and *Strategist* Action Logics become more prevalent, and which constitutes the worldview that informs *Sense-and-Respond*.

Toward this end, we will, in the following chapters, address perhaps the central question of this whole book:

How can we grow our minds?

PART III

The Deliberate Growing of Minds

In Part III, we explore what it would look like to grow our (and others') minds, and what it would take to create the conditions in which this can happen. We first introduce what the research in facilitating inner growth can tell us. From this, we establish a baseline set of principles on which we can then build a set of key design principles for creating and nurturing what I call a *deliberately developmental ecosystem*. What are the key features of such a deliberately developmental ecosystem? What are the key qualities of the practices and conditions in such an ecosystem? These are among the key questions fully addressed in Part III.

Being Deliberate About Development

Let's take a moment and briefly reflect back on all that you've read so far.

From the beginning, I've been saying that *Sense-and-Respond* organizations are a product of *Sense-and-Respond* leadership, which, as we're defining it, is an *everywhere* phenomenon, not just something that happens at the top. The kind of leadership we're talking about here shows up in individuals; it shows up in relationships; it shows up everywhere across the organization. It is what I've been calling "small-l" or everywhere leadership.

In the book's introduction, I defined "small-l" *Sense-and-Respond* leadership as that which happens when individuals, everywhere, are willing to take responsibility for their world, are guided by a deep sense of inner purpose, are willing to recognize and evolve beyond the limitations of their current Action Logic profile, and have the capacity to create not just new things (e.g., products and services), but new ways of *thinking*, new ways of *relating*, and new ways of *organizing*—all in order to think and act effectively in the face of VUCA.

When such a leadership capacity arises throughout an organization (though, not necessarily in every single person)—that is, when it becomes an *everywhere* phenomenon—a more solid foundation of capability is laid down for accessing and setting the conditions for a broader organizational agility. As was said earlier on, *Sense-and-Respond* organizations emerge from *Sense-and-Respond* minds—from the *inside out*.

At the source of *Sense-and-Respond* leadership, therefore, is the complexity with which one is able to make sense of one's world—both cognitively *and* emotionally—and the deeper, *inner*, Action Logic and meaning-making structures that determine that sensemaking. Our inner development unfolds through a sequence of Action Logic stages, each such stage organized around a more complex, diverse, and contextually rich meaning-making schema than the previous stage. As we develop, we grow the number of Action Logics we are able to access at any given moment and, in effect, grow an ever-richer *vocabulary* of Action Logics from which we may draw. In this way, we gradually advance through stages of increasing complexity in our meaning-making. With the development of an ever-richer Action Logic vocabulary—and our advance through stages of increasing meaning-making complexity—comes growth in our capacity for skillful action and adept behavior.

Such growth—both *vertical* and *horizontal*—is key to developing our capacity for *Sense-and-Respond* leadership. Such a capacity rests in our ability to activate within ourselves the developmental vocabulary of late *Achiever*, *Individualist*, and beyond—that is, to ground ourselves within a Postmodernist worldview. Without such a deeply grounded inner capacity, our power in the face of VUCA is severely diminished—a diminished power that is manifested both at the individual and at the organizational level.

We Must Be Deliberate About Inner Growth

What we know is that most people in most organizational settings don't yet have the capacity to readily activate within themselves late *Achiever* and *Individualist* Action Logics, nor are they able to exhibit the skills that those later-stage Action Logics enable. In fact, what the developmental psychology research shows is that the center of gravity for most people within most workplace environments rests predominantly within *Expert* or *Achiever*—the center of the Modernist worldview and of the Predict-and-Plan model of organizational management that so predominates today's organizations.[30] This should come as little surprise: It stands to reason that organizations whose predominant management paradigm rests in Predict-and-Plan—and

---

[30] For instance, Bill Joiner and Stephen Josephs estimate that within most organizational settings, approximately 45% operate predominantly from an *Expert* Action Logic stage, while 35% do so from an *Achiever* stage; only about 12% operate predominantly from *Individualist* and beyond (the remaining roughly 8% operate primarily from *Diplomat*). Note that this doesn't mean that others outside that 12% are unable to access within themselves those later-stage Action Logics; it merely means that only about 12% have those as their developmental center of gravity. Note, too, that these distributions change with different populations within a given organization; for instance, we're likely to see more people operating at *Individualist* and beyond as we enter the upper echelons of senior organizational leaders. See also Anderson and Adams, *Mastering Leadership*, for similar conclusions, based on a database of tens of thousands, and also Rooke and Torbert, "Organizational Transformation as a Function of CEO's Developmental Stage."

the Modernist worldview that it reflects—would promote and activate Action Logics congruent with that paradigm and that worldview.

In order to fully grasp the implication of this notion and why we need to think about it, it will be helpful to briefly consider the social factors that come into play in a person's inner development. Social environments regulate the prevalence of, and activate the emergence of, particular Action Logic vocabularies. This is as true of the elementary school—an environment intended to activate and nurture particular Action Logic vocabularies in children—as it is of the college and university, which serve to do the same with respect to young adults. It is also true of modern organizations in which people work, whether it is a bank or a police department. Organizational environments that are heavily grounded within a command-and-control kind of culture, for instance, tend to create conditions that activate and sustain earlier Action Logics, such as *Opportunist, Diplomat,* and early *Expert.* In a similar way, organizations that are centered within a Predict-and-Plan culture tend to generate conditions more favorable to the activation and sustaining of *Expert* and *Achiever* Action Logics.

We can see this dynamic concretely when we consider, for instance, the drivers behind employee recruitment and retention. Companies tend to hire, retain, and reward people who are best able to activate within themselves—and to act skillfully from the perspective of—Action Logics that are most resonant with the dominant culture which that company promulgates. When they work well, hiring processes are entirely congruent with the dominant organizational culture and the worldview on which that culture is founded, as are the policies and practices that determine compensation, bonuses, and promotion. This is how companies consolidate their effectiveness as organizations—by creating structures, systems, and cultural conditions that strengthen and solidify particular Action Logics and Action Logic vocabularies.

Now, while organizational environments determine particular Action Logic vocabularies, the reverse is also true: The Action Logic vocabularies which a given social environment most powerfully activate serve to maintain the status quo which defines that very social environment. The causation is circular and inherently reinforcing. Those Action Logics favored in an organizational culture become the very grounding of that culture, reinforcing and strengthening that culture through the predominant meaning-making schema those Action Logics generate, and the kinds of habits, beliefs, values, and practices that those meaning-making schema produce. In this way, you could say that organizational culture arises through reinforcing psychological, behavioral, and relationship patterns engendered by a human system's predominant Action Logics—while, at the same time and by the very same process, those predominant Action Logics are made all the more predominant through reinforcing structural, situational, and systematizing patterns of the organizational culture; in other words, a self-reinforcing circular loop.

What we need—those of us who wish to claim our leadership in a VUCA world—is a way in which we might deliberately re-orchestrate this dynamic in order to bring about the emergence of a new kind of **organization**—a new kind of culture—by bringing about a new kind of **mind**, and vice-versa. What worked throughout the second half of the 20th century is becoming increasingly untenable as we continue onward into the 21st century. The Predict-and-Plan organizational culture, and the predominant Action Logics congruent with that model—primarily *Expert* and *Achiever*—flail in the face of VUCA.

In order for organizations to operate effectively in this VUCA world of ours, we need to create conditions that are deliberately intended to promote and stimulate the ability for people to activate within themselves, and in each other, late *Achiever* and *Individualist* vocabularies and beyond. This is not to say that *everyone* in an organization needs to have a center of gravity that is grounded in those later-stage Action Logics. Rather, it is to say only that some number of people, across all levels and from all walks of life within a given organization—from product delivery team-members to top-level executive leaders, from QA engineers to customer service reps—are able to access and activate within themselves qualities, and congruent skills, that reflect the capabilities of those later-stage Action Logics.

How many people, or what percentage of a given population, this will entail will of course depend on the organization and the nature of the business, market, and technological challenges it faces. Peter Block—teacher, consultant, and author of numerous books on leadership and organizational change—used to say that in order to create conditions that favor deep systemic change in an organization you only need a quorum of about 20% of a given population who are able to embody the capabilities and qualities congruent with the desired change.[31] As long as some number of those people hold top-level leadership positions, such a quorum is sufficient; these people become powerful catalyzers of change by virtue of their passion, their ability to influence others, and their capacity to fully embody not only a new way of *doing*, but a new way of *being*. To be sure, there are other factors that come into play—factors that will be explored more fully in Part V, *The Role of Organizational Leadership and Management*.

In order to create conditions that deliberately promote and stimulate the ability for people to activate within themselves, and in each other, late *Achiever* and *Individualist* vocabularies and beyond—to develop within themselves, that is, the capacity for *Sense-and-Respond* leadership—we need to change the way in which we design organizational environments to one where we value the growth of people's *inner* capabilities as much as we value the growth of people's *outer* competencies.

In the following pages, we investigate what it means to do precisely that: to be *deliberate* about growing the capacity to activate, within ourselves and in others, inner Action Logic vocabularies reflective of late *Achiever, Individualist* and beyond. Here, I use the term "deliberate" to describe an approach to organization development[32] that focuses specifically on leveraging the power that our inner meaning-making schema exerts on human performance, and how we can help raise the level of our performance by raising the complexity of our inner meaning-making. In *Evolvagility*, performance specifically means the ability to perform intelligently and skillfully in the face of VUCA—the very conditions we face in any organizational setting or industry in which people create new products, especially those involving high tech, and in which markets are ever-changing and ever-evolving.

---

[31] There are some studies—notably those from Stanford University—that tell us that when only 5% of a given population—whether an organization or a society—accepts a new idea, it becomes *embedded*, and when 20% adopt the idea, it becomes *unstoppable*. See Everette Rogers, *Diffusion of Innovations* (Free Press, 2005). Also see the audio book by Peter Block, *The Right Use of Power: How Stewardship Replaces Leadership* (Sounds True, 2002).

[32] As laid out in Kegan and Lahey, *An Everyone Culture*, in which the authors coin the phrase "deliberately developmental organization."

In being deliberate about inner development, we're talking about creating *conditions* that help promote and evolve the inner meaning-making capacity of individuals, collectives (two or more people who are in some way working together on a common goal), and organizational systems. We're also talking about adopting *practices* and creating *occasions* that work together to support this development. Let's take a moment to consider these in turn.

Conditions refer to our environment and may take the form of expectations, commitments, or challenges. For example, we may now be expected to regularly give each other feedback, which at once raises the possibility of greater openness in our relationships, while also helping us see more clearly the impact we have on others (of which we may ordinarily be unconscious). Or perhaps we make commitments that *stretch* what we currently see as possible for ourselves, for example, "I commit to giving two public talks per quarter in order to help me move past my fear of public speaking." A commitment works when it is communicated to another person, who will hold me accountable to the commitment I've made; a commitment that I make to myself has little power. Challenges force us to up the level of our game. For example, one could ask an Agile software delivery team to increase their velocity by 30% over the next quarter, while also increasing one of their quality metrics by 20%. If posed as a *developmental* challenge, not a *performance* challenge, it can help us think very differently about how we work, not force us to work faster.

Practices are the things that we *do*. As we practice a new skill, we experience a shift in the inner meaning-making apparatus by which we make sense of things and relate to others in our world. Practices have the developmentally catalyzing potential to psycho-activate inner development. For example, when people learn professional coaching skills[33] their view of themselves and others shifts. They now start to see people (including themselves) less as fixed entities, and more as being in an ever-unfolding process in which who they are is ever-changing and evolving. They also are more apt to rec

---

[33] I use the term "professional coaching skills" in the way we have adopted the term within Agile Coaching Institute's programs: It refers to coaching as it is defined within the International Coach Federation (ICF), and as it relates to an entire profession, from personal "life" coaching to "executive" coaching.

ognize the fact that their perspective on things is always and only but *one* perspective.

Giving "impact feedback" is another example of a practice.[34] Giving and receiving impact feedback activates a significant shift in mind, which is a greater sense of responsibility for impact on others, and a greater degree of personal openness and vulnerability to share with another—in a potentially difficult moment—one's own inner thoughts. It also induces a frame of mind in which we take responsibility for our *own* experience, and for caring enough about the integrity of our relationships that we are willing to risk having a potentially difficult conversation for the sake that integrity.

Occasions are temporary events that are designed to catalyze some new insight, whether for individuals or for an entire group. A training event is one common kind of occasion. Graduation or award ceremonies are special occasions that have specific symbolic power by celebrating growth in people's developmental journey.

Throughout the remainder of Part III, our quest will be to address the following questions:

> *What are the practices, conditions, and occasions we need to create in order to facilitate, and even accelerate, development within ourselves and in others?*
>
> *How do we activate within ourselves and each other Action Logic vocabularies that characterize late Achiever, Individualist, and beyond?*

---

[34] "Impact feedback" is a way of giving another person feedback that is based on one's *experience* of a particular behavior. A common format for giving *impact feedback* is: "When you said/did X, the impact on me was Y." An example: "When you repeated my name several times just now, [the impact on me was that] I felt like I was being reprimanded." This important skill will be covered in some depth in Part IV.

Pointing the Way: Research-Based Concepts

Let's review what is already known about how to create the levers and structures that can help us fashion environments that facilitate development—within ourselves, within others, and across human systems. There exists a fairly rich body of research that builds on the theories of meaning-making and Action Logic described above, but which focuses specifically on what it takes to facilitate environments that deliberately foster the growth and development of the meaning-making and Action Logic schemas within individuals.

Here I want to introduce three specific research-based concepts. The first concept presents the notion of a developmental *holding environment*. A *holding environment* is a social and structural setting deliberately designed to foster developmental growth. The second concept points to the importance of the deliberate design of *facilitative structures* for fostering developmental growth. Here "structures" refer to organizational conditions, constraints, and explicitly defined practices that we create with the intention of fostering developmental growth. The third concept brings these two ideas directly into the arena of organizational life in the form of *liberating structures*. Let's now take a walk through each of these.

The Developmental Holding Environment

Inner development can be fostered and accelerated when it occurs within a deliberately designed *holding environment*. Reflecting the research of Robert Kegan (who in turn based his theory on the work of pediatrician and psychologist Donald Winnicott), a *holding environment* is a deliberately designed structure that is defined by specific kinds of relationships, by individually held developmental goals (around which there is usually a supportive *accountability* relationship), and by events and arrangements (such as recurring coaching conversations, collaborative work projects, and so on).[35]

---

[35] For more on the notion of "holding environment," see Kegan *The Evolving Self.* For a slightly different take on the notion, though closely related to the way I am developing it here, see Ronald A. Heifetz, Alexander Grashow, and Marty Linsky, *The Practice of Adaptive Leadership: Tools and Tactics for Changing Your Organization and the World* (Cambridge Leadership Associates, 2009).

A *holding environment* can be understood as a kind of a psychological container for promoting inner development. The purpose of the *holding environment*, as Kegan describes it, is two-fold. First, to help people develop toward, and into, a later stage of development (*vertical* growth). Second, to support them in growing and expanding the skills and practices related to their current predominant stage—which, as was discussed above, has the effect of deepening and consolidating their current predominant stage, particularly when it has been newly acquired (*horizontal* growth).

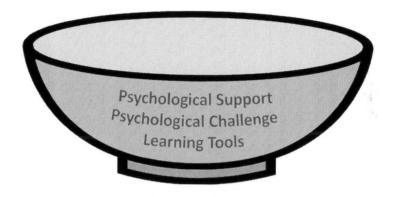

Figure 9: Holding Environment

According to Robert Kegan, three conditions must by met in order for a *holding environment* to support inner growth:

1. **Psychological Challenge.** The situations and circumstances in which one finds oneself need to pose some kind of challenge that has a *developmental edge*. Typically, these are situations or circumstances that present problems whose solutions require inner capabilities that are just slightly beyond one's current center of gravity. (Problems whose solutions require inner capabilities that are too far beyond one's current center of gravity are both needlessly stressful and developmentally ineffective.) Examples include a promotion that brings on new role-related challenges, or a project whose complexity forces the person to "think outside the box" in some genuinely new and somewhat personally challenging manner.

   Any such challenge can be posed as a new skill or competence to be learned (an example of *horizontal* growth). Or, it can take the form of a kind puzzle or riddle—perhaps framed as a job assignment given by one's developmentally minded boss—which can only be solved by stepping outside of one's familiar or comfortable way of thinking or acting—that is, a genuinely *developmental* challenge (an example of *vertical* growth).

2. **Psychological Support.** Stepping out into developmentally challenging situations requires support structures. Such support has the effect of emotionally bolstering where a person is already at; encouragement for taking those (perhaps tentative) steps toward what might be next, developmentally; and reassurance that whatever mistakes they may make along the way are okay. This is where relationships become significant, developmentally.

3. **Learning Tools.** These are specific tools that help the person advance developmentally. These can be in the form of new distinctions and practices, or training in new skills or techniques (especially those that engender some kind of state experience—a concept I'll come back to later on, in the section *Deliberately Facilitating Inner Development*), all of which help people accomplish work-related tasks in ways that introduce greater capability, nuance, and complexity of impact. That is, they help people bring to bear more complex meaning-making and Action Logic schemas.

Developmentally Facilitative Agents

The concept of *developmentally facilitative agents* builds on the notion of the *holding environment* by identifying specific qualities that define such an environment. In his research, Paul W. Marko defines a *facilitative agent* as a set of conditions which, taken together, act to promote, or otherwise *facilitate*, developmental growth.[36] *Facilitative agents* are defined in terms of conditions, occasions, or practices which, in some way, cause us to shed some aspect of a previously held assumption, belief, or worldview—a shedding that causes a shift within our inner meaning-making schema.

---

[36] Paul W. Marko, "Exploring Facilitative Agents that Allow Ego Development to Occur," in *The Postconventional Personality: Assessing, Researching, and Theorizing Higher Development*, ed. Angela Pfaffenberger, Paul Marko, and Allan Combs (State University of New York Press, 2011).

Figure 10: Facilitative Agents

As Marko points out, *facilitative agents* abound throughout history, from the teachings and practices of Buddha, to the Christian conversion experience, to the peak experiences chronicled by psychologist Abraham Maslow, and even in near-death experiences, whose more frequent occurrence in recent decades has been aided by the miracles of life-saving medical technologies.

In each such case, some deliberately crafted practice, condition, or occasion presents to us (or rather *within* us)—usually over the course of time—a *disorienting dilemma*: a moment when something inside us realizes that the assumptions and beliefs we've been holding (or, more accurately, have been *holding us*) are no longer adequate for coping with what is now in front of us. One of two things happens: Either we develop strategies of *assimilation*, in which we continue to try to make the outside world fit with our inner beliefs, understandings, and assumptions, or we choose to alter something in our beliefs, understandings, and assumptions—to *accommodate* some aspect of our own inner meaning-making schema—in order to more adequately meet what is in front of us. Only with this latter strategy is it possible for a developmental shift within us—whether small or large, whether completely life altering or only minimally so—to happen.

Four qualities are required if a *facilitative agent* is to promote developmental growth:[37]

1. A *facilitative agent* must present developmentally catalyzing practices, conditions, or situations that are, in some way, ***disequilibrating***—which is to say that they must challenge some aspect of a person's deeply held assumptions, habits, or beliefs in such a way that they start to see their essential inefficacy. Specifically, researchers have found that the appropriate disequilibrating effect happens when the practice, condition, or situation activates Action Logics that are one to two stages ahead of the center of gravity of a given human, or human system. Too close to one's current center of gravity, and the level of disequilibrium is insufficiently strong to generate the *disorientation* needed to prompt a developmental shift. Too far away from one's current center of gravity, and the level of disequilibrium becomes overly stressful or is dismissed as too "far out."

2. A *facilitative agent* must present developmentally catalyzing practices, conditions, or situations that are personally ***salient***—which is to say they are seen as inherently related to matters people actually *care* about, and which are seen as obviously relevant to the work at hand.

3. A *facilitative agent* must present practices, conditions, or situations that are ***emotionally engaging***—which is to say they draw people in, not just intellectually, but *emotionally*. To be clear, we're not talking about having an emotion here or there. Rather, when we say that a facilitative agent needs to be emotionally engaging, we mean that that it must activate an emotional connection to something deep within a person—that it somehow connects one to their deeper life's journey.

4. A *facilitative agent* must present practices, conditions, or situations that ***occur within an interpersonal context***—which is to say that they happen within the context of something we are doing with

---

[37] John Manners, Kevin Durkin, and Andrew Nesdale, "Promoting Advanced Ego Development Among Adults," *Journal of Adult Development* 11, no. 1 (January 2004).

others, and within the context of our relationships with those others. A developmentally catalyzing environment that is constituted only of solo activities—such as meditation, when done solely in isolation away from a longer-term meditation community— are powerful means to facilitate growth. However, there seems to be a need for the interpersonal dimension as well.

The notion of the *facilitative agent*, and the conditions for its use, tell us there is both an art and a science to designing any kind of environment that promotes inner growth and development—whether at the level of an individual, a team, or an entire organization.

Developmentally Liberating Structures

Building on the more general idea of the *holding environment*, and reflecting the structural orientation of *facilitative agents*, **liberating structures**[38] bring the practices and distinctions of deliberate development specifically into the organizational setting.

Developed by William Torbert and founded on the principle that organizational performance is predicated on the developmental capacity of an organization's members, *liberating structures* are organizational structures—composed of specific practices and conditions—that are imposed by management in order to deliberately support developmental growth as it relates to salient organizational situations and challenges.[39] In this sense, they are a kind of developmental contract between management and performers that are aimed, not at increasing employee performance per se (though that is the ultimate benefit to the organization), but rather to deliberately create an environment of developmental challenge.

---

[38] Note that the notion of "liberating structures" here is something entirely different from the more popular notion, and related practices, of the liberating structures for facilitation, as documented in the book by Henri Lipmanowicz and Keith McCandless, *The Surprising Power of Liberating Structures: Simple Rules to Unleash a Culture of Innovation* (Liberating Structures Press, 2013).

[39] William Torbert, *The Power of Balance: Transforming Self, Society and Scientific Inquiry* (Sage Publications, 1991).

Liberating structures, when effective in fostering development, exhibit several important qualities:

- **Deliberate Irony.** When it is effective, a *liberating structure* presents a situation, condition, or constraint that, in some way, is apparently contradictory. The effect is that some aspect of one's current meaning-making schema is challenged. To give an example, years ago I was coaching a mid-level manager who, at one point, challenged all eight Scrum teams in his organization to increase their internal velocity. (Velocity is an Agile software development term that refers to the amount of work a team is able to complete within a single two-week iteration, or "sprint" as it is called in Scrum.) He called for a 50% improvement over the next two quarters (six months), while maintaining all current quality metrics, and while keeping a sustainable pace (no more than 40 hours/week).[40] The intention behind this call was not about trying to get the teams to work faster (though that might have been a side benefit), but to present a situation that would challenge the teams to think differently about how they work.

- **The structure includes constraints that short-circuit habitual patterns of coping**. To continue with the example, one thing that happened is that many of the teams tried to increase their velocity by taking shortcuts in code quality, resulting in more bugs. It was therefore stipulated that frequent paired programming code reviews occur. This was an imposed constraint, which at once made it hard to hide bad code, while at the same time encouraging paired collaboration. Paired programming was new to these teams; but we felt that if team members were forced to practice it—though in the relatively limited application of reviewing code—it could become a new, and developmentally stretching, practice which many would come to like, which is what actually happened.

- **The structure has embedded within it an explicit promise by management to remove whatever impediments the teams run into that inhibit their ability to realize the goal of the structure.**

---

[40] Note that each team had its own measure for velocity and that the 50% increase applied to that team's current average velocity.

A *liberating structure* can't work if it doesn't have the form of a *social contract*, which implies that both parties in an agreement—and a *liberating structure* implies an agreement between management and performers—have a part in the agreement that they must uphold. In the case of our running example, managers were required to stay apprised, on a nearly day-by-day basis—even, in some cases, hourly—of impediments to the teams' ability to accelerate their performance, and they were required to do everything possible to resolve those impediments. If managers failed to do this, they were just as subject to strong questioning from performers as performers would be by management if they were not evidencing progress toward the 50% increase in their velocity.

- **The structure is designed to be a dialog and an empowering exchange between management and performers.** The purpose of this dialog is to expose potential incongruities between the conditions and tasks management imposes and its espoused reasoning behind those conditions and tasks. In our running example, the way this looked was that the senior manager of the group sponsored monthly breakfasts in which all were invited to have a dialog with that senior manager, and others on the senior management team. The breakfasts were relatively sumptuously catered, adding incentive to the invitation for all to attend. Senior management set the tone of these gatherings by admitting to the mistakes and incongruities they themselves saw in their own behavior; then, they invited those who were present to give additional feedback in what they were seeing as incongruous behavior.

Liberating structures tend to elicit behavioral cycles of conflict and growth. A conflict cycle arises when people respond within the context of a *liberating structure* in habitual and familiar ways (assimilation). Rather than generating a shift in their own meaning-making, they hang on to the old ways, trying to fit the new situation to an already existing inner schema. The resulting behaviors have the effect of coming to be at odds with the new situation.

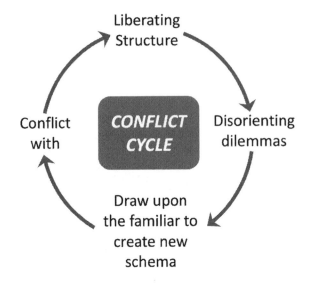

Figure 11: Conflict Cycle

For instance, in the earlier scenario, some team members tried to game the system in a variety of ways: They snuck in extra work hours; they tried to take coding shortcuts; and they sought to find ways to inflate their velocity numbers. In such situations, it should be assumed that the source of this misbehavior is not ill-intended; rather, such behaviors are viewed simply as ways of coping with what is essentially a *developmental* challenge for that person, or for those people. As such, it is a form of *assimilation*. The role of management at this point is to keep the heat on, provide an environment in which developmental reflection is common and frequent, and channels of open and honest communication remain ever-open.

In contrast to the conflict cycle, a *growth* cycle happens when people respond within the context of a *liberating structure* in ways that promote inner development and growth. In a growth cycle, people overcome their experiences of disorientation and confusion, adjusting something in their own meaning-making schema (which is a form of *accommodation*) in order to perform in ways that are congruent with the new, more complex situational environment.

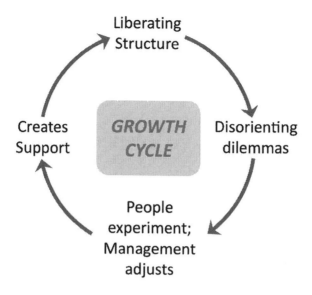

Figure 12: Growth Cycle

Going back to our scenario, a number of shifts started to happen over time. Among these were that team-member collaboration deepened: They saw themselves as true members of a team who needed to work together if they were to deal with the kinds of dilemmas that this condition demanded of them. Team members got better at thinking outside the box and finding solutions to problems that forced them to examine and adjust their assumptions.

Both cycles—*conflict* and *growth*—are equally valid responses. In fact, in some ways, the conflict cycle can be seen as a genuine attempt to deal with the new reality posed by the *liberating structure*: It reveals deeper and authentic patterns that are present in the organization that this *liberating structure* simply is uncovering.[41] In this regard, the conflict cycle might in fact be better in the sense that it can raise awareness of larger institutional

---

[41] As an aside, Agile frameworks such as Scrum can be understood as a kind of *liberating structure*, once the developmental challenge that Scrum elicits is recognized and made explicit through the addition of practices and conditions that deliberately foreground and highlight the developmental challenge.

conditions that are otherwise hidden, kept under wraps by the apparently good behavior and high performance by the organization's people.

Deliberately Facilitating Inner Development: Foundational Principles

My own work in facilitating and catalyzing transformational growth in human systems—whether as a coach, consultant, or workshop leader—has been strongly influenced by Kegan's notion of the *holding environment* and by the kinds of ideas exemplified by *facilitative agents* and *liberating structures*.

Over the years of integrating these concepts into my own work with organizations and systems—and in reflecting on and thinking deeply about what I am learning along the way—a small handful of principles have come to inform my work and how I think and talk about it. Three such principles are central to what I believe it takes to facilitate—and certainly to *accelerate*—the inner growth and development necessary for *Sense-and-Respond* leadership.

Inner development is an inherently ecosystemic phenomenon.

Typically, organizations tend to approach human development and growth by focusing solely on the individual. Employees declare personal developmental goals, with a strategy for getting there, marking progress along the way. This can work somewhat, because inner growth and development is an individual phenomenon. However, as we have seen, much of how inner growth happens resides within the kinds of relationships we have, the challenges we face, the expectations others have of us, the institutional norms that condition how we behave, and the social practices in which we engage with others. Inner growth is closely tied to the social and institutional contexts in which we work.

It is this reasoning which has led me to adopt the term *ecosystemic* to describe how I think about the process of inner growth and development—both our own and that of others.[42] Within the context of a developmental *ecosystem,*

---

[42] For many years I have taken an *ecosystemic* or *environment design* approach to

individuals openly share their developmental challenges and aspirations with each other and engage in the deliberate design of the ecosystemic environments in which they work together. Consequently, the structures, expectations, and practices of those environments themselves come to facilitate developmental growth. In this way, the work people do in service of broader business and organizational goals goes hand-in-hand with their own developmental growth. Indeed, businesses and organizations benefit from the individual growth of their members.[43]

The notion of the *holding environment* points to the more general principle that inner development is a whole human endeavor in which a mere learning environment is, by itself, insufficient. **Learning** (along the *horizontal* axis of inner growth) happens within an *institution*; **development** (along the *vertical* axis of inner growth) happens within an *ecosystem*.

You can think of elementary school and high school as *ecosystems* for developing children and young adults. Of course, a big part of this is the institutional aspect related to learning: curricula, theories of childhood learning,

---

organizational level Agile coaching. My work was informed early on by my study of complexity science; systems thinking (with Peter Senge); social science (particularly work by Karl Marx and by the sociologist, Max Weber); and by the work of Thomas Leonard (who first introduced me to the idea of "designing environments" as a professional coaching intervention practice). Starting with my early work coaching Agile teams, I noticed how much learning and growth can happen when I focused on creating the right kinds of social, ideational, and even physical environments with people, building directly on what I considered to be the environmental design orientation of Scrum. I quickly started to bring these environmental design principles into the broader organizational sphere. There is great deal of social science research that supports the idea that human behavior is conditioned by the social, biological, and physical environments in which they find themselves, and that in order to effect human psychological change, you need to design (*ecosystemic*) environments such that they support the kind of change you are looking for. See bibliography section, "Ecosystemic Design" for specific references.

[43] The suggestion that organizations should focus as much on people development as they do on product and service development is one of the main arguments that Kegan and Lahey make in *An Everyone Culture*.

the activities and exercises by which learning is facilitated. But beyond that is the larger *ecosystem* of the child's development: playground politics, friendships, classroom etiquette, the regulating and structuring routines of day-to-day life, etc. All of these things constitute a very natural and socially organic ecosystem that facilitates the child's development.

As individuals move into adulthood, many go on to university and from there move on to professional work within a modern corporate, or semi-corporate, environment. These experiences—college and the professional career—provide ecosystemic environments that promote yet further development.[44]

But, as we move into middle-to-late adulthood, our social environments no longer reliably provide the right conditions for continued development. Inner growth frequently slows or halts altogether. Either that, or individuals endeavor to manufacture their own *holding environments*—in the form of special relationships, particular types of work or job roles, personal development programs, and so on—in order to support their own (and perhaps others') developmental growth. Such individuals choose to grow by their own energy and initiative. But not all (in fact, most don't) choose the path and life required to grow in this manner.

Evolvagility sees the role of the 21st century organization as providing *holding environments*—in the sense of *developmental ecosystems*—that help people to grow the complexity of their Action Logic beyond that which currently predominates in the Predict-and-Plan organizational environment. This happens within an organization when the creating and designing of deliberately developmental environments becomes a big part of the day-to-day work which people naturally do, and when it becomes a central part of long-term organizational strategy.

Inner development happens through the accumulation of temporary *state* experiences.

A "state experience" is one that provides a momentary glimpse—whether for an individual or a group—into a new meaning-making possibility, in

---

[44] In his book, *In Over Our Heads*, Robert Kegan uses the term "curriculum" to refer to the nature of just such a developmentally catalyzing social environment.

such a way that it leaves a lasting emotional imprint. A state experience can last for just a couple of minutes, a couple of hours, or several days; however, by definition it is a *temporary* experience.

It's worth taking a moment, at this point, to make a distinction, as Ken Wilber does,[45] between states and stages. A "stage" refers to the meaning-making and Action logic schema that forms an individual's developmental center of gravity. In this sense, the stage that constitutes one's inner center of gravity is relatively *persistent* (even though, as we've said, one might regress downwardly or progress upwardly between stages, but—short of a major physical or life-circumstance calamity—only for a short while). And the ability to consistently incorporate the meaning-making of a later stage is **hard-won**; it can take years or even a decade to achieve, especially when left to one's own devices—and for the later stages, one may never get there (at least not in this lifetime).

In contrast to a stage, a "state" is a *temporary* condition, which can last anywhere from a few minutes to days. It happens when an individual has a powerful insight related to exposure to a particularly powerful or inspiring (at least to them) idea, or set of new practices, whether in a workshop, a coaching session, or any similarly catalyzing occasion. We usually call such a moment a state *experience* because it typically has both an emotional and cognitive impact on us. That impact can be very intense—It's no wonder we often describe such an experience as a high.

Of course, such momentary highs fade over time. This is often regarded as the main drawback of workshops and of the state experiences they engender. They can provide powerful experiences—but those experiences always fade and then we're back in the real world. But, in my view, this momentary high—and the insights and experiences that feed such a high—is precisely what is so powerful about a state experience. This momentary high is a point of key leverage—state experiences are powerful precisely because of the emotional imprint left behind by that high. That imprint is neurologically associated with exposure—no matter how brief—with a new meaning-making schema. While something—specific details and information, for

---

[45] For a clear explication of the distinction between stage and state, see Ken Wilber, *Integral Spirituality: A Startling New Role for Religion in the Modern and Postmodern World* (Integral Books, 2007).

instance—may be lost over time, the *imprint* is not. And that imprint holds a memory that is directly associated with ideas and distinctions that can be refreshed and grown.

If leveraged in the right way, that emotional imprint—and the insights and ideas it relates itself to—can provide the energy to drive genuine and sustained developmental growth. A series of state experiences can be engineered, acting like an indoor rock climbing wall in which one can pull oneself up the wall one support at a time—state by state. [46]

Inner development can be activated through the growing of new skills and the introduction of new challenges.

Inner growth occurs, in part, through the learning of new practices and skills, and through being confronted with new *challenges* related to those practices and skills—all of which happens along the *horizontal* plane of inner growth. When those practices and skills derive from a later-stage Action Logic than that which is our currently prevailing center of gravity, those new practices, skills, and challenges can have the effect of *psycho-activating* developmental growth toward that later-stage Action Logic (along the *vertical* plane of inner growth).

---

[46] Picture retrieved 11/13/18 from https://pixabay.com/en/photos/climbing%20wall/, labeled for reuse.

"Psycho-activating" refers to changing something in one's mind through the introduction of something from *outside* the mind. A hallucinogenic drug is the most commonly thought-of example of this. But, at least as common in practice, is the psycho-activating of inner growth by teaching people (whether children or adults) new skills and practices.

When we teach children to share their toys, for instance, we're helping them to develop for themselves a practice that has a psycho-activating potential. At first, children may see little to be gained from sharing their toys (such is the developmental center of gravity in which they live internally). But then, with time, they start to see that the practice of sharing toys can, in the longer run, benefit them—if for no other reason than that, at some point, another child will share *their* toys. Of course, it usually isn't until much later that a significant developmental shift happens, which translates into an experience of satisfaction in doing something that makes another person happy. But it *is* a shift—and one that, at some point and in some way, had at least one psycho-active trigger in the practice of sharing.

In a similar fashion, when we teach adults the basic coaching skill of asking powerful questions—as opposed to offering advice or one's own opinions— at some point another kind of developmental shift starts to happen. As we learn this skill, we start to realize that others really *do* see the world differently than we do. The capacity for genuine *curiosity* in others—the way *they* think, the way *they* see the world, what *they* aspire to—comes alive in us, as does a deeper regard for others more generally. An inner shift happens.

Psychologist William Perry likened the introduction of developmentally catalyzing practices to Trojan Horses. On the one hand, a new set of practices have practical utility that can be used at and applied from a person's current developmental perspective. Yet, at the same time, that set of practices carries within it developmental "soldiers" that at some point will exit the horse (those practices) and fan out across the "city"—in this case, the city of the human mind and the various ways it makes meaning of various aspects of one's life.[47]

---

[47] William Perry, *Forms of Intellectual and Ethical Development in the College Years: A Scheme* (Jossey-Bass, 1999).

Taken together, these principles remind us of the complex and non-linear nature of inner development, of the fact that inner development is both an individual and a relational phenomenon, and that inner development is as much as about development (along the *vertical* axis) *per se* as it is about the skills and competencies we *learn* (along the *horizontal* axis). In the next section I introduce a more methodical framework to help us think through how we might begin to make real such an attitude, and how we might outfit such an approach.

The Deliberately Developmental Ecosystem

We have covered a lot of territory in order to create a foundation for where we're going next. The ultimate aim is to learn how we might create conditions that enable people to activate within themselves, and in relationship with others, qualities and capabilities congruent with later-stage Action Logics: late *Achiever, Individualist* and beyond. Doing so creates the cultural grounding necessary to achieve the capabilities of the *Sense-and-Respond* organization.

It is my firm belief—and it is the grounding assumption of *Evolvagility*, and of the work on which this book is built—that developmental growth can only happen within social and organizational settings in which situations, occasions, and conditions are deliberately designed to activate and stimulate that growth. Furthermore, those situations, occasions, and conditions must build on a foundation of what has already been learned about how to help people grow developmentally.

Such a design has the effect of creating a kind of developmental *scaffolding*. A scaffold[48] is a temporary structure which is erected on the outside of a

---

[48] Photo retrieved on 11/18/18 from Microsoft Word picture library's Creative Commons.

building, allowing us to stand at different levels of height in relation to the building, so that we might do some kind of work on it—whether that be simply painting its exterior, or gutting its interior.

Within the context of growing ourselves, and others, as *Sense-and-Respond* leaders, I imagine a similar kind of temporary mental scaffolding structure, but one that allows us to access different heights of our own self.

Where we are going next is to lay out a design process by which we might promote and accelerate inner development within, and across, a human system, through the creation of a kind of developmental scaffolding, and thereby create conditions that favor the emergence of genuine and sustainable *Sense-and-Respond* leadership capability.

This design process, which is ongoing, is the product of many years synthesizing research with on-the-ground, trial-and-error practice. I have come to call this approach *deliberately developmental **design***. In a similar vein, I refer to the developmentally catalyzing conditions that such a design is intended to generate the *deliberately developmental **ecosystem***. This reflects a way of working with human systems that I have increasingly adopted over the years and has been inspired more recently by Kegan and Lahey's terminology—*the deliberately development organization.*[49]

In the following pages, I shall introduce the idea of the *deliberately developmental ecosystem*, by revealing its main design features; the spheres of personal and interpersonal engagement that yield various developmental practices; and finally the developmental moves that determine the specific aim of any potentially developmental practice or condition. As we go through each of these you will no doubt hear echoes of the ideas and principles that we have covered recently, ones that I have been explaining throughout this book.

This initial work will lay the final groundwork for us to go, in Part IV of Evolvagility, more deeply into the kinds of actual practices and conditions that can engender a deliberately developmental ecosystem.

---

[49] Kegan and Lahey *An Everyone Culture.*

Features of a Deliberately Developmental Ecosystem

A *deliberately developmental ecosystem* can occur at any level of scale—it is not limited to the enterprise level of an organization (it is in this sense that the work presented here differs, specifically in its scale, from that of Kegan and Lahey's work). For instance, a *deliberately developmental ecosystem* can occur within a business partnership of just two people, in which the two people in the partnership see their partnership for its developmental potential as well as in service of whatever endeavor they are partnering on. It can occur within the context of a team, whether it is a software delivery team or an executive leadership team. It could occur within the context of a developmental cohort: A group that comes together for the express purpose to grow themselves (and each other). It could also occur within the context of a product group or a department, or at the level of an entire enterprise.

Regardless of its scope, there are specific aspects of the *deliberately developmental ecosystem* that I want to highlight. First, it is **developmental**, in the sense that its intention is to be a vehicle for *inner* growth, with an emphasis on *vertical* growth. Secondly, it is **deliberately** developmental, in the sense that we are intentional in the design of that ecosystem so that, indeed, it fosters development. And, finally, it is **ecosystemic** in that it constitutes a *complex* (in the sense that the literature in "complex adaptive systems" describes it)[50] community of interacting human systems which leverage the holistic and emergent conditions that uniquely arise within a social ecosystem.

Let's explore each of these aspects.

---

[50] For a concise but still useful description of the term "complexity," see Snowden and Boone, "A Leader's Framework for Decision-making". For a more in-depth, but also very good primer on Complex Adaptive Systems and its application within the organizational context, see Robert Axelrod and Michael Cohen, *Harnessing Complexity: Organizational Implications of a Scientific Frontier* (Basic Books, 2000). For greater depth and insight on complexity and management, see Ralph Stacey, Douglas Griffen, and Patricia Shaw, *Complexity and Management: Fad or Radical Challenge to Systems Thinking?* (Routledge, 2000).

It is Developmental

A *deliberately developmental ecosystem* is deliberately **developmental** in that, first, its focus is on the developmental dimension of human capability—whether at the level of the individual or the collective. This is somewhat different from the more common scenario of a mutual support group in which people are, for instance, giving each other feedback on one another's individual behavior and performance—an environment in which the exclusive focus is on helping each person improve their outer game. While such a behavioral focus is still important, what we want to bring into particular focus here is the *developmental* dimension of each individual's behavior and performance.

Within the context of a *deliberately developmental ecosystem*, instead of helping each other improve their own individual behavior and performance, we see people helping each other uncover the internal meaning-making and Action Logic schema—manifested by the kinds of assumptions, beliefs, and interpretations people hold—that underlie and inform individual behavior and performance. Together, they explore the ways those internal schemas may be enhancing or inhibiting individual behavior and performance.

An additional feature of the *deliberately developmental ecosystem*—and a consequence of its specifically developmental focus—is that we come to be just as attentive to the developmental qualities of the relationship system in which we find ourselves as we are to the individuals who constitute that relationship system. That is, in addition to developmentally growing one another individually, we are also committed to developmentally growing ourselves **as a relationship system.** (Note that such a system can be a relationship of just two people, or it can be a team of seven, or a department of 30). Given this, we can say that a *deliberately developmental ecosystem* is one in which:

- *I* grow (development at the level of the *individual*)

- *We* grow (development at the level of the *relationship*)

- The **systems around us** grow (development at the level of the *ecosystems* around us)

It is Deliberate

A *deliberately developmental ecosystem* is **deliberately** developmental in that there is an intended design to the conditions that support and empower developmental growth throughout the ecosystem. This design is manifested through the existence of:

- A **shared intention** (Why are we doing this?)

- A **shared vocabulary** (What new categories and distinctions do we need to have?)

- **Thinking tools** (What models and theories will we leverage to help us think in new ways?)

- A set of **social practices** (What are the things we do, the conditions we hold, and the kinds of events and ceremonies we engage in—which, in some way, serve to help us grow and develop ourselves?)

Let's walk through each of these briefly, starting with *shared intention*. A shared intention is an explicit declaration of why we are here and what we are doing. It is one aspect of the deliberately developmental ecosystem that reminds us of the explicitly developmental focus of this occasion. The nature of the shared intention can be suggested by questions such as:

- What is it that we might not be seeing?

- What developmental shift are we wanting to create for ourselves, and why?

- Where are we currently stuck, and what underlying assumptions, beliefs, and expectations are we holding that might be keeping us stuck?

Shared vocabulary refers to the words we use together; specifically, lingo or jargon that helps us create for ourselves new categories for thinking. New categories give us new perspectives and new ways of viewing of our world. In this sense, they have the potential of psycho-activating the emergence of new meaning-making structures, as they come to be called for by the situation.

DISTINCTIONS: CREATING OUR WORLD BY NAMING IT

In creating a new *vocabulary*, we're coming up not merely with new words, ideas, or concepts. We're also coming up with new *distinctions*.[1] A distinction makes something that had previously been unnoticed in the background jump out and become "distinct."

A *distinction*, in the way we're using the term here, helps us see something we couldn't see before. As an example, the word "pointer" has a certain meaning in the programming world. Technically, a pointer is a data structure that points to the location, in computer memory, of some piece of data, or another data structure. But, as such, a pointer is not just that data structure; it also distinguishes the notion of indirection in programming language parlance: A concept—or a *distinction*—that leads to a whole collection of concepts and ideas that help programmers understand more complex ideas and develop more complex programming constructs.[1]

In a somewhat similar fashion, the word "assumption" points to a concept that means "a thing that is accepted as true or as certain to happen, without proof."[1] But assumption is more than a mere word; its use opens up a whole new world of potential action and impact. For example, when we create a practice called *examining our assumptions*—in which we critically and objectively examine those things we have accepted as true or as certain to happen—we begin to see things we couldn't have seen had we not engaged in that practice. Most critically, it now becomes possible for us to see where our acceptance of things as true or certain have led to errors, some of which have had serious consequences.

Without the distinction "assumption," we would not have the practice called "examining our assumptions." And, without the practice called "examining our assumptions," we could not possibly have seen that our thinking of certain things to be true, but were not, was at the source of major errors, having significant impact on our performance as an organization. That practice of "examining our assumptions"—and the outcome it can generate—is made possible entirely by that single word—that single *distinction*—"assumption."

Agile delivery processes—such as Scrum and Lean Startup—introduce new vocabularies with *distinctions* such as "Scrum Master," "Daily Standup," and "Minimum Viable Product (MVP)." Such distinctions introduce wholly new mental categories that orient completely new worlds of possible action, and thereby have a significant impact on organizations and even entire industries. This is true of virtually every professional field of endeavor. Distinctions are what make it possible to think, and *create*, newly.

In many ways, and on many levels, *Evolvagility* introduces a vocabulary that is key to deliberately developing ourselves and others. Without the word "development"—and the way in which the distinctions it introduces orients how we understand the nature of mental and emotional processes—none of the practices we will dive into in Part IV would make any sense, let alone help us actually *develop* ourselves in any deliberate manner.

The phrase **thinking tools** is somewhat similar to *vocabularies*, except whereas a vocabulary consists of individual words that point to distinctions, thinking tools defines more richly-developed models and theories that help us see—and to be able to leverage, through practice—bigger-picture concepts.

One way that Scrum teaches us about how a *Sense-and-Respond* team might work, for instance, is through the definition of a model (e.g., the iterative sprint cycle model) and a theory (a theory of self-organization, which holds that—under the right conditions and with the right kinds of structures—when left alone, a team can organize and manage *itself*, and in so doing, produce results that far exceed those of teams that are traditionally managed). These act as *thinking tools* that help us see an otherwise familiar project management process in an entirely new light.

In a similar vein, *Evolvagility* teaches us how the principle of *Sense-and-Respond* can be applied to sensemaking itself—both at the individual and relationship system level. It does this by drawing upon a theory of mental and emotional development and a model of Action Logics of ever-increasing complexity that adults move through as they grow in their own development. These thinking tools frame a set of practices to help people grow their capacity for *Sense-and-Respond* leadership. As is the case with Scrum, and the models and theory it advances, the theory and model advanced in *Evolvagility* help us understand an otherwise familiar domain of activity—in this case, how we approach the growing of any new kind of organizational capability—in a completely different way.

The models and theories of Scrum and the model and theory of *Evolvagility* define a small assembly of thinking tools that provide a conceptual arc around which we can wrap our thinking, and around which we can grow practices.

Finally, there are the **social practices** in which we engage. These include the three concepts I introduced earlier in Part III: Practices, Conditions, and Occasions.

The **practices** we adopt that shift our inner meaning making; the **conditions** in which we operate help us shift or challenge us to improve and grow; and events and ceremonies are the **occasions** that catalyze our new insights.

It is Ecosystemic

A *deliberately developmental ecosystem* is fundamentally a human ecosystem, in that it constitutes a community of interacting human systems. A human system can be a dyad (a relationship of two people), a team, a department, or even, in the case of an industry, an entire enterprise.

Regardless of its size or scope, a human ecosystem is, in essence, a *social* system. As such, the boundary between the thoughts, feelings, and emotions of an individual and those of the larger social system can be blurry. On the one hand the thoughts we have, the feelings we experience, and the aspirations we hold all have a social basis in our relationships, and in the broader social settings in which those relationships live. That is, individual consciousness is conditioned by relationships and by the broader social environment one finds oneself in (or one *puts* oneself in).

And yet, at the same time, the complexity, nuance, and adaptability of the behaviors, practices, and skills we manifest together *as a collective*, and as a larger *social system,* are the product of the level of complexity of each person's *individual* meaning-making and Action Logic schemas. My ability to engage in, and contribute to, the evolution of highly collaborative and relationally-intelligent relationship systems, will be a product of the complexity of meaning-making I am able to hold, especially as it governs how I see and understand other people and my relationships with them.

Individual consciousness and social capability are thus mutually constitutive—they *co-emerge* together. This means that, as an individual making meaning of my day-to-day, moment-by-moment world, I both **create** and am **created by** the social ecosystems in which both I, and it, emerge, together.

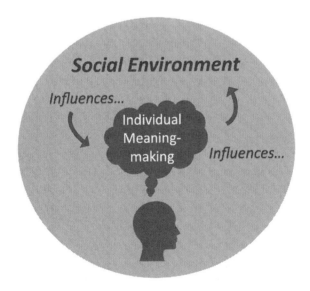

Figure 13: Social Environment

This mutually determinative co-emergence of self and system is the primordial ground of inner growth. Inner growth always arises within, and necessarily requires, an ecosystemic environment for it to unfold. Meanwhile, that environment is always enhanced, and to a great extent, *defined*, by the quality of growth that happens within in it, and by the complexity of mind which that growth yields.

This deep quality of *co-emergence* between individual *self* and social *environment* is at the heart of what I mean by *ecosystemic* and is one of the key orienting distinctions behind the approach to catalyzing inner growth within an organizational context that I am about to promote. It is for this reason that we can say that *Sense-and-Respond* leadership is both an *individual* and a *social* phenomenon.

Deliberately Developmental Spheres of Practice

Given the ecosystemic nature of inner development I am advocating, we can now explicitly draw up the social spheres across which development happens, and across which it manifests. These spheres are: *Self, Relationship,* and *System.*

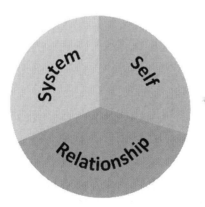

Figure 14: Three Deliberately Developmental Spheres of Practice

We've been touching all along on the idea that developmental growth happens both within the *individual* and a *relationship* arena. Now, as we seek to understand the nature of a *deliberately developmental ecosystem*, we want to explicitly delimit them as such, since, as we'll see in a while, each sphere yields distinct and separable *deliberately developmental* practices. The articulation of these different spheres helps us to set our developmental focus. Sometimes the focus is on growing ourselves, or others, *individually.* At other times, the focus is on developing ourselves as a *relationship system.* At still other times, the focus is on developing the inner capacity of an entire department or organization. Different deliberately developmental practices apply to different spheres.

Let's briefly scan each of these spheres just to clearly and definitively demarcate them.

Self

As we've been saying throughout the book, from within the *Self* developmental sphere, our focus is on the complexity of the sensemaking—and the *Action Logics* that underlie it—that we are able to *individually* bring to any given situation. Arising from this is the recognition that often the complexity of the situations we face in a VUCA world are simply beyond our capacity to make sense of, leaving us swimming in the chaos or, as Robert Kegan has put it, "in over our heads."[51] In order to be able to lead in the face of VUCA, we need to be prepared to "upgrade" the complexity of the inner software—the Action Logic—on which is built our own, *individual* capacity to make sense of the complexity we are facing in the world.

Relationship

In the *Relationship* development sphere, the primary focus is on the complexity of sensemaking that we generate through deliberate relationship and engagement with others. By deliberate, I mean that we bring skillful practice in how we communicate, how we coordinate, and how we collaborate with others. Skillful practice is both a pre-condition for, and the very context of, deliberate relationship and engagement. Under such conditions of intentional and skillful practice, relationships and relationship systems (e.g., teams and groups) become the primary means by which we grow and develop, both individually and organizationally. That growth and development, in turn, becomes the very foundation of high performance in organizations.

---

[51] Kegan, *In Over Our Heads.*

System

In the *System* sphere, we are talking about the larger systemic sphere in which we live and work. We're not talking about an entire enterprise, necessarily. What we are referring to here is the immediate sphere in which we have some ability to influence outcomes, but which may include people, events, and situations that cannot be experienced in real time.

For example, an Agile delivery team falls closer within the *Relationship* sphere because (a) it is common, and relatively easy, to get the entire system together in the same room (even if that room is teleconference line); and (b) the events and situations that affect how we were work happen in close proximity to us, both in time (we don't have to wait for something) and in space (though with a globally distributed team, this can be hard). In such a case, we think of the team as a different kind of social entity than the broader department in which a variety of interrelated functional groups are housed, all of which share a common departmental purpose and set of goals. Such a department would be an example of an *organization system*.

Though presented here as distinct *spheres* of developmental focus, I want for us to see them as inextricably linked and mutually catalyzing.

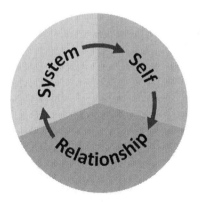

Figure 15: Development within each of the three spheres is mutually catalyzing

The complexity of our inner *meaning-making*—at the individual level— fuels the developmental capacity of our relationships and relationship systems. Meanwhile, within the very same context, the developmental capacity of our relationships forms a *holding environment* that fuels and supports the growing of our individual meaning-making complexity.

117

By the same developmental unfolding, the complexity of the way in which individuals are able to construct *meaning*—and the complexity and capacity of the relationships individuals engage in—determines the ability of the broader social and organizational systems in which they find ourselves to sense and respond effectively in a *VUCA* world. And yet, at the same time, those very same social and organizational systems impact the developmental capacity within both the individual and relationship spheres.

This brings us back to the point made just now regarding the *ecosystemic* nature of inner growth, which is that individual development necessarily occurs within a relationship and systemic context. Ordinarily, we think of individual growth and development as standing on its own—as separate and distinct from social context, as something we can measure and assess in isolation from the broader social context. What I'm saying here is that individual development and growth both catalyze, and are catalyzed by, development and growth in our relationships and systemic environments. *We need all three spheres.*

Deliberately Developmental Practice Moves

It is tempting to think—especially given the emphasis on developmental ascendency that has characterized much of the tenor of this book so far—that inner growth is *always* about developmental advancement, about moving upward along the *vertical* axis of growth.

However, in actuality, much—if not most—of inner growth is about *horizontal* growth. It is about acquiring and sharpening the skills and competencies that are congruent with one's current developmental profile, one's current meaning-making and Action Logic schema. In fact, sometimes it is appropriate to intentionally take a step *backwards*, developmentally.[52]

---

[52] Many of the ideas in this section derive from, and are inspired by, similar ideas found in the audio program by Rob McNamara, *Elegant Leadership: Commanding Influence: Your Development for Greater Mastery at Work*. The program is available from Ten Directions at https://tendirections.com/elegant-leadership/commanding-influence/. Also in Cook-Greuter, "Nine Levels of Increasing Embrace in Ego Development" and in the chapter on "change" in Beck and Cowan, *Spiral Dynamics*.

It can be helpful to have a vocabulary that describes the different moves that one can make, in terms of inner growth—whether for oneself or for others—and to be clear about which kind of move is best suited to the moment. Three such moves can be discerned: One can **stretch** upward developmentally; one can **consolidate** where they are already at, developmentally (e.g., by growing new skills and competencies, or sharpening ones they already have); or one might **step back**, which is to *intentionally* (that word, "intentionally," is important here) allow oneself to developmentally revert somewhat, and in some way.

Next, let me explain the kinds of practices and conditions that might elicit each developmental move.

Stretch

A developmental stretch is one that takes us into, or toward, a more complex, more nuanced, more contextually rich meaning-making capacity, or Action Logic stage.

I call it a "stretch" because it typically evokes some kind of *disorienting dilemma*: A moment (which may last far longer than a moment) in which some aspect of our developmental equilibrium is disrupted—a moment that challenges some deeper assumption, belief, or preference such that we experience confusion, disorientation, or anxiety.

Now most of the time, when faced with such a moment of disorientation, we move quickly to try to regain our equilibrium through some means of assimilating the situation to an already familiar state. If we succeed in doing so, we're back to status quo. Unless we somehow stay in that place of disorientation and sustain the discomfort of being there, there is no developmental stretch; it is only a brief visit. In this way, it is similar to a Hatha Yoga move; if we don't hold the pose, we don't get the stretch. And—in a manner similar to Hatha Yoga, where we sometimes need to use a strap to maintain a pose and hold the stretch—a developmental stretch often involves the placement of some kind of structure that holds us there long enough for the new developmental opportunity to gain some traction within our psyche.

It might be helpful to think of a developmental *stretch* as a huge rubber band, one end of which is wrapped around your waist and the other end of

119

which is pulled by some kind of structure that plants itself ahead of where you might be currently at, developmentally. That structure could be a relationship, a condition, a commitment, or vision that in some way acts to pull you forward toward a more developmentally evolved version of yourself through a combination of challenge, support, and relevant learning tools. Such structures are essential in counteracting the strong pull that existing structures exert—structures that include current habits and practices, relationships, and the force of organizational, societal, and even family culture.

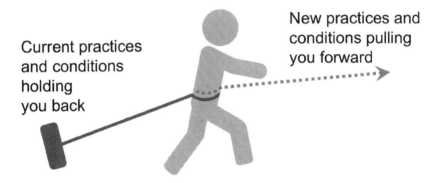

Figure 16: Deliberately Developmental Practices and Conditions Act to Pull You Toward Your Developmental Stretch[53]

As was said earlier, the people and institutions that accompany our growing up and the early parts of our adult life all constitute environments in which situations arise, sometimes with greater frequency than at others, that stretch us developmentally. So, while it can often be difficult, and even painful, to sustain those periods of developmental stretch, most of us (though not all of us) usually do so, either because we are somehow forced to (socially or otherwise), or because we see that our current ways of dealing with a given situation—or others like it—simply no longer work. In many of these instances throughout life, the conditions of a given environment, or the support we receive from within that environment, or the practices and skills we learn while within that environment, equip us for dealing with the challenges of that environment.

---

[53] Adapted from Senge, *The Fifth Discipline*.

Stretching, therefore, is how we develop ourselves (and others). Pretty much all that we've been covering in the early sections of Part III—from the notion of the *holding environment* to the notion of *facilitative agents* and *liberating structures*—apply to the developmental Stretch move.

Consolidate

Much of what constitutes inner growth takes the form of what developmentalists call developmental *consolidation* or translation. A *Consolidate* move is one in which people grow by learning and practicing new skills or competencies that are related to, and in some way, reflect some aspect of their developmental capacity. It is this phenomenon of developmental consolidation I was referring to earlier (in the section titled "The Dialectic of Inner Growth") when I described the process by which the learning of new skills such as the professional coaching skill of asking powerful questions. Though this learning occurs along the *horizontal learning* axis, it inevitably strengthens and deepens developmental growth along the *vertical* axis.

The primary means by which a *Consolidate* move is engendered is teaching and mentoring. Another primary means is through the introduction of conditions and structures that in some way introduce a constraint on how people are to do things.

Let's think through an example of what this might look like. Consider what happens when someone has grown within themselves the inner capacities of an *Expert* Action Logic. Among the things that happen for people as they move into this stage of meaning-making is that they are able to reside solidly within their capacity for abstract thinking and formal operations. This translates into a drive toward mastery, particularly craft mastery—as in, for instance, software development, highway engineering, political craftsmanship, medical practice, etc.

As a person deepens their craft mastery—as they become highly skilled (and highly valued) software developers for example—they are also solidifying the cognitive aspects of the deeper meaning-making and Action Logic that got them where they are. That solidification makes it possible for that person to begin to expand their drive for expertise into other fields. The software developer, for instance, might now start to get seriously interested in business process engineering, or in scaled Agile, where his or her proclivity for abstraction finds a larger, wider field.

These are examples of some of the ways in which developmental consolidation happens, and how, through exercise of the *Consolidate* move, we can deliberately help that process of consolidation along.

Step Back

There are times when the most appropriate developmental move is to step back. Some of us can become rather addicted to developmental growth, or at least what we *think* is developmental growth. We go for the thrill of rapid internal change and the adrenalin rush that those moments of disorientation and disequilibrium give us. We become personal development junkies.

But this has little to do with real developmental growth (in fact, it could be evidence of someone who has gotten stuck in an *Expert* Action Logic loop, wherein the subject of their *expertise* is personal development). As Rob McNamara points out, developmental growth is a longer-term game.[54] And though, yes, in this book we are indeed talking about *accelerating* development and growth, we're not talking about developmental speed dialing.

In fact, part of the process of inner growth is being deliberate about the pace and the unfolding of one's inner growth. It entails an increasing capacity to discern what next steps will best serve one's particular path. At times, it means taking the plunge into a Stretch move. At other times, it means standing back and staying put, developmentally, in a mode of Consolidation. At still other times, it means a deliberate step backward in our development. Deep, sustainable development is naturally a process of developmental *progression* and *regression*—moving ahead a bit, and stepping back a bit, then moving ahead just a bit more, and so on.

Another consideration here is that along any developmental growth path, one may have several developmental projects focused on a particular area in one's life where one has a commitment to growing oneself. (I'm calling it a *developmental* project even though such a project typically involves both *vertical* (developmental) and *horizontal* (learning) growth.) For instance, I

---

[54] See McNamara, *Elegant Leadership*.

might have a personal developmental project to be able to stand in my authority in the decisions I make, and another one focused on being better able to stay present and clear in meeting situations that otherwise fill me with anxiety, and a third one about being more emotionally available to my family.

There are times, however, when I might need to let one developmental project slide, when there is a felt need to bring greater developmental focus and intensity to another area. For instance, if I am promoted to a significantly more demanding leadership position, that might be a good opportunity to bring particular focus to that second project—being able to stay present and clear when in anxiety-provoking meeting situations—letting the other two slide, at least somewhat. These are all examples of the developmental move called *Step Back*.

In the next part of the book I will build on the design principles just covered in order to lay out one possible set of practices by which you might establish a *deliberately developmental ecosystem* within your own organizational environment.

PART IV

The Design of a Deliberately Developmental Ecosystem

In Part IV, we walk through the key elements for establishing the practices and conditions of a *deliberately developmental ecosystem*. These elements are key to catalyzing the emergence of the inner qualities—at the level of individual, relationship, and organizational system—that are at the heart of *Sense-and-Respond* leadership capability.

Part IV provides a practical foundation on which you can begin to grow your own *deliberately developmental ecosystems* from which people throughout an organization might grow and develop within themselves, and in each other, the capacity for a deep and sustainable *Sense-and-Respond* leadership capability. Along the way, I offer sample applications to guide you as you work through your own design process.

The design elements I present here consist of *practices* and *conditions*. The practices are framed around—and are designed to facilitate developmental growth across—the three practice spheres of *Self*, *Relationship*, and *System*. In tracking across the three spheres, the practices I present provide a comprehensive foundation for the growing of a *Sense-and-Respond* leadership capability at the level of individual, relationship, and system—the foundation for a deep and lasting organizational transformation.

In addition to practices, I describe key conditions you will want to establish in order to support the developmental potential that the practices offer, and to create the kind of social environment conducive to the growing of a deliberately developmental ecosystem.

Evolvagility Practices

Evolvagility provides a scaffolding that supports the activity of *Deliberate Sensemaking*, whether that ecosystem is that of a two-person partnership, a seven-person team or twenty-person department—and whether that ecosystem has a brief one-hour tenure or endures for the course of three years. In this part of the book, I describe, in some detail, the practical details of this scaffolding.

> The intention of Evolvagility, as a set of practices and conditions, is to promote and accelerate developmental growth—specifically the capacity to activate the vocabularies of late Achiever, Individualist, and early Strategist Action Logics—as it might occur across the spheres of Self (Individual), Relationship and System.

At the heart of the model is a reminder that the ultimate activities we are engaged in here are the activities of *Sensing, Sense-Making,* and *Responding.* The arrows indicate this is an ongoing, cyclical activity. These activities constitute the very essence of what we mean by *Sense-and-Respond.*

Moving outward from the center of the model, we find the Action Logic layer, but here reflected across three *spheres* of developmental engagement and focus: *Self, Relationship* and *System.* This explicit foregrounding of the *Action Logic* layer highlights the emphasis I am placing on the centrality of our Action Logics to the quality and complexity of our *Sensemaking*—whether at the level of the individual, relationship or organizational system. When we bring focus to those Action Logics—and the power they have over our capacity for making sense of what we are sensing and for how we might respond in any given situation—we are laying the groundwork for the practice of *Deliberate Sensemaking.*

Moving outward further, we find eight fundamental deliberately developmental practices. The practices pertain roughly to each sphere—*Self, Relationship,* and *System,* with two of the practices crossing between two adjacent spheres, as depicted by the dark grey coloring of their respective boxes.

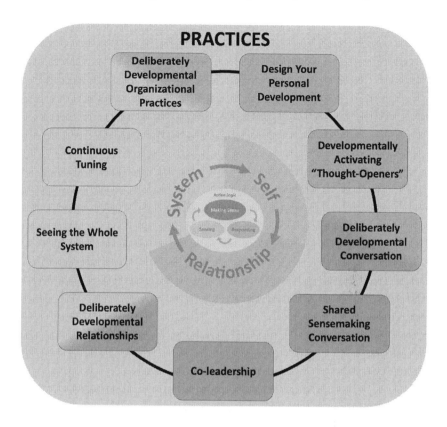

Figure 17: Evolvagility Practices

Practices are activities and actions whose practice is intended to *psycho-activate* inner development and growth, specifically within an organizational setting. The practices presented here are ones that I—and others—have introduced into a number of organizational, coaching, and training settings, and in a variety of combinations and renderings. They are the product of years of research, personal practice, and countless experiments; and they build on a rich body of research from the fields of executive coaching, developmental theory, and organization development.

There are many practices that I do not include here. Most notably, meditation and mindfulness practices—which come from, or are derived from, a centuries-long tradition from the East—which, nevertheless, I have seen, both in myself and in others, to be indispensable in catalyzing inner growth and development. There are also other contemporary practices, derived from the developmental research tradition and applied within the organizational setting, that are similarly powerful, and which I encourage the reader to also investigate and study.[55]

Many of the practices presented here have the effect of stretching us developmentally; in this way, they are designed to activate inner development. Some of the other practices, by contrast, have the effect of consolidating where we are already at developmentally—helping us develop new skills and competencies that increase our effectiveness in a VUCA world while at the same time further stabilizing and strengthening our core developmental stance. Additionally, a given practice can have both effects at different stages or even at different moments in our developmental journey.

In the following pages I will describe each of the practices. Note that it's not possible to fully teach each practice here; rather, my intention is to provide enough description to help point you in the right direction, and to give you a sense of how you might apply it yourself.

Design Your Personal Development

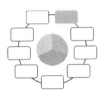 If we are to be deliberate about people's development—to not leave developmental growth to chance and to circumstance—then we need to be deliberate about *our own* development. This sounds obvious, but it bears emphasizing: In environments in which I've seen inner growth contributing to overall organizational performance—specifically *agility*—two conditions prevail. First, individuals are very deliberate about

---

[55] Among these are the deliberately developmental practices, which I have referred to a couple of times already, documented in Kegan and Lahey, *An Everyone Culture*. Also, I would encourage the interested reader to study the "Immunity to Change" process, also created by Kegan and Lahey, which brings a developmental perspective to a process by which people uncover the inner habits and commitments that people often hold—for the most part unconsciously—that thwart their best commitments. For more on this process and the theory behind it, see Robert Kegan and Lisa Lahey, *Immunity to Change: How to Overcome It and Unlock the Potential in Yourself and Your Organization (Leadership for the Common Good)* (Harvard Business School Publishing Corporation, 2009). One final resource I would recommend here is Jane Allen and Heidi Gutekunst with William Torbert, *Street Smart: Awareness and Inquiry-in-Action* (Amara Collaboration, 2018).

128

their inner growth, and they have taken on specific practices in order to purposefully engage in their own development. Second, individuals are very public about their developmental challenges and opportunities, and actively create social environments in which they work together to grow the inner capability they need to call upon in order to transcend the limitations that underlie and otherwise condition those challenges and opportunities. Those who are deliberate in this way about their development adopt the following practices:

- They reflect upon and grow a sense of connection with deep purpose and vision

- They have a deliberately developmental game plan

- They create a social, or *relationship*, structure that acts as a mini-*holding environment* for their growth

Let's examine how each of these might look in practice.

Sourcing Yourself in Vision and Purpose

As Bob Anderson and others often point out, being connected to our mission and purpose in life helps us avoid becoming overlay entrapped in sour reactions.[56] Creating and connecting to our own personal vision—for our work in the world, for our relationships, for our lives—is a way to bring tangibility and specificity to what is otherwise the intangible aspirational dimension of our selves. It brings to life—by giving it attention and focus—that part of ourselves from which arises our most noble instincts, our deepest longings. Ultimately, it connects us to what one might call our *soul's purpose*.

One might voice one's personal vision or purpose in many ways. These can include something that is written down—whether a short catch phrase or a longer essay. It can also include the capturing of a particularly evocative image or photo. Or, it can take the form of a collage that one composes from scratch. Whichever form it takes, the very process of rendering for ourselves some expression of a deep vision or purpose activates the emergence of a deeper intelligence, one that penetrates beyond the rational mind

---

[56] See Anderson and Adams, *Mastering Leadership*.

as it reaches down toward our deepest longing, and our deepest aspiration in life.

We don't often bring focused attention to this part of our inner life, and this attention-giving strengthens new and different parts of our brain. Neural science teaches us that the very activity of giving attention to certain connections in the brain—which is what we're doing when we give focused attention to the creation of a vision—has the effect of strengthening those connections.[57] This strengthening of new neural connections is enhanced through the creation of something tangible, something we can touch, look at, or otherwise *sense*. The process of making a tangible artifact both reflects and helps us connect to our deeper vision, and becomes a means by which we quite literally create something new in ourselves. By such a process, the artifact we create becomes a kind of talisman—an object that, in its evocation of our deeper self, comes to have an almost magical quality in its power to help us connect to that deeper world within us, and a world beyond the hold of a purely rational and analytical thinking—a world where intuition lives.

The rendered vision—as that which we can put our hands on, whether it is something we read or just gaze upon—becomes a reminder that we come back to when we get lost; it is the center we bring ourselves back to when we've gotten knocked off kilter. In coming back to it (for instance, you might have it tacked onto the wall in your workplace, or taped on a bathroom mirror), it re-familiarizes us with that deeper vision. It engenders associative connections, firing, and effectively strengthening, those deeper neuronal connections that got created. The *You* that is evoked in the process becomes a deeper you. A *You* that, over time, if frequently drawn from and returned to, becomes as real as anything else about you.

Rendering Your Own Vision. The following template is intended to help you start the process of rendering an expression of your inner vision, your deeper purpose. You can use this to guide you in that process, whether you

---

[57] See Mohab Costandi, *Neuroplasticity* (Massachusetts Institute of Technology, 2016); and Norman Doidge, *The Brain That Changes Itself: Stories of Personal Triumph from the Frontiers of Brain Science* (Penguin Books, 2007).

are rendering it in the form of a text, a collage, or whatever medium you are drawn toward.

Organizational Context
▶ What do I envision for my broader organizational setting?

Relationships
▶ Who are the kinds of people I want to impact? Partner with?

Models
▶ Who are the world leaders, whether living or dead, whether famous or unknown, who I envision myself being like?

World Context
▶ What do I envision for the world in which I live? For my community? For my country? The planet, even?

Figure 18: Vision Template

The process of capturing and rending a vision takes some time. Over the course of some weeks or even months, it is something you'll want to come back to it from time to time. The process of capturing one's vision is an ongoing activity, certainly not to be finished in a single sitting.

In working with this template for the first time, set aside a period—at least one hour—and find a quiet place that inspires you, that naturally connects you to that deeper place in you where dreams and aspirations feel most natural. Begin with one of the two questions on the left: What do I want to **Create**? Who do I want to be **Be**? Allow your mind to wander; let it become a receptor to messages, whose sources may be unknown to you. Capture whatever words or images come to mind. Don't worry if they don't make sense. In fact, in a way, it can be better if they don't make sense. What you're trying to do here is activate a deeper *intuitive* intelligence, not just a *logical* intelligence.

After some time, you might find your imagination wandering. You might begin, for instance, by asking yourself: Who are the kinds of people I want to impact? Who will I need to partner with? Who are the *kinds* of people I need to be around? Record your answers in the *Relationships* section.

Then, you might allow your attention to move toward *Organizational* context, asking yourself the question: What do I envision for my organization? This is a key question even if you don't hold a position of organizational leadership—having such a vision for your workplace organization empowers you to expand the range of impact you see yourself having.

From here, you might think of expanding into the broader world you live in—the *World Context* of your community, your country, the world at large—by asking yourself, and reflecting upon, the question: What do I envision for the world I live in? You might, along the way, be considering: Who are the leaders (whether living or dead) who truly model the leadership qualities I myself would want to bring?

Remember, this is an ongoing process. As you begin this process, you may get ideas as you go about your day-to-day life and want to jot them down. Your emerging Vision grows from the midst of the day-the-day world you live in, just as that emerging Vision affects the way you go about living in that world.

Your Deliberately Developmental Game Plan

Once you have begun the process of creating and rendering for yourself your Vision, you might begin to think about your developmental journey, where you currently are on that journey, and where you would need to go if who you are to be congruent with who you need to be in order to truly live in the spirit of your Vision. As you think about your developmental journey, it can be helpful to have a developmental *goal* as well as a game plan for getting there. The following template may help you create your goal and game plan:

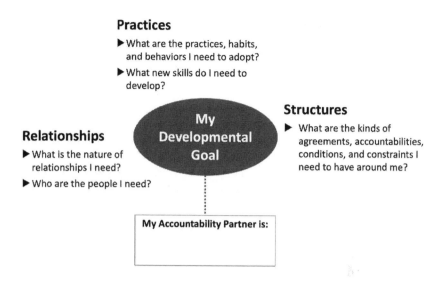

Figure 19: Game Plan Template

It is best to start with a *developmental goal*. A developmental goal is related to something you want to be able to do or accomplish, but more importantly, it points to someone you are able to *be*. For instance, rather than the professional goal of "leading a large organizational change effort," a more developmentally oriented goal might be "to be able to lead within a larger organizational change context." The difference between these two seems small, but it is crucial: The second statement is more developmentally oriented; the goal is to be *able* to lead within an organizational context. This focus on what you are *able* to do emphasizes the inner, developmental dimension of your effort.

In order to leverage that *developmental* potential for you, your developmental goal needs to constitute either a developmental *Stretch* or a *Consolidation* move. For example, you may want to get better at mentoring other people, and the consequent developmental stretch is to become less attached to how you think others should behave and what you think others should be interested in learning for themselves. (This developmental capacity has shades of both the *Individualist* and *Strategist* Action Logics.) An example of a consolidation move might be to improve your mentoring or coaching skills in order to become better able to attune yourself to the needs and interests of those who you wish to mentor. In either case—whether through developmental *Stretch* or through developmental *Consolidation*—your developmental goal needs to be one that requires you to expand or grow something in yourself.

Your developmental goal could take the form of a new role, whether a lateral move into a completely new area of the business or an upward move in which you would be situated in a more complex, and therefore more developmentally demanding position. Or it could be the taking on of a new project that poses new developmental challenges for you. Whatever the nature of the specific avenue you take, once you have a developmental goal, ask yourself:

> *What are the things I would need to be able to do? In order to be able to do those things, who would I need to be?*

Some variations of this question of yourself might be:

- What would I need to be able to tolerate emotionally, in order to be with the new levels of complexity, confusion, and other people's anxiety?

- How would I need to be able to think in order to embrace the greater complexity of the situation?

- In what ways would I need to be able to relate with others?

- What would I need to change about how I view other people? Specific people?

- What stories do I make up about the situation, about myself, and about others? How might those stories be constraining, or limiting me? What new stories might I invent that could be more useful here?

- How do I need to alter the relationships I have with people to create a foundation for greater workability, collaboration, and shared alignment?

For instance, you might have as a goal to lead a larger organization, program or department—and you can honestly say that this would be a stretch for you. Now, ask yourself: What would I need to be able to do? Who would I need to be? What stories about myself (for instance, about my own inadequacy) would I need to give up? What relationships would I need to cultivate? What stories would I need to give up about those specific people?

You could also think of a developmental goal in terms of a specific Action Logic stage you'd like to be able to occupy more fully. As when creating your vision, allow this to take some time.

Once you've established a developmental goal for yourself, think about creating for yourself a *holding environment*: What kinds of relationships and structures do I need to create around myself to support my movement toward achieving this developmental goal? What accountability structures[58] do I need to create?

You also want to think through what new practices you need to adopt: What new habits and behaviors might I need to now assume; what new skills and competencies do I need to develop?

A key ingredient in your development game plan is an ***accountability partner***. Accountability partners each hold accountability for the other, mutually. This is someone with whom you share your developmental journey on a rather intimate basis. Each of you knows, and holds as sacrosanct, the other's aspirations and vision. Each of you is aware of the other's traps, peccadillos, and self-destructive patterns as well as the other's great gifts and abilities. You make promises and commitments to each other that are related to your visions, to your developmental goals, and to your game plans.

Create a Relationship System That Acts as a Developmental Holding Environment

Building on the importance of having an accountability partner is of even greater importance when becoming part of what we will call a *deliberately developmental relationship system*. This system can be just you and one other person—you and your accountability partner, for instance. In addition, if

---

[58] An accountability structure is an arrangement you make with someone else in which you hold each other accountable for the promises and commitments you make—promises and commitments that typically serve to stretch you in some way.

you are a member of a team, you can constitute that team as a *deliberately developmental relationship system*. The nature of a such a relationship system points to the fact that while the inner growth and development necessary for *Sense-and-Respond* leadership capability is indeed individual, the process of inner growth and development is also necessarily social: In order to grow and develop, we need others—we need *relationships*. You will learn more about this when we get to the *Relationship* practices.

Developmentally Activating Thought-Openers

 As we design for ourselves a vision for who we want to be in the world (and in our organizations) and what we want to create—and as we formulate developmental goals and a game-plan for realizing those goals—we need a great number of structures and conditions that provide the necessary challenge, support, and tools—the *holding environment*—to catalyze the developmental growth needed to realize those goals and to be congruent with that vision.

The remaining practices in the deliberately developmental environment we are designing are intended to do just that. The first of these developmentally catalyzing practices is related to the opening up of our *thinking* (and when I use the word "thinking" I refer both to the cognitive and to the emotional realm). Here we introduce a thinking tool that I call a **Thought-Opener.**[59]

A *thought-opener* is an articulated thought, idea, or distinction that is designed to get you thinking in a new way. A thought-opener can sometimes have the effect of generating a kind of state experience—it can inspire you or annoy you, or it can simply be something that is puzzling. It can have the effect of pulling the rug out from underneath you—that is, out from underneath the way in which you normally think about things.

In the work we are doing to grow *Sense-and-Respond* leadership capability, we want to bring about conditions that help people to grow and strengthen their capacity for holding *Individualist* and *Strategist* Action Logics—to

---

[59] The idea of "thought-openers" derives from a similarly developmentally catalyzing set of thought forms found in Laske, *Measuring Hidden Dimensions*; and in Basseches, *Dialectical Thinking and Adult Development*.

grow their capacity, that is, to be able to think and act from a *Postmodernist* worldview. Developmental thought-openers are tools to help us do this.

The notion of developmental thought-openers builds on the idea of developmental scaffolding, introduced earlier; they invite us to think differently about familiar—or even unfamiliar—matters by asking ourselves the question: What would it be like if I thought like *this*? The main thing to remember with thought-openers is that they are not useful as statements of truth per se. Rather, we want to think of them as thoughts to dwell on or think about—in a manner similar to how Zen disciples meditate upon a Zen *koan*—in order to open up in you some new way of thinking. The point of the thought-opener is not related to their truthfulness, but to what they do *in you*.

Thinking Personae: Pluralist, Ecologist, and Visionary

The thought-openers presented here are organized around three different thinking qualities, or *personae*, if you will. Each thinking persona exhibits a certain way of thinking about and relating to the world—it takes on a particular quality of thinking that is endemic to the *Postmodern* worldview characteristic of *Individualist* Actions Logics and beyond.

The *Pluralist* thinking persona recognizes diversity and plurality of perspectives, and values that diversity and plurality as a way to both see the larger context, but to also include as many voices as possible. This thinking persona sees the need for collaboration, for relationship, and for partnership. By its inner logic, intelligence arises from the chaos and messiness of human engagement and interaction.

The *Ecologist* thinking persona takes a systemic and socially contextual view of the world. From the perspective of the Ecologist, everything is constituted through the interaction of *complex systems*. The view of the Ecologist is, hence, ecosystemic and is especially at home in the larger social and organizational frame.

The *Visionary* thinking persona takes the perspective that our intelligence, as individuals and as social systems, comes from the degree to which our actions are sourced by deep purpose and vision. The Visionary persona is all about creating our world—our capacity for authorship of the circumstances around us. One specific characteristic of the Visionary is that it sees the egoic self as contingent, as that which eventually dissolves in the face of the force of the larger self that finds its home in an expanded sense of cosmos.

The Thought-Openers

The thought-openers are grouped by *persona*. They reflect several aspects of the Action Logics: **Cognitive** (how we think); **Affective** (how we relate to and experience our feelings and emotions); and **Relational** (how we perceive and understand other people and our relationships with them). Some are more oriented toward one or another aspect than others.

Each of the thought-openers is posed as a statement, followed by a question, or sometimes, a small set of questions. You could work with these thought-openers either as individual solo work, or within the context of a *deliberately developmental conversation*; both are explained and discussed in the next section.

As individual solo work, you can think of these thought-openers as a kind of thinking dictionary. There are a number of ways in which you could approach working with these individually—there is no single approach that is right or best. For instance, when challenged or stuck in—or even when you are excited by—a situation or condition, you might, when you have a quiet moment for reflection, scan this list and allow your eye to be caught by one or another thought-opener. Another way to use these thought-openers is to choose one or another persona you'd like to focus on and choose a thought-opener reflecting that persona. Still another approach, if you happen to have a more methodical bent—and are especially ambitious—is to simply start at the top and work your way through each one in sequence (which you would pursue over the course of many, many months).

THOUGHT-OPENERS

Pluralist Persona

- Who I am is a process of unfolding. How might I characterize, or otherwise describe, that unfolding?

- I am composed of multiple selves, no single one of which is any more true about me than the others. What are some of those selves in me? Which of these do I most often push away, or otherwise deflect (both positive and negative ones)?

- Reality is composed of perspectives. Any situation or challenge, when seen through the lens of different perspectives, yields a very different range of possible approaches or resolutions. For this current situation, what might be a different perspective to hold it in? And another?

- Collaboration is the means by which work gets done. It is what allows me to think and work beyond the limitations of my own favored perspective. How might collaboration help in this moment? How might my blind attraction to collaboration actually hinder me?

- The creation of adaptive approaches and solutions to the situations and challenges we face depends on a high degree of diversity of perspective. What perspectives might I, or we, be missing out on right now? How might I (we) increase the diversity of perspectives in this moment?

- There is a difference between what happened and what I made up about what happened. All too often, we conflate the two: What I make up about what happened becomes, for us, what happened. For any given situation, ask yourself: What can I describe about what happened that is true and simple and does not interpose my own layer of what I make up?

- Whatever it is that seems to be happening in that other person—their emotions, their hang-ups, their limitations—is a reflection of what is happening in me. What emotion or energy that I experience coming from another person might I have projected onto them? How might I phrase that emotion or energy so that it is no longer from the third-person perspective (they/them) but is instead from the first-person perspective (I/me)?

Ecologist Persona

- Our thinking and behavior are determined by the social situations and milieus in which we find ourselves; individual consciousness arises in relationship with others. In what ways might my thinking be a product of (a) my relationships, (b) my upbringing, and (c) my work environment? Can I free myself from that entanglement?

- For any situation or challenge there is always a larger context we are not seeing, but if we could see it we would have greater insight. What might that larger context be for this situation?

- The character of every situation and challenge is determined by its relationship to something else. What might be that relationship, and what might be the something else for this situation?

- At any given moment, every situation occurs within a larger process, or unfolding. If we wish to impact a situation, we need to be able to see the larger process in which the current situation is but a momentary snapshot. What might be the larger process in which this current situation arises?

- In social systems, cause and effect is not readily observable, either because of time (cause and effect may be separated by long periods of time); locality (cause and effect may be separated by large spatial distances); or complexity (cause and effect may be hard to sort out in complex situations, because we cannot see the entirety of a situation). How can I (we) see the non-linear cause and effect of this situation or condition?

- You can't change a human social system; you can only create conditions in which it becomes possible for that system to choose to change itself. What is the nature of change we want for this system? Can I (we) let go of that in order to find out what the system itself wants? What is the nature of the conditions we might create to help that system come to be able to choose for itself?

- Situations are inherently messy. When I expect things to be clean and understandable, that is me trying to impose my own mental model of order on something or someone else. It probably won't be a good match. Can I stay solid and stable in the midst of messiness or chaos?

Visionary Persona

- I am the author of my life, and all that happens is a product of what I create in me, and around me. What might I author in this moment? What might I take responsibility for that I am currently not?

- My picture of the world is never complete—I must learn to live and to act in the very creation of that which is ever-incomplete. Given that I (we) don't know, what might we create in this moment?

- I am, in all that I do, anchored by a connection to deep purpose and vision. What is my purpose? What is my vision?

- My inner feelings and intuitions are as much a source of information as my cognition (thoughts). What is my sense in this moment? What do I intuit? What impulse do I have right now? Where in my body am I feeling it?

- Anything observed must include the consciousness of the one observing it. In what ways is my own way of thinking, framing, and understanding determining this situation? In what ways might my wish to be comfortable influence how I am seeing this situation?

- Who I am as a recognizable self is ever in flux; it is contingent on the social and technological system I find myself in. It is also contingent upon the situations and relationships I find myself in. Moreover, it is, ever-unfolding, ever-evolving. The notion that there is a static "me" that is unchanging—the me, for instance, that I may discover when I go out to "find myself"—is largely an illusion. In this situation, this relationship, this social setting what is the part of me that is recognizable, and what is the part of me that seems foreign?

- My vision holds a world beyond me, beyond this situation, and beyond us. It stretches beyond this organization, this country, even this planet. It spans across this lifetime, and even beyond. What can I envision 100 years from now? 500 years from now? 1,000 years from now? Who would I need to be, how would I need to think, in order to hold such a vision?

Whichever approach you take, and whichever thought-opener you choose to work with, you will start by reading the statement, letting it settle for yourself. Jot down any thoughts that arise as you consider the statement. Then, read the question (or the set of questions) that follows the statement you just read. Jot down two very different responses to the question—capturing two different reactions to a question activates different kinds of thinking by helping you explore, mentally, some aspect of the polarity inherent in many of these thought-openers. Once you've captured your response to the question(s), put it all down and go back to your day.

Then, in the evening when you have time to reflect, go back to that thought-opener again, and repeat the process (don't look at what you might have jotted down earlier). Then—and only then—read what you wrote earlier. Jot down any remaining thoughts you might have. Then, set it all aside. Don't get hung up by the content of what you wrote—in fact, you could even throw it away. The point isn't what you wrote. The point is what happens in your brain by just going through the process of thinking through a salient and familiar situation through the lens of the statement and question that constitutes that thought-opener.

The other way to use thought-openers, as I mentioned, is within the context of a deliberately developmental conversation. Let's go there next.

Deliberately Developmental Conversation

 We now begin to enter into the realm of practices that happen in relationship with others. The first of these is the *deliberately developmental conversation*. A deliberately developmental conversation is a kind of coaching conversation in which the focus is on helping another create greater awareness around the nature of their inner meaning-making and Action Logic schema, and how the quality and depth (or lack thereof) of that meaning-making might impact how and what they are able to *Sense* and what manner of *Response* they might take.

This is somewhat different than most professional coaching conversations because here we explicitly emphasize another person's *developmental* growth, and the manner in which a person's meaning-making might be shaping, or even defining, the challenges that person is having.

Focused Listening and Powerful Questions

Deliberately developmental conversations have a solid foundation in professional coaching practices. *Focused Listening* and *Powerful Questions*[60] are particularly salient.

The practice of Focused Listening recognizes two fundamentally different kinds of listening: "Level I" and "Level II".[61] Level I listening is what we do most of the time—it is a form of internal listening. When we listen to another person at Level I, we are either referencing what they are saying to ourselves—(for example, "That reminds me of what happened to me," or "Why is she telling *me* this?" or "That is soooo not what I would do!")—or we are simply not paying attention to what they are saying at all, and are thinking of other things. When we listen from Level I, our attention and focus is on ourselves and our own needs. Much of the time (perhaps most of the time), this is appropriate—it's what gets us through the normal, practical aspects of day-to-day life. However, Level I listening is not useful for deliberately developmental conversations.

Focused Listening—or Level II listening—is different than Level I in that here, our focus is genuinely on the other person. Our attention is like a laser shining on that other person. When listening from Level II, we think about the other person, not ourselves. We wonder, what's important for them? What is meaningful about what he just said? With Level II listening, our listening itself becomes a form of coaching intervention. It becomes a container into which that other person's speaking takes on deeper significance for them. When a person has an experience of being listened to in this way, she typically finds herself with a deeper connection to herself and a greater attunement to her own thinking and feeling process.

---

[60] The phrases "focused listening" and "powerful questions" refer to practices developed by the founders of the Co-Active coaching methodology and the Coaches Training Institute (CTI). For more information, visit the CTI website http://www.coactive.com/.

[61] The terms "Level I" and "Level II" listening refer to terms developed by the founders of the Coaches Training Institute (CTI).

The other foundational professional coaching skill that grounds the practice of a deliberately developmental conversation is the use of powerful questions. Powerful questions[62] reflect a more general—and *foundational*—coaching principle, and that is an emphasis on asking questions that deliberately evokes in another person a new angle or a different way of thinking about and relating to a given situation. This is contrasted with the more ordinary kind of question that seeks information—or the similarly ordinary practice of giving advice and making suggestions, which is appropriate for an explicitly mentoring conversation, but less so in a coaching context.

You can think of powerful questions as the speaking correlate of focused listening; they are questions which I might pose to another, not for me to get information for my own use, but to help the other person get something clearer for themselves, to have an insight for themselves, to be able to take a different perspective for themselves, to see more clearly a path forward for themselves.

Powerful questions are short and open-ended (they don't elicit Yes/No answers). Some examples of powerful questions include:

- What's possible?

- What have you learned from what you tried?

- What's important about that?

- At the beginning, how did you want it to be?

Did you notice that none of these questions include the word **why**? "Why" questions tend to send people to a more logical, or more historically focused place. They can also invite defensiveness. Powerful coaching questions are intended to keep people in the present, and to maintain a more expansive frame of mind.

---

[62] For a short description and a number of examples of powerful questions, visit http://www.coactive.com/ee_newsletter/images/uploads/31-Powerful-Questions.pdf.

Deliberately Developmental Conversation Moves

Deliberately developmental conversations build significantly on these practices. As is the case with any conversation in which the focus is on growing capacity in another person, the foundation of any deliberately developmental conversation is focused listening—actually being present with another person, both for who they are and for who they might be.

But the nature of the questions we ask within a deliberately developmental conversation have a slightly different emphasis than that of the powerful questions just described. The most important difference is that the developmentally oriented question presumes—and often draws upon—a shared vocabulary of distinctions and concepts that have their source in the developmental paradigm we've been exploring in this book. For instance, you might—within the context of a deliberately developmental conversation—explicitly reference specific Action Logic terms within any given question. An example of such questions could be: What might be the predominant Action Logic that informs the way you are thinking about this? How might that Action Logic limit how you are seeing this? What might be a different Action Logic from which you can look at this?

Questions such as these are designed to explicitly invoke the meaning-making dimension of the person's way of seeing and relating to the situation. It does this by explicitly referencing a specific vocabulary and a specific body of distinctions directly related to the developmental paradigm we want to invoke. As was said earlier, vocabularies (and distinctions) are key to catalyzing new ways of thinking since they generate new categories—and, as such, trace new neural connections—in people's minds. In addition to whatever other benefits arise from the coaching nature of the conversation, the developmental vocabularies and distinctions we introduce within a deliberately developmental conversation themselves act as catalyzing agents in another person's development as well as our own.

Practically speaking, you can think of deliberately development questions as falling into four overlapping categories.

Probing Questions. Probing questions help the other person probe into the underlying meaning-making they may be bringing to the current situation under discussion. Examples of probing questions are:

- What did you make up about that?

- What is the most significant thing about that?

- What in your thinking makes [the situation] seem the way it is?

- What if what that other person did [which was upsetting to you] made perfect sense? What might be the nature of that sense?

Provoking Questions. Provoking questions help to stimulate the other person to possibly generate a different perspective on the situation for themselves. They are intended to evoke a kind of cognitive disorientation in order to shift the ground of the other person's sense-making (and quite possibly our own). Questions derived from the thought-openers introduced above are good candidates.

- For this current situation, what might a different perspective be? What's another? And another?

- What might you take responsibility for in all of this, that you are not?

- How is this even a problem for you?

- The character of every situation and challenge is determined by its relationship to something else. What might be that relationship, and what might be the something else for this situation?

Supporting Questions. Supporting questions help the other person to see and connect to some deeper capability they already have, or to look around them to see where they might go for support. They are designed to help the other person discover—or *re*cover—their own inherent resourcefulness. Here are a few examples:

- What's a way of looking at this that connects you to your deeper vision?

- What is your intuition telling you?

- You know "self-confidence" can be arranged. What can you do to arrange to get self-confidence?[63]

Reflecting Questions. Reflecting questions help the person explicitly reflect on their own meaning-making and Action Logic. For example:

- How might you describe the nature of the perspective that has you see it that way?

- What assumption might you be making about that?

- What needs to shift in how you are making meaning of this?

- How might this look from the perspective of [Action Logic]? What might be different if you were to look at this from the perspective of [different Action Logic]?

Asking questions is not the only conversational move in a *deliberately developmental conversation.* The other moves are Acknowledgment, Articulation, and Reframing.

Acknowledgement. Acknowledgement is a verbal recognition of a quality in another which you see, but which they may or may not see in themselves. A couple of examples:

- I acknowledge you for the courage it took to stand your ground with me just now.

- I acknowledge you for the generosity of spirit it takes to allow others on the team to take credit for those things that you did.

Articulating What's Going On. This is a classic coaching move in which we reflect back to another person something we are noticing. It could be something we're noticing *in them.* An example might be "You have now said 'I'm frustrated' three times. What do you make of that?" Or it could be something you're noticing in yourself. For instance, "I notice myself feeling a little anxious in this conversation," or "I'm finding myself getting sleepy in this conversation." In either case—whether reflecting on

---

[63] "Self-confidence can be arranged" is from Thomas Leonard, *The 15 Frameworks: Hallmarks of the Certified Coach* (Coachville.com, 2002). It is available here: http://www.wellcoach.com/memberships/images/15_Frameworks1.pdf.

something we're seeing in the other person, or in ourselves—it is a way of holding up a mirror on the conversation and allowing for both you and the other person to stand back and reflect on the process of the conversation, or to take a different angle on the conversation.

Reframing. Every thought, opinion, and articulation assumes a particular context. For instance, if I ask you for some water, it would be safe for you to assume that I meant a glass of water, not a bucket or bowl. That context defines the frame in which I (and presumably others) understand what I am saying.

Often when we are stuck in a particular situation—that is, when we are having difficulty finding a desired resolution to an aspect of a given situation that is problematic for us—it is not so much the situation itself as it is the *context*, or the *frame*, in which we are holding it. Sometimes simply finding a different way of framing the problem or situation dissolves whatever problematic quality we want to resolve—that is, by creating a different frame, the problem seems to all but vanish.

Reframing is a deliberately developmental conversation move that helps another find a different frame. A reframe is most commonly offered in the form of a question. Many provoking questions are effectively reframes, for example, "Why is that even a problem in the first place?" or "What if crying were an expression of *courage* rather than of *weakness?*"

Challenging. Pointing out to another where there is an incongruence between what they say they are committed to, and how they actually show up, is an act of profound service—so long as we are careful to keep the "I" in the equation. A couple of examples:

- You say that you want my honest feedback, and yet on three occasions in this conversation when I told you what I think, I experienced my feedback being devalued by your saying "Well, that's just *your* opinion."

- I have twice asked you a direct question about what happened in the conversation you had this morning with Sally, and both times when you responded I find myself more confused than before.

Shared Sensemaking Conversation

 A deliberately developmental conversation tends to be a one-directional conversation, in which one person helps another generate for themselves some developmental insight into themselves, and in which the focus tends to be on one person. By contrast, a *shared sensemaking conversation* is one that is multi-directional; one in which the focus is on the sensemaking capacity of the *collective* (whether two people, three people, a team of eight, or a group of twelve).

Shared sensemaking conversations happen when two or more people have a conversation around something that is important, typically something related to a work situation. What differentiates this kind of conversation from an ordinary one is that the focus of shared sense-making is on deepening the quality of our *shared* understanding, not just of the situation at hand, but of the ways in which our assumptions and beliefs—both individually held and shared among us—limit and/or benefit how we perceive and talk about that situation. *Shared sensemaking conversations* are among the primary vehicles in which we engage in the practice of Deliberate Sensemaking.

Shared sensemaking conversations focus on:

- The situation; the "topic" of the conversation

- The nature of the meaning-making and Action Logic that determines how we think about, and relate to, the situation

- Our process as a relationship system; the patterns of interaction and communication that define the quality of our shared sensemaking

The Topic

For it to catalyze a deliberate sensemaking conversation with developmentally catalyzing power, the topic around which a *shared sensemaking conversation* orients itself must exhibit the four qualities found in a *facilitative agent*, which we discussed earlier (see the section "Developmentally Facilitative Agents" in Part III).

1. **Disequilibrating**: The topic must have something about it that is *edgy*, that is in some way disconcerting, in the manner in which it challenges a collective's deeply held assumptions, habits or beliefs.

2. **Salient:** The topic is one that those engaged in the conversation have not merely an interest in, or even a passion for—though these are important—but one which truly matters in their day-to-day work together. For example, a topic related to reversing global climate change is made salient by the fact that a company's entire product line contributes in some significant way to global climate change.

3. **Emotionally Engaging:** The topic needs to be something people truly care about.

4. **Interpersonal:** The topic must be one that requires the coming together of a collective—that is, it is a topic that cannot be seriously thought through (and certainly not resolved) by a single person in isolation.

The Meaning-Making and Action Logic Context

The qualities of disequilibrating—salient, emotionally engaging, and interpersonal— make the topic of a *shared sensemaking conversation* ripe for developmental richness. In fact, you could say that any time these four qualities arise in any kind of situation or condition you can count on the fact that there is great potential for developmental growth.

In most problem-solving processes the dimension of consciousness and meaning-making are given little or no attention—they are so far in the background as to be virtually invisible. Given the Postmodern worldview that informs the way *Sense-and-Respond* people work, and specifically the practice of shared sensemaking, the dimension of consciousness and meaning-making are pushed into the very foreground.

In other words, though we are committed to finding a solution to a given challenge, we also recognize that sometimes the solution is to be found precisely in the very manner in which we are holding the challenge (the topic) in our minds. So, in a *shared sensemaking conversation*, we value inquiry into the nature of our own assumptions, beliefs, habits, and attitudes, and the ways in which these play a part in the very constitution of the topic or situation at hand. In light of this, we ask ourselves questions like this:

- What are the hidden beliefs that inform how we are thinking about this situation?

- What assumptions do we hold?

- What's important to us about this? Why do we care?

- What stories and narratives do we draw on, subliminally, to help us make sense of this situation?

- What is the nature of the metaphors that frame the ways in which we understand what's going on (Sensing)?

- What's the nature of the thinking that determines how we conceive which actions might be a best fit for a given situation (Responding)?

- Given all of this, what's an experiment we might try (Responding)?

We might also mine the thought-openers for some questions.

The Protocol of a Shared Sensemaking Conversation

A *shared sensemaking conversation* has a particular protocol, roughly following the *Sense—Make Sense—Respond* flow that is at the heart of the *Sense-and-Respond* operating system:

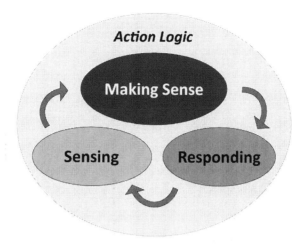

Reprise of Figure 4d: The Sense-and-Respond Human Systems Operating System

The process starts with **Sensing**. We pose some of the same questions we posed early on in the book: What are we seeing? What information do we have? What could we be missing? In what ways might we need to adjust our filters, and our modalities of sensing, so that we can see what we might be missing?

Then, we continue as we did earlier in the book: based on what we're sensing, we start to **Make Sense** of what we're sensing. What might this be telling us? About the organization? About us? About me (as a leader)? What's confusing? What's strange? What's hard to take? What's hard to understand? What *in us* makes it hard to understand? What does this confirm or disconfirm? What seems to be missing?

As we continue, we begin to inquire into the Action Logics that may be informing our way of making sense, and even our way of relating within this particular collective. We may pose for ourselves questions such as:

- What are the beliefs that inform our thinking?

- What worldviews? What assumptions?

- What's important to us? What are we committed to?

- What stories and narratives do we draw on, subliminally, to help us make sense of a given situation?

- What is the nature of the metaphors that frame the ways in which we understand what's going on (Sensing)?

- What's the nature of the thinking that determines how we conceive which actions might be a best fit for a given situation (Responding)?

- In what ways do personal, and *shared*, histories determine what's possible and what isn't?

As we continue the process of shared sensemaking, our **Response** to the kinds of questions just posed draws us back to our **Sensing**, and the cycle continues.

Sensing Versus Making Sense

Within the context of *shared sensemaking*, there is an underlying heuristic that is key to the workability and effectiveness of the shared sensemaking conversation. Individuals must come from their subjective experience—their *sensing* (what they know, what data they have, what metrics are available, and, perhaps, even what *feelings* they have)—as opposed to their interpretations—their *making sense*. The *making sense* part is what happens collectively, collaboratively.

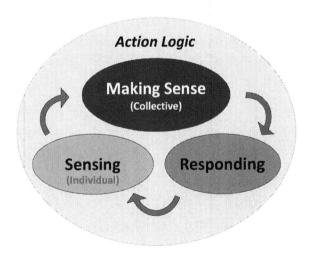

Figure 20: Individual and Collecting Sensemaking

This is what makes *shared* sensemaking different than *individual* sensemaking. With the latter, both sensing and sensemaking occur within the same mind; with the former, sensing is conducted by individuals, while sensemaking is what is done collectively.

This general requirement points to a distinction between "what happened" and "what we make up about what happened." I have found this to be a useful distinction to reference within the context of the *shared sensemaking conversation* because it helps people see how automatically we jump from sensing (what happened) to making sense (what we make up about what happened). It is this jump that causes us to mistake our *interpretation* of what happened with what *actually* happened.[64]

This conflation of interpretation and actuality can be especially problematic in a collective context due to the tendency of interpretations—of the stories we make up and the beliefs we come to hold—to become further cemented when held collectively. And it is that cementing of interpretations and beliefs that form the very edifice of shared culture.

Shared sensemaking is a key practice for growing *Sense-and-Respond* leadership as an everywhere phenomenon. It has *tactical* import in that it provides a deep approach to collective problem solving. It has *developmental* import in that it provides an avenue in which, through the process of problem solving itself, it has the effect of growing human developmental capability—both within the individual context and within the collective context. Finally, it has broad *organizational* import in that it can enable a breaking loose from limiting and deeply entrenched cultural patterns through the practice of examining and transforming previously unexamined assumptions and beliefs.

---

[64] Chris Argyris' "ladder of inference" points to similar phenomenon by which we cognitively jump from raw experience to full-on interpretation in a matter of milliseconds. For more, see "The Ladder of Inference: How to Avoid Jumping to Conclusions" at https://www.mindtools.com/pages/article/newTMC_91.htm.

AN EXAMPLE OF A SHARED
SENSEMAKING CONVERSATION

Here's an example of what this all might look like. You have a product team consisting of a couple of Product Managers, a couple of Agile-team Product Owners, and a Director of Product Management. Their topic is that, despite robust demand over the previous three years, during the course of the last year there has been declining demand and interest. Product enthusiasm is low as evidenced in a downward trend in social media buzz, and sales are way down.

The shared sensemaking process starts with *Sensing*. People ask themselves, and each other, the same kinds of questions we just considered: What are we seeing? What information do we have? What are we missing? What might we not be seeing? They admonish each other to stick to "what happened," noting their tendency to jump to interpretation, or making sense.

Then, at some point, they begin to switch to a different mode of questioning. This begins the collective *Making Sense* part of the conversation. They ask themselves, collectively, some powerful questions. What's the most confusing part about this? What's the strangest part? What might this be telling us about the organization? About us? This last question seems to hit a nerve, prompting them to turn to some of the kinds of questions more directed toward revealing the underlying meaning-making and Action Logic that might be at work here:

What beliefs do we hold about this product? What assumptions? What are we committed to? What stories and narratives do we draw on, subliminally, to help us make sense of a given situation? What's the nature of the thinking that determines how we conceive which actions might be a best fit for a given situation (Responding)?

These questions prompt a conversation that reveals a deep assumption and an unexamined belief. The assumption is that the product is already popular and successful and doesn't need as much of the kind of thoughtful attention they gave to it earlier on. The underlying belief they uncover, through further, very disclosive, conversation, is that they can't possibly give all the attention required of every product they held in their portfolio—there is simply not enough bandwidth.

As the conversation continues, they ask themselves a key question—one that often has the effect of revealing deeper Action Logic frames. They ask: What are the common terms we are using to describe this situation when we talk about it? When they reflect on their conversation, and jot down on a flipchart some of the common words, they note a vocabulary that seems to reflect for them a powerful Expert Action Logic orientation—words and phrases like bandwidth, not enough, we can't do it all, and overwhelmed.

As they realize how possessed they are by a limiting vocabulary, they then ask themselves a powerful question: If we could have it how we want it, how would that be?

After some brainstorming together, they come up with the following phrase:

> We want to love *all* of our products *all of the time*.

Then, more deliberate sensemaking reveals yet another assumption: In order to give each product the attention and love they each deserve, they *themselves* would have to do it. The underlying, unexamined belief here is that only they themselves could understand enough about the customer to make the kinds of decisions necessary for each product.

Once they clearly see the nature of their own assumptions and beliefs, and how they have limited their perception of what is possible, they see an obvious solution. Since their product development teams are all Agile—though some are more mature and capable than others—what if they brought those teams together with some of the actual customers, on a regular basis, and let the teams themselves make more of the product business decisions, based on what they learn from these actual customers and their respective Product Owners? This would not only break the stalemate of their own capacity limitations, but it could serve a secondary—and perhaps even more powerful—effect, which would be to more fully empower their product development teams by giving them responsibility in areas which tie more directly to the business.

This could lead, finally, to an experiment they can try—the *Respond* phase of this sensemaking conversation. They decide to try their idea out with two different development teams to see what happens over the course of the next two months.

Co-Leadership

 Co-leading is shared sense-making in action. It arises in a situation or event in which (usually) two people are called upon to lead *together*. Co-leadership is a relationship dance in which the activity of *Sense-and-Respond* happens *in the relationship*. When done skillfully, the result of co-leading is a far greater intelligence and capacity to *Sense-and-Respond* within the leadership and facilitation of highly complex social situations.

Co-leading occasions result in increased intelligence, which is gained when two people are leading together in a synergistic and collaborative fashion. This is particularly evident within the context of group facilitation or of a workshop (in particular, workshops that are *transformative* in nature, hence requiring the holding of a safe emotional container). However, co-leadership doesn't only have benefit in a group setting; there are many other occasions in which the situation itself can benefit from the increased intelligence and available skill of an effective co-leading dance. For instance, management situations can benefit when two managers come together in co-leadership. A similar benefit is gained when business partners learn to partner as co-leaders.

Co-leading requires particular relationship skills which, when exercised, can be powerfully catalyzing and developmentally psycho-activating. It is yet another way in which individual development happens within a relationship context.

Sense-and-Respond leadership is the capacity to dance with what is happening at any given moment—in the face of volatility, uncertainty, constant change, ambiguity—and in the face of the consequent anxiety we feel. Co-leading makes it easier to navigate this kind of real-time dance: two people can be attentive to (Sense) and act (Respond) in the moment with greater intelligence than one. But this presupposes that the two are dancing *together*. And, dancing with another—in the moment—requires an ability to let go of attachment to one's own agenda and to the need to be in control. So, while co-leading can ease the challenges required of being able to dance in the moment, it also brings its own challenges.

The Stake

The co-leaders' *stake* is the stabilizing force in the adaptive dance I'm describing here.[65] A stake is a statement of what we assert to be true and necessary for a given occasion, in the standing for which we create for ourselves a deeper purpose for our being here, for this occasion. A stake is not a goal. A goal is a milestone toward a specific *end*: increased profit, faster time-to-market, greater customer value—these are all goals. Having a goal is important, but we also need to articulate our stake.

For instance, in facilitating a one-day workshop to help a management team deepen their capacity to take greater risks in their decision-making processes, I and my co-leader might articulate this stake: From danger comes opportunity. As you can see, this is not a goal. Rather, it is a provisional

---

[65] Henry Kimsey-House and David Skibbins, "Leadership: What's Your Stake," *New European Economy Magazine* (Winter 2010).

truth—provisional because it is specific to this occasion—which acts as an anchor in every moment-to-moment action we take, in every split-second decision we make. At any moment, in our co-leading dance in that moment, our split-second decisions and actions are informed by our stake.

In this sense, a stake acts metaphorically as a stake in the ground that allows us to *Sense-and-Respond* without the need to have to predict what might happen in order to be able to plan what we might do. As long as our dance remains grounded in our stake, it can take whatever direction we in the co-leading dance see it wanting to take, depending on what we are sensing—both in the situation we are leading and in our relationship with one another.

It is the Relationship That is Leading

Our stake is one way in which we ground what would otherwise be an ungrounded co-leadership dance. The other anchoring point in a *Sense-and-Respond* co-leadership dance is the fact that the two of us are dancing *together*. In fact, one way we often describe what's going on is that it is not us, as individuals, who are leading; rather, it is the relationship that is leading. Leadership takes place within the context of the dynamics and the patterns of our interactions. Those dynamics and interactions themselves can be highly evocative and catalyzing, especially in a workshop or group facilitation situation. When something goes awry in what we're doing, or within the environment in which we are leading, we look to what might be going on in *our* relationship, and course-correct there, rather than trying to figure what might be going on externally.

What seems to happen, when we lean in to the relationship, is that a different kind of intelligence emerges. An intelligence that has its source not just in the individual intelligence of any single person, but in the intelligence—and even *wisdom*—that seems to emerge when we trust in the power of the relationship.

Such a manner of co-leading requires a high degree of trust and a capacity to let go of our individual pre-conceived notions of how things should go, and of our attachment to our preferences for how we wish things would go. In fact, I personally know of no better way to grow the inner developmental capacity for *Sense-and-Respond* leadership —a Postmodernist mindset and capacity grounded in the *Individualist* Action Logic and beyond—than practicing, and becoming masterful in, the art of co-leadership.

Deliberately Developmental Relationships

All of the Relationship practices just discussed—the *deliberately developmental conversation, shared sensemaking*, and *co-leading*—are greatly aided by—and in fact, can really only happen within the context of—a **deliberately developmental relationship**. This is a relationship in which the context of the relationship is the quality, depth, and intelligence of the relationship itself. Distinctions and practices—drawn from the body of practices introduced across both the Self and the Relationship domains—are deliberately employed in order to create a social environment in which inner growth and skillfulness is valued just as highly as the business outcomes we are brought together to create.

> When we declare a relationship to be deliberately developmental, we establish a basis of integrity, mutual respect, and mutual commitment to both our own and the other person's inner growth. This basis becomes the solid foundation on which our relationship grows, and on which we, as individuals, grow as well.

In this way, the *deliberately developmental relationship* is the relational context which makes possible the *Relationship* and the *Self* practices we've just been talking about. By the same token, it is those practices that solidify the deliberately developmental context of that relationship. In this way, the relationship itself becomes the kind of powerful *holding environment* that we described above.

Figure 21: Deliberately Developmental Relationship

The notion of a *deliberately developmental relationship*, and the emotional and relational container (the *holding environment*) that it engenders, forms the context in which the other Relationship practices—the *deliberately developmental conversation, shared sensemaking conversations*, and *co-leading*—find their effect. Without it, none of those other practices would be possible.

Seeing the Whole System

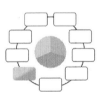 We are now moving into the *Systemic* sphere, which is the domain of sociality in which we talk about social systems or, more simply, "systems." Unlike relationship systems we've talked about thus far, a social system is one in which it is impossible to have the whole system in the room. Because of this, they are uniquely impacted by discontinuities that characterize social systems due to the difficulty in bridging them. And yet, being able to see the whole of an organizational system—discontinuities and all—is a key ability if we are to expand beyond our most immediate relationship systems, and bring about, or otherwise catalyze, broader *Sense-and-Respond* capability within an organization.

This is extremely rich territory, and it involves a great many frames for thinking. In Part V, we will explore in some depth the role of organizational managers and leaders in facilitating the emergence of *Sense-and-Respond* organizational capability in ways that pertain directly to organizational systems. For now, we focus on the nature of the activity that smaller groups—

whether fully constituted teams or ad hoc work groups—can do together to come to be able to see, and effect change in, the organizational systems of which they are a vital part and by which they are so often impacted.

Discontinuities of the Organizational System

Organizational systems are characterized by discontinuities in their ability to be seamlessly unified entities. Their complexity can, at least in part, be explained by this. These discontinuities manifest themselves as distances that separate individuals and collectives from one another. When we look, we can discern at least four kinds of distances in an organizational system: Focus, Perspective, Time, and Space.

The most obvious kind of distance is *Space*—which is that people are not in the same physical space at this moment, or their location in different places makes it difficult, and certainly impractical, to bring *everybody* together.

Time is also a kind of distance. You might think of this as pointing to the fact that people live and work in different time zones, which can make it difficult to bring people together. But the more significant systemic aspect of time is that organizational systems exist in, and unfold over, time. Organizational systems—just like any system—have a history, and the nature of that history has an effect, often hidden, on what is happening *now*. It is hard enough to reflect on, and consider the effect of, time on a relationship system, such as a team, that is able to come together more easily. It is much harder for a larger organizational system, due to the fact that the span of time tends to be much longer as social systems get larger; but also due to existence of the other distances which characterize those larger systems.

Focus relates to the fact that, in a larger organizational system, different parts of the system are focused on different tasks, and exist in different organizational settings, each of which is constituted on the basis of the tasks they are organized around. Those people who are focused on accounting, for instance, are not terribly interested in, or concerned with, the kinds of challenges and tasks that those in marketing are focused on. In a larger system, it is natural for human systems (and is developmentally consistent with the *Expert* Action Logic that prevails in most organizational settings) to want to focus primarily on their area of expertise, their social milieu. By contrast, in a smaller system—such as an Agile team of seven people—it is easier to bring people with different areas of focus together. This is not just because the other distances are smaller (e.g., space and time), but because it is easier for the smaller system to organize themselves around, and focus on, a common task. For instance, though its team members may come from different areas of focus, an Agile team is often given another, often overriding, focus as defined by the project or product goal that the team is working on. This project or product goal serves as the unifying focus for the team.

Perspective can bring about another kind distance between people in an organizational system. Perspective relates to how people see the world, and correlates to a number of factors, including the area of focus (people who work together in the same focus area tend to share perspective), culture, economic status, and, yes, developmental profile. For example, people operating primarily at the *Expert* Action Logic tend to hold a different perspective than those operating primarily at *Achiever*. The differences in perspective among non-allied groups present significant challenges to communication, and certainly in collaboration. A great number of gaps—in vocabulary, in knowledge, in emotional dispositions, in developmental capacity—have to be navigated in order come to a place where shared understanding, shared alignment, and shared commitment can happen.

Seeing the Whole Organization

These distances make it very difficult to see an organizational system in anything like its entirety. In fact, I would dare say that we can never really see an organizational system in any definitive way. Organizations are inherently complex and non-linear and are therefore unknowable in any definitive or final sense of the term. All we can do is make informed guesses, act on the basis of those guesses, and then iteratively inspect and adjust as we go along.

This stance is in stark contrast to the more commonly held belief—which is, ultimately, a product of the prevailing Modernist worldview, captured by the *Expert* and *Achiever* Action Logics—that tends to see the world as an immense clockwork, with predictable linear cause-and-effect. For those who are steeped in this mindset, the approach to broader organizational work that I advocate here may be somewhat challenging indeed.

The standard methods we have for examining the nature of organizational systems, and for improving them, have limited impact on overall organizational change. While I would not ignore them—because they do have some important contributions—we need to augment them with a new set of methods, and, ultimately, a new methodological thinking that leverages the holistic and non-linear nature of whole systems. You could say that it is precisely such methodological thinking that pervades the entirety of this book.

There are a number of methods for helping large organizational systems come together.[66] While such work is key to facilitating broad organizational and systemic self-awareness and change, there are also ways in which smaller, self-organized, and developmentally oriented, groups can work together to be able to see, and hence instigate small adjustments to, the organizational systems of which they are a part.

Organization Modeling

One such method, inspired by the practice and methodology of *systemic constellations,*[67] I call **organization modeling**. Our aim with *organizational modeling* is to visualize some aspect of an organizational system in order to see it more clearly and, perhaps more importantly, to explore our own hidden biases as it relates to that system. Organization modeling is much simpler than systemic constellations. For one thing, we're not trying to uncover the deeper psychological currents of a system. Nor do we believe that we are endeavoring in any way to change the system through the enacting that unfolds in the constellation.

As is the case with any kind of constellating method, organization modeling is done with a small group of five to seven people. Preferably, participants are actually part of the organizational system you are investigating; to be

---

[66] See Peggy Holman, *The Change Handbook: The Definitive Resource on Today's Best Methods for Engaging Whole Systems* (Berrett-Koehler Publishers, 2007).

[67] For a really good and eye-opening introduction to systemic constellations—and to the nature of human systems more generally—see John Whittington, *Systemic Coaching and Constellations: The Principles, Practices and Application for Individuals, Teams and Groups* (Kogan Page, 2016).

effective, you need people who have some skin in the game—people for whom any topic related to the system will generate both *salience* and *emotional engagement*. You will need a room with some space for people to stand and move short distances, and the process requires about 30–45 minutes.

To get started, someone in the group volunteers to be the modeling Host. The Host is the person who has a particular organizational situation that either poses a challenge or an opportunity, and whose dynamics are in some way complex, confusing, or ambiguous. The situation must be currently alive, not one that existed in the past—that is, the situation must have salience and some degree of emotional energy for the Host.

Once the Host and the situation have been determined, the Host selects individuals to physically stand in as—or *model*—elements of the system in which that situation is currently playing out. Those elements could be anything from specific *roles* in the organizational system, to specific *individuals*, to organizational *functions*, to particular *teams* or *departments*, to structures (such as a hardware platform) and organizational policies (such as an HR policy)—any element that constitutes what the Host sees as a key element in the system in which the chosen situation is seen to activate.

The individual *models* are physically arranged in the space by the Host in such a way as to reflect how she or he sees the systemic and structural qualities of the system being modeled, and the interrelationships among the elements. For example, people may stand nearby or far away from one another, face each other, stand sideways, or be back-to-back. The Host arranges the people in such way as to reflect the current system and the interrelationships of its elements.

Once the initial spatial configuration of the elements of the system have been set, the facilitator of the session invites each of the models to say what their experience is like, as they sense into the felt quality of the element they are modeling. Typically, their descriptions reflect the current state of affairs in the system. Once we have heard from each model, the facilitator asks the Host to reposition one or two elements in the system in such a way as to address, or repair, the problem verbalized earlier by the Host and then individually by the models. Next, the facilitator then asks each model to physically reposition themselves in the constellation in a manner in which they somehow feel moved to do, based on their new orientation. The Host is then asked to reflect on what that does to his or her understanding of the system.

The process concludes with a reflective debrief in which the Host deepens their learning about this particular systemic situation, and in which each participant (as well as any observers) reflect on their learning around systemic dynamics, more generally.

> *Organization modeling is a way of learning more about a human system, while also exposing our own preferences and assumptions, and how those preferences and assumptions not only color how we see the organization (and revealing our biases in the process), but generating new insights as to how we might go about approaching the system in a more open and more informed place.*

Organization modeling is a method of systems learning that observes the inherent non-linear and essentially complex nature of human systems. It is an example of the kinds of newly emerging human technologies for understanding and engaging with human systems.[68]

Continuous Tuning

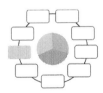 We have just investigated a way of thinking about how we might come to be able to *see* organizational systems that attempts to account for their inherent discontinuities and non-linearity. In doing so, I shared with you a specific method for helping us better see such an organizational system, in all of its non-linear glory. Now, armed with greater insight into the nature of a specific organizational system, we have a theory of that system on the basis of which we can think through how we might

---

[68] For an introduction into this kind of approach to working with human systems, see Anne Rød and Marita Fridjon, *Creating Intelligent Teams*, (K R Publishing, 2016). You can also learn more about these ideas, and about the powerful training programs they offer by visiting https://www.crrglobal.com/orsc.html.

endeavor to help that system move toward greater congruence with its aims and goals.

I want to emphasize at this point the importance of including actual organization players—people who have skin in the game—in all of these systems practices and processes. Ultimately, we're talking about helping a system see *itself* and to change itself in whatever manner is right for itself.

The philosophy that informs this kind of thinking is well captured in Deborah Rowland and Malcolm Higgs's book *Sustaining Change*,[69] in which are observed the following principles:

- Organizational systems change is governed by the establishment of a few rules in relation to which people are encouraged to experiment and self-organize

- Engagement in change is voluntary

- Organizational leaders and managers can only *create the conditions for change*—they cannot direct the manner of change

- Change processes are oriented around self-organizing "cells"

Informed by such a philosophy, I propose an approach to organizational systems change that is aligned with the very nature of *Sense-and-Respond*, an approach that I am calling *continuous tuning*. This is about making small adjustments within a system and observing the effect.

One image comes to mind when think of this manner of systems intervention, and that is the image of a piano tuner. With each turn of the screw for a given string, the tuner listens carefully; not just to the immediately adjoining strings, but to a number of other strings across the entire keyboard. The same is true when tuning an organizational system: we make a small adjustment in one part of the system, and then observe the impact over the entire organizational system.

---

[69] Deborah Rowland and Malcolm Higgs, *Sustaining Change: Leadership That Works* (John Wiley & Sons, 2008).

The Action Learning Tool

In the following, I want to introduce an **Action Learning** tool that enacts this tuning approach. Action Learning is an organization development (OD) tool used to help a system iteratively and incrementally learn by *acting* within an organizational system, while at the same time having their actions be informed by what they are *learning*. What I particularly like about this tool is that it is iterative and incremental, and it can be used anywhere and everywhere within an organizational setting.

In my experience, the tool works best when people everywhere—at all levels and across all organizational functions—learn how to use this tool and then take it up as they investigate, uncover, and resolve organizational issues that impede their ability to do good work. Coupled with its use by management and leadership working at the organizational level (which we will cover in some depth in Part V), this tool provides a powerful *Sense-and-Respond* method for gradual, self-managed organizational change and transformation.

An Action Learning process is something that takes place over the course of some weeks, since the cycle involves a learning/reflection stage (typically done within a single session of 30–90 minutes) followed by an experiment/action stage (which can last anywhere from a day or two, to a week or two). In general, an Action Learning process—spanning multiple iterations—for any given question, challenge, or situation should last no longer than six weeks. Beyond that span of time things start to get stale, and there is a greater chance for habitual, culturally induced patterns to dull the sharpness of the work and of the people conducting it.

The Action Learning process is conducted by an ad hoc team from the organization—called an Action Learning "cell"—which is assembled (or better, *assemble themselves*) specifically for this purpose. The people who form an Action Learning cell are typically composed of people from a variety of walks of life, but who are drawn together around a shared concern. As people learn how to do this, it is useful to have someone who can mentor and coach them (much like Agile teams have an Agile Coach to help them get up and going). As was said above, the work of an Action Learning cell is typically no more than a few weeks—and the scope of their work is purposely kept small and close so as to avoid having this work take up a

169

disproportionate amount of people's time. Once the work of a cell is completed (however they define completed), the cell disbands.

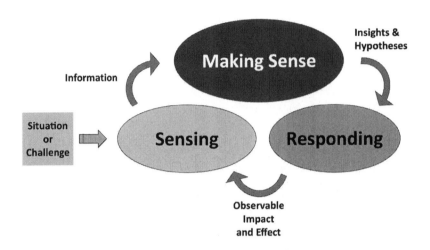

Figure 22: A Sense-and-Respond Action Learning Model

Figure 22 depicts how one might model the *Sense-and-Respond Action Learning* process. Let's walk through the elements of this process.

The Action Learning process begins with a **Situation** or **Challenge**. Typically, your Action Learning cell will have already done some work around *Seeing the Whole System*. For instance, they might have conducted an *organization modeling* session to bring into greater relief aspects of the system or situation (or its own biases, preferences, and assumptions regarding the situation or system) prior to beginning the Action Learning process. But this is not at all necessary for an Action Learning cell to be productive in their work together.

In general, it is good for the situation or challenge statement to be expressed as a complete sentence—for example, "Our business and engineering managers have a hard time agreeing on priorities and we believe that might be impacting the product development teams' ability to stay on track with their delivery release schedule." Short phrases or words leave things open to misunderstanding, misinterpretation, and confusion.

As you move into the **Sensing** phase, you start to ask yourselves, as a team, questions to help you gain more information. Among the questions you might pose at this point are:

- What information do we have?

- What behaviors are we observing?

- What are the kinds of organizational structures, policies, or systems at play?

- What seems really challenging about this situation for other people? For ourselves?

- How do we feel about the situation? What judgments and assessments might we be having?

The next phase in the process is **Making Sense**. Here you move into a more reflective mode and ask questions which have the following quality:

- What information might we be missing?

- In what ways are the behaviors impacting the situation?

- In what ways might those organizational structures, policies, or processes be impacting the situation?

- What does the nature of the challenge say about the organization? About us?

- How might our own feelings, judgments, and assessments be affecting how we're seeing this situation?

As is so often the case with this kind of work, the point is not necessarily to come up with concrete answers, per se, but rather to stretch and expand your own thinking about the situation. Where you are ultimately going is toward the formulation of a *hypothesis* on the basis of which you might formulate an experiment. This reflects a kind of *inspect-and-adapt* thinking as applied to the process of organizational research and continuous change.

As you formulate a hypothesis or two, or render an insight for yourselves, you enter the **Respond** phase where you think about what experiments you might try, based on what you are learning. The nature of the experiments we are considering at this point are intended to accomplish a number of different kinds of outcome:

- Get more information

- Gain greater insight

- Effect a small change or make a small improvement as it relates to this particular situation

- Communicate with someone who has the power to impact the situation

There is a slight nuance here, because the point is not necessarily to come up with some improvement for the organization. Though one intention may be to introduce an experiment that could effect small (or even a *large)* change, the intention also is that whatever action you take helps you gain more information, or render for yourselves a deeper insight.

With such an experiment—or small set of experiments—posed, cell members then disperse and do whatever work they've agreed to do in order to carry out whatever experiment the cell has committed to. Once that work has been done, the cell members come together once again— armed with new information, insights or actions taken—to move through another *Sense—Make Sense—Respond* cycle.

At some point cell members declare the process complete. This usually happens when they achieve some intended goal, or when they feel that they have reached a new level of insight—which they are obliged to share with relevant other stakeholders in a meaningful way—in relation to the statement (of the challenge or situation) that kicked off the cycle in the first place.

Action Learning as an Organization-Wide Practice

Action Learning, in the way I am describing it here, is conducted not just by an organizational management or leadership team on behalf of an entire organization, but by any number of ad hoc teams who self-organize themselves around a shared interest, passion, or concern. Action Learning teams are typically self-selecting (though it is usually a good idea to have someone who is experienced and skilled in facilitating the process to act as the process coach and facilitator for a given ad hoc team, certainly while that team is learning the process).

I have found the practice of Action Learning, practiced in this way, to be a very powerful catalyst for organizational learning and improvement for a number of reasons. First, when practiced in the cross-functional and highly participative manner described here, Action Learning has a higher probability of solving institutional challenges and issues which top-down, top-down directives are less good at doing. One reason for this is that when people are allowed to frame the problem, they are more likely to *own* it and are more likely to find ways of solving it that are more creative and more likely effective.

Second, when practiced in the way described here, Action Learning becomes a cultural practice and, as such, has the effect of raising the level of general organizational awareness and collectively-held competence. Organizational improvement comes to be truly owned by *everyone*.

Third—and perhaps most importantly—the very process of participating in an Action Learning team—or cell—can itself be developmentally catalyzing. The nature of the process requires a certain degree of self-examination as well as examination of the relationship space in which the team works. This inward examination explicitly points to the Action Logics currently at work within those individuals, and within that particular team. As such, Action Learning becomes one of those practices that, by its very practice, have the effect of psycho-activating inner growth, both at the individual level, and at the level of the relationship system involved.

When done well, Action Learning simply becomes part of what people do on a day-to-day basis. Sometimes a cycle might last a couple of days, sometimes several weeks. Not everyone in a given organization is involved in an Action Learning cycle at all times—some tend to be more involved than others. Nevertheless, when done well, Action Learning becomes another *everywhere* phenomenon, further deepening and expanding the developmental impact, which is the very essence of *Sense-and-Respond* leadership.

Deliberately Developmental Organizational Practices

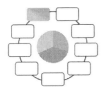 We now move into a territory in which individual and relationship practices exert an impact more broadly across the organization landscape. While these practices can be, and often are, exercised within the relatively intimate environment of a deliberately developmental relationship or in any kind of deliberately developmental ecosystem, the value they bring is amplified when they come to be practiced organization-wide—that is, when they come to be a part of the routine fabric of day-to-day organizational life.

In Part V, I will discuss the role of organizational leadership and management in supporting and empowering these practices. For now, I want to delve into the specific practices themselves.

Developmental Feedback

Leaders everywhere—whether they sit at the top of the organization or as team members committed to their team being excellent—have an intention for the kind of impact they want to make on others and on the world around them. People who think and act from later Action Logics—those who have deliberately put themselves on the path of *Sense-and-Respond* leadership—want to know if their *impact* is congruent with their *intention*.

By contrast, people who think and act from earlier Action Logics, and are not truly on a path toward *Sense-and-Respond leadership,* have little interest in seeing that gap. In fact, they feel threatened by that gap, and by anything that someone might say to reveal that gap, because the information blows the cover of self-delusion that often is a hallmark of the leadership quality of those who have not yet made the commitment to, or done the work to, grow their inner complexity of mind.

Feedback is what helps us see the gap between our intention and our impact.

As we grow toward later Action Logic stages, feedback becomes increasingly important. We recognize, more and more, that there is often a very big gap between our intended impact and our actual impact. As leaders, we want to be informed, perhaps even *constantly*, of that gap. That is the value of feedback.

Unfortunately, the manner of feedback that is all too often practiced fails to provide the information that is most useful to us. Most of the time it comes in the form of an admonition of how you should or shouldn't be and is packaged as though it were a statement of fact about another. Such a notion of feedback presupposes a Cartesian model of communication, in which there is a sender and a receiver; when I give you feedback, I am *sending* you information with the expectation you will *receive* it. This puts undue pressure on the receiver of the feedback to accept it as valid, even when they feel—perhaps even legitimately—that it is somehow hard to receive, whether because it is emotionally hurtful, cognitively incongruent (with how they see themselves), or just simply hard to reconcile with the context of their relationship with the giver.

But feedback is always as much about the giver as it is about the receiver. In effect, we're talking about one human being telling another what they think of that other; and the "what they think" will always be a product of the inner meaning-making of the feedback giver, whether or not she or he is aware of it. Nevertheless, when in the throes of the classical model of feedback, we persist in treating feedback as a sender-receiver phenomenon.

By contrast, within the context of small-l *Sense-and-Respond* leadership, we transcend the Cartesian sender-receiver model of feedback; instead, we want to see feedback as an authentic form of communication that occurs within a developmental and relational context and which emanates from a genuine commitment to one another's growth and to the integrity and authenticity of our relationships.

Two feedback protocols that provide a powerful practice frame for becoming skillful in giving and receiving feedback along the lines I am promoting here are:

- *Situation-behavior-impact* feedback (or simply *impact feedback* for short)

- *Observation-story-assumption* feedback (or simply *what I make up*, for short)

Impact Feedback

Impact feedback[70] is based on the premise that feedback is not about telling another person what they did wrong, or what they should or should not do. Rather it is about telling another person what you observed them doing and what your *experience* was. The protocol is [what happened] + [my experience] + [silence]. Here are some examples:

- When you stopped me mid-sentence (*what happened*), I found myself feeling embarrassed and confused (my *experience*—which is the *impact* on me)

- When you kept hopping around in your slide deck during your presentation (*what happened*), I got worried that you might have been lost, and I started to lose confidence in what you were doing (my *experience*—which is the *impact* on me)

- When you keep arriving late to our regularly scheduled meeting (*what happened*), I get frustrated and start to feel like this isn't very important to you (my *experience*—which is the *impact* on me)

One key here is to give your feedback as a short phrase—as short as possible—and then *shut up*. Stop talking; allow for the impact of your feedback to settle for that person. Wait for them to process it and respond to you.

It is important to be careful to avoid offering a suggestion for how they might change their behavior. Offering a suggestion implies that you know what the source of the behavior is (what the problem is) and that you have an insight as to how they might change or improve something that they themselves haven't thought of—both of which are likely to be based on erroneous assumptions. This often leads to a diminishment of trust and a

---

[70] The situation-behavior-impact feedback model was developed at Center for Creative Leadership and reflects an approach to feedback, and communication more generally, which is derived from the practice of non-violent communication. For an easy introduction to situation-behavior-impact feedback (SBI), see "The Situation-Behavior-Impact Feedback Tool: Providing Clear, Specific Feedback" at https://www.mindtools.com/pages/article/situation-behavior-impact-feedback.htm.

feeling of defensiveness—neither of which helps the other person to best leverage the feedback.

In general, your feedback to another person (or, if you're the one *receiving* the feedback, the feedback you receive from another person), though it may be true for the giver of the feedback, cannot be regarded as *true* in any universal sense of the term. Feedback is simply information, not truth. The point, then, with feedback, is to get as much as (and give as much) as you can—without becoming obnoxious about it—because it is all about getting as much information as possible. Some of the information will be valid; other information will be less so.

This leads to another key aspect of impact feedback: When you are the giver, your feedback may elicit any number of reactions—from dull reception, to no reception, to argument. Your job is to let go of your attachment to the rightness or legitimacy of the feedback once you have given it, and to not argue for it. If the feedback you give to another fails to resonate with that other person, but you feel a strong need to stand firmly by your feedback, letting go of it, at least for the moment, has the effect of giving the other person some time and inner space to settle the impact of the feedback for themselves.

Another approach for when the feedback fails to land for the receiver is allow it to move toward a kind of *shared sensemaking conversation* in which the two of you (or however many of you there are) are actively and deliberately making sense of the feedback and its impact. An example of what this might look like:

Giver: When you interrupt me, the impact on me is that I get rattled and lose my train of thought.

Receiver: Well, the problem for me is that when we're having a hard conversation, you often talk for very long stretches, offering two or three thoughts in which each thought builds off the other. After a while I get frustrated because I can't follow it, and then I start to tune you out.

Giver: Wow! I am so sorry: I had no idea that I was doing that. I wonder if it would be helpful if I were to slow down a bit, particularly at those moments?

Receiver: Hmmm. Actually, I think if you could pause a bit between sentences, to allow me to get it, that might help.

Here, the feedback conversation moved quickly toward the opening of a *shared sensemaking conversation* in which the two people negotiated how they might be together in a difficult conversation. Such a conversation is likely to lead to subsequent experimenting in which each person tries something new—leading to more impact feedback and probably further shared sensemaking. It is by such a process of co-creation, kicked off by the initial impact feedback, that greater relationship intelligence is generated, and relevant Action Logics—particularly those that are post-*Achiever*—get strengthened.

What I Make Up

This leads to another protocol for giving and receiving feedback, which explicitly emphasizes the collaborative and co-creative possibilities that feedback might offer. It has the following format:

1. Here's what I *observed*.....

2. Here's what I *make up* about what I observed....

3. Here are some *assumptions* I might be holding—and an *Action Logic_orientation*—that may be determining how I see what happened and how I see you.....

4. How do you see it?[71]

A couple of examples:

*   When you stopped me at mid-sentence (what I *observed*), what I made up was that you think I talk too much, in general. This feeds into a kind of self-criticism I have about being too talkative and that that's what you were addressing. That just might be my *Diplomat* Action Logic showing up—a desire to please others at all costs. What thoughts do you have about what I'm saying?

---

[71] This feedback protocol is similar to one I learned from the faculty of the Coaches Training Institute (CTI).

- When you kept hopping around in your slide deck during your presentation (what I *observed*), what I made up was that you were lost. My assumption is that one should follow slides in an orderly manner, and here you were jumping around. I got so preoccupied with how wrong you were doing things, that I stopped paying attention for a while. I guess that was my inner *Expert* talking to me. Now, looking back, I realize that I might have completely missed the point of what you were saying. What do you think?

This form of feedback is more about initiating a conversation that creates more transparency, openness, and trust. In this regard, the orientation of this protocol is around building and deepening relationship and generating, together, a shared sensemaking. It becomes a way to explore one's own inner processing, and the meaning-making that underlies and informs it, while at the same time exploring some of the assumptions and expectations of the relationship itself. With this protocol, the conversation is no longer about the feedback itself but about the meaning-making that informs that feedback and the relationship that is the context of the feedback.

When feedback is practiced in a deliberate manner—as is the case with the two practices just introduced—it becomes a catalyst for growth and development both at the individual level and at the relationship level. When exercised throughout an organization, such practices generate, as well, broader organizational capability. Petty resentments—the result of withheld communication and feedback—are lessened and, as a consequence, relationships are strengthened. Moreover, when people are given skillfully delivered feedback, they learn to better see, and thereby close, gaps between intended impact and actual impact—a significant stimulant to developmental growth.

Feedback as I am describing it here generates an intimacy and trust that has the natural effect of deepening authentic relationship. This deepening of authentic relationship arises partly from the increase in positive feelings that such feedback can generate. But, perhaps more significantly, people come to realize that relationships are not at all *accidental*, but that relationships can be enhanced through deliberately developed skillful means—that relationships can be deliberately developed.

We All Own and Even Celebrate Our Mistakes

Perhaps the single biggest energy drain, and the source of the greatest number of errors and challenges that plague organizations, is what organization and management scholar Chris Argyris calls "organizational defense routines."[72] These are routine behaviors that everyone displays but no one talks about. For example, we cover up our mistakes, our inadequacies, our misjudgments, and failures either by hiding them or blaming others for their occurrence.

The cost of this routine behavior—multiplied thousands of times across the organization—has many consequences. First, covering up errors makes it impossible for us to correct them—and all of those uncorrected errors become a source of significant organizational dysfunction. Meanwhile, the routine behavior zaps our energy and attention, and reduces our capacity to be authentic with one another, because we so often interact within a space of unacknowledged subterfuge. Finally—and perhaps most significantly for an organization aspiring to be a *Sense-and-Respond* organization—the covering up of errors enforces and enables an attitude toward mistakes that basically says they're bad and that we should not make them. Consequently, we hold ourselves back from taking bold or risky actions, or actions that might be perceived by others as wrong or stupid, for fear of making mistakes.

Evolvagility, in contrast, teaches us to own and even *celebrate* our mistakes. It helps us to relate to mistakes both as things that naturally happen in the course of our day-to-day lives and as possible signals of movement into our own developmental stretch zones. Toward this end, it can be beneficial to have specific practices that help us acknowledge our mistakes, to declare the inner development and learning they might engender in us, and to celebrate them for the learning and development they do engender. This is another example in which practices—when taken up and genuinely exercised—can form the basis for the evolving not only of individual minds but of organizational culture more broadly.

---

[72] In *An Everyone Culture* Kegan and Lahey point out that in most workplace settings, people actually have *two* jobs: one that they are paid to do and the other one related to their efforts to hide their errors and weaknesses; to look good.

One practice for acknowledging and learning from our mistakes is something called the "Failure Bow." I learned this from the improvisation artist and teacher Matt Smith.[73] Typically when we make a mistake, we try to hide it because we are, in some way, ashamed of ourselves, and we endeavor to hide this from others. The problem with this strategy is that the mistake may never get revealed—and hence finding its remedy can be elusive. But what's more, in hiding the mistake and the shame we feel about it, we effectively hide *ourselves*; we take ourselves, even if only for a moment, out of the game.

The failure bow is designed to counteract this behavior and this tendency to hide from our mistakes. Instead, we actively and very publicly declare our mistake by announcing the mistake we made, and then say something about what we learned from it and how we intend to clean it up. Finally, we take a bow. In so doing, we generate a playful regard and attitude that has the effect of counteracting the negative response to our mistakes.

Another example of an organizational practice is something I call *My Biggest Mistake*. The format of this practice is to state: "My biggest mistake in the last [period of time] is...... and what I learned is...... " This practice, when done well, has an almost ceremonial quality to it. When someone has completed sharing their biggest mistake—whether today, in the last week, the last three months, or the last year—they are acknowledged and recognized both for owning up to the mistake and for the learning they created for themselves as a result.

I have seen this work quite well. For example, during an Agile team's biweekly retrospective, one or two team members would take a turn at it. For each person, at least two other people were invited to offer an appreciation to that person, again acknowledging them for owning up to the mistake and for the learning they created for themselves (and possibly others on the team). Such recognition works best when the person giving it is speaking from their own genuine experience of the person being recognized, as

---

[73] To learn more about the "Failure Bow," watch the TEDxBellevue video by Matt Smith, "The Failure Bow." It is available on YouTube here: https://www.youtube.com/watch?v=cXuD2zHVeB0&feature=youtu.be. For more on Matt Smith and improvisation, visit: http://www.mattsmithimprov.com/?page_id=143.

opposed to simply making something up in order to be nice. Another example of this practice was during a large departmental or program retrospective at the end of a release. They broke themselves into smaller groups of between five and seven people, with each person taking a turn. After everyone in the small groups had a turn, a sampling of individuals was invited to share theirs with the whole group.

While this practice can feel awkward at first (as does any newly adopted practice), after a while, when practiced widely throughout an organization, it has the effect of normalizing mistakes and destigmatizing error. This destigmatizing of error refocuses people's attention and energy on learning and growing from their mistakes, contributing significantly to their inner growth and development. Moreover, people start to see the value gained when more and more mistakes and errors get revealed, as opposed to being covered up as ordinarily happens.

Evolvagility Conditions

In addition to practices, a *deliberately developmental ecosystem* is supported by several environmental *conditions*. These conditions serve to guide people through day-to-day activities and interactions. They act as principles of conduct and as constraints on our actions. They are what make it possible for the practices of *Evolvagility* to have their intended impact.

Designed Alliance: Defines a set of agreements and protocols that create an environment of safety, trust, and challenge necessary for this kind of work

Accountability: Defines a set of distinctions by which people are able to stretch themselves and each other both in the outcomes they generate and in the developmental growth that informs the quality and impact of those outcomes

A Rigorous Focus on Developmental Growth: Within the context of a deliberately developmental ecosystem, we need to regularly connect and reconnect to the concepts and distinctions—and to the emotional rigors—that differentiate developmental growth from simply getting better behaviorally

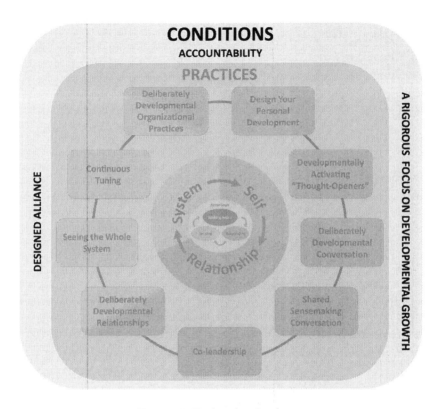

Figure 23: Evolvagility Conditions

Designed Alliance

The term *designed alliance* comes from the world of professional coaching. It defines a set of agreements and protocols to help us be clear about intention and purpose, and to create an environment of safety, trust, and challenge necessary for the developmentally oriented relationship system— whether between two people or among those within a larger collective such as a team or group—flourish.[74] A designed alliance tends to be deeper than

---

[74] For more on designed alliance within the context of a coaching relationship, and from the perspective of the co-active coaching model of Coaches Training Institute, see "Designing an Alliance" available at https://coactive.com/learning-hub/fundamentals/res/FUN-Tools/FUN-Designing-Alliance.pdf. To learn more about co-active *leadership*, see Karen Kimsey-House and Henry Kimsey-House, *Co-Active Leadership: Five Ways to Lead* (Berrett-Koehler Publishers, 2015).

the more prosaic set of norms by which members within a team, for instance, are bound by a set of rules that they are expected to follow. This is because the designed alliance goes beyond logistical agreements to address the psychological and emotional needs of an intentional relationship, and to pave the way for people to solve many of the kinds of challenges that can arise in such a relationship.

The word "alliance" points to "a union or association for mutual benefit"[75] and, perhaps more significantly, toward a shared alignment around a common goal. The word "designed" indicates an intention that those who enter into the alliance are committed both to its creation and fulfillment and to the collaborative process by which that design is held and honored.

The designed alliance begins with alignment around the **intention** or purpose of the deliberately developmental ecosystem we are entering into. Whether it is a single conversation or an ongoing structure, being clear around the intention helps us know when we are complete, when we have drifted off topic, and when we are truly off the mark in terms of our goal, versus feeling discomfort when the heat gets turned up, as it often can within any kind of developmentally oriented conversation or engagement. As I said earlier, the nature of an *intention* can take the form of questions such as: What is it that we might not be seeing? What developmental shift are we wanting to create for ourselves, and why? Where are we currently stuck, and what underlying assumptions, beliefs, and expectations are we holding that might be keeping us stuck?

The designed alliance continues with alignment around the **qualities** a given collective will hold. This is where people ask questions like: What are the kinds of things we need in order to flourish together in this particular ecosystemic situation? This is where things like humor, understanding, and rigor might figure in.

As a pair or group continues in the design of their alliance, at some point they begin to move toward a set of agreements. This part of the process begins with individuals declaring what they anticipate they might need in the relationship. One person, for instance, might need a lot of moral support given the particular developmental challenge they are facing personally,

---

[75] From the definition of "alliance" given on my MacBook Dictionary.

while another person might request that her feet be held to the fire. Yet another person may explicitly request that he be allowed to slow things down, from time to time, to allow the various parts of his thinking process to catch up.

The next part of this conversation centers on what each person intends to bring to the relationship in order to **support** its flourishing and to support the individual needs just declared. This might include things like patience (for one who might ordinarily wish for things to go faster), being direct (perhaps for someone who ordinarily might tend to beat around the bush), and empathy. It could also include particular informal roles that people will take on, such as time-keeper, note-taker, and meeting convener (the person who schedules meetings or other events).

This naturally leads toward the creation of a set of **agreements** to be held by the collective. As these agreements form, special attention is given to possible edge cases—moments when the group drifts from the spirit of their alliance either by breaking explicitly designed agreements, causing a disruption to the functioning of the group, or by drifting away from the very charter of the deliberately developmental ecosystem, which is to keep the focus of the work of the group pointed toward the developmental intention around which that work is aligned.

A designed alliance is a living thing, not a one-and-done. Breakdowns often occur in any relationship system, and in those predicated on the deliberately developmental charter that the practices and conditions of *Evolvagility* serve to further, all the more so. Such breakdowns are often occasions to revisit the designed alliance and make updates as needed.

A designed alliance differs in scope, depending on the scale and scope of the relationship system that constitutes the deliberately developmental ecosystem. Typically, a deliberately developmental ecosystem entails a relationship system whose lifespan is many months, or even years—as is the case, for instance, with intact project or product teams. In this case, the process of initiating a designed alliance calls for at least an hour or two. Sometimes, however, the ecosystemic environment is one whose lifespan is relatively far shorter. For a single, one-off, conversation, the conversation for designing an alliance might only require a few minutes—if for nothing else, to become clear as to the purpose and the contours of the more general conversation.

Regardless of the scope, the intention of the designed alliance remains the same: to create an atmosphere of shared alignment, safety, and trust in order to do the work that the practices of *Evolvagility* ask us to do.

Accountability

The deliberately developmental ecosystem that is catalyzed by the practices and conditions of *Evolvagility* provides a *holding environment* that is at once *disequilibrating, salient, emotionally engaging*, and activated through *interpersonal* engagement (the *facilitative agents* I described earlier). One of the conditions by which *Evolvagility* brings about such a *holding environment* is the condition by which people hold each other *accountable*.

In order to understand the notion of accountability most applicable within the deliberately developmental context of *Evolvagility*, we need to undo some of the assumptions and understandings we currently hold about what accountability is and how it can operate. In a traditional management setting, people are held accountable by their managers for generating particular results and for upholding certain behaviors and attitudes. The consequence for failure is usually felt as some form of rebuke or punishment—whether a minor ding on a performance review, or a major sanction—to be generally avoided, if at all possible. The overall effect is that it creates an atmosphere of compliance and general obedience to a behavioral, performance—and even a *cultural*—norm.

Though it is often couched in terms of a person's development, such a common notion of accountability has the primary effect of controlling people's behavior and directing their energy and efforts toward the realization of important management goals. This is certainly a sensible way to think of it within the context of a Predict-and-Plan organizational environment and management philosophy. But it has the effect, ultimately, of leaving people disempowered and disengaged, since the thing for which they are being held accountable—and the impetus and energy on which it is built—comes primarily from outside of themselves.

Evolvagility promotes a notion of accountability that diverges considerably from the legacy of the term we've become so accustomed to in traditional Predict-and-Plan settings. This new notion of accountability is one in which people are accountable not just for what they say they will do, nor even for what they say they want—which constitutes a deeper, more meaningful notion of accountability. Rather, this new notion of accountability is one in which people are also accountable for who they might become, developmentally.

Another differentiating factor here is that individuals *themselves* choose that to which they declare themselves accountable—no one can hold another person accountable to that which that other person has not chosen to be accountable, not a manager and not an institution. As that which an individual chooses for themselves—and as that which relates to both the realm of *doing* and the realm of *being*—accountability is the means by which an individual manages their own *integrity*—integrity to themselves, to others, to the institution, and even integrity to the larger world of which they see themselves as being a part.

There are several factors in the management of people's accountability within a deliberately developmental ecosystem that make it work well. A **declaration** is when someone announces the beginning of a new state or condition. A **promise** is when someone declares a future state for which they take personal responsibility—and for which they are willing to be held accountable. **Holding** oneself or another accountable necessarily carries both a *challenging* and a *supporting* aspect—in which sense it acts as a kind of *holding environment*.

Declaration

By definition, a declaration is "a formal announcement of the beginning of a state or condition."[76] For example: I now declare you husband and wife. With the uttering of this phrase, nothing has changed in the physical universe (at least not according to classical physics); and yet *everything* has changed in the lives of those two people. In this sense, its utterance creates a future that would otherwise not have existed. Gandhi's declaration "India will be free" is another example; again, nothing in the physical universe has apparently changed, and yet the course of a civilization is altered forever.

---

[76] From the definition of "declaration" given on my MacBook Dictionary.

What changes is the nature of the *commitments* and *behaviors* that a declaration calls forth. A marriage, for instance, calls forth new commitments regarding communication, cooperation, and interaction. It now becomes important to communicate with the other person in a manner that is supportive and which seeks to understand. Marriage also calls forth new behaviors; for example, one can no longer think only of oneself—one must now take into consideration the needs and preferences of the other person. In this regard, a declaration has the effect of changing both individual behaviors and the social environment in which those behaviors are conditioned.

For a declaration to work it must be *public*—a declaration made silently to oneself has less binding power than one made in the presence of others. When you make a public declaration, it changes not only how you now see yourself; it also changes how others see you and how, consequently, they interact with you and behave with you.

Some examples of declarations might be: "We are a team in which all people become their very best"; or "When this group is together, no one gets let off the hook"; or "In our partnership, we both challenge each other and support each other."

Promise

Closely related to the notion of a declaration is the notion of a *promise*. A promise is a declaration of something specific that one will do. For example, "I will be there at 11," or "I promise to just sit and listen to what you have to say." A promise is similar to a declaration in that it announces the beginning of a state or condition," except with a promise the promise-giver is on the hook for its fulfillment. The promise-giver is not only saying "This shall be," as is the case with a declaration. Rather he or she is saying "This shall be" and "I am accountable for making it happen."

A promise has several aspects: The specific thing being promised, a specific date/time by which the thing being promised will be completed, and a mechanism to make known the actual outcome of the promise (whether or not the thing being promised was done by promised date/time). A common way of articulating this is:

- What?

- By When?

- How will I (we) Know?

Much like a declaration, a promise changes the nature of the commitments and behaviors that the promise calls forth. If I promise to lose 20 pounds, there is the inherent commitment to that promise and to the behaviors that support that promise. In light of that commitment, for instance, it would be wholly inappropriate to eat donuts for breakfast every morning. Also, as is the case with a declaration, the power of a promise is most fully leveraged when the promise is made *publicly*.

It is important to understand the notion of a promise as it exists within the *deliberately developmental* context. In this context, a promise is not just about what one will *do*, but who one will need to *become*. For example, a product development team promises that they will increase their delivery speed by 50% over the course of the next four months, without working overtime and without lowering quality. Note, first of all, that there is both a *What* and a *By When* in this promise. Note also that the team has explicitly closed off two potential loopholes to their promise—working overtime and taking shortcuts that could result in the reduction of quality. Note too that this is a promise that has been made publicly—which means that their success or failure will be open for scrutiny by others.

The effect of such a promise is that the team will need to find new ways to be effective. They will need to lean down their processes; ferret out and correct inefficiencies; improve communication and collaboration practices among themselves; have more open and transparent conversations with product stakeholders; and be willing to give potentially disappointing news in a timely fashion. All of these behavioral changes will have a psycho-activating impact—the new practices, habits, and customs they need to adopt to realize this promise will force them to change things within themselves, both individually and as a team. They will need to *become* a different team and the people on the team will need to *become* different people.

In many ways, a *promise* is a kind of *liberating structure* (see the section on "Liberating Structures") in that it becomes a kind of forcing function for growth—whether by forcing people through a kind of **crisis** (in which, for some period of time, they struggle in the effort to assimilate the new situation that the promise presents to habitual reactions—the *conflict cycle*) or through a kind of **liberation** (in which they accommodate to the new situation that the promise generates through the adoption of new attitudes, practices, and behaviors—the *growth* cycle).

High-performing individuals and teams of every stripe often make audacious promises in order to force themselves to up their inner game, and to liberate themselves from the tyranny of wrong habits and behaviors. This is particularly common in the world of sports whether or not they actually realize the promise is less important than the changes inside themselves that the publicly-declared promise catalyzes.

> The key to the power of a promise is that **the purpose of a promise is not to keep the promise, but to make it in the first place, and then to live into what's necessary to keep it.**

It is the *living into the promise*, and the inner capabilities that that living into calls forth, that is the driving force of the promise—not whether or not one has actually *kept* that promise. From a developmental perspective, compulsively *keeping* the promise at all costs, including the cost of whatever developmental growth might happen, ultimately drains the developmental power of the promise (and is often the expression of an over-zealous *Expert Action Logic* orientation). And yet, at the same time, to treat the keeping of the promise cavalierly—as though it doesn't matter whether we keep it—just as surely drains the power out of the promise. The power of the promise is therefore to be found in the dialectical tension between these two poles—between the keeping of the promise and a willingness to let go of one's attachment to the keeping of it.

Holding Accountability

It is with this understanding of the nature of the declaration and of the promise that we bring our attention back to the notion of accountability and what it means to *hold accountability* for others.

One holds accountability for another just as one holds the raising of a child. It is a holding that **challenges** the other to live into whatever new capability is called for by the promise they've made—a challenging that can take some degree of fortitude and perhaps even courage as you stand alongside that other person's *promise* rather than their psychology. That is, you stand by the promise of who they say they want to be rather than the psychological tricks they have habitually used in the past to keep them stuck.

And yet, at the same time, holding accountability entails a *holding* that empathically **supports** the other as they navigate the inner torrents necessary for passage to the other side of whatever self-imposed beliefs, stories, or unacknowledged fears might be holding them back from realizing a more fully realized version of themselves. Such a support is a kind of *compassion*, which is a willingness and ability to step aside from whatever frustration or disappointment you might have for this other person in order to see them in the light of the struggle they may be encountering.

Holding accountability for the promise (or declaration) of another means to hold that promise with the same dialectical posture with which we ask the maker of the promise to hold for themselves: a balancing of *challenging* with *support*, and the emotional and relational finesse such a balancing dance calls for. In this way, holding accountability for another itself occasions developmental growth for the one—or *ones*—doing the holding.

The holding of accountability has a certain kind of structure and protocol. First there is the making of the promise itself and a declaration of the developmental opportunity that that promise makes possible. Then, there are the requests and structures that might be needed to support the fulfillment of that promise.

Here's an example of how this structure might be generated over the course of a brief conversation.

HOLDING ACCOUNTABILITY - EXAMPLE CONVERSATION

Me: I promise to stand solidly in my authority as we navigate the hard decisions we have in the coming weeks. The possibility I see for my development is to move beyond my inclination toward passivity and letting others decide when faced with hard decisions and to have a greater tolerance for whatever bad decisions I might make.

Partner: What might impede your ability to live into that promise? What escape hatches do you see yourself possibly taking in order to avoid having to make potentially hard decisions?

Me: Good question. One thing I can see right off the bat is that I can see myself becoming quiet and somewhat glum, which might prompt others to step forward and decide in that moment.

Partner: So, if I'm with you at such a moment, how would you want me to be in order to hold you to account?

Me: Hmmmm. Well, I would want you to not jump in. Or, better yet, I would want you to insist on there being a pause and then explicitly and directly ask me what I would want to do. I suspect that won't be easy—for either you or me. But that's what would support me in that moment.

Partner: Yes, I will do that. Now what about those times when I am not there in the moment? What are other ways in which I might support you?

Me: What if we check in at the end of the month and I can tell you how it went?

Partner: That feels like it would be too long. I'm afraid too much time might pass. I suggest that we check in at least once a week, say, during our weekly check-in meeting?

Me: Yes, I can see that. OK. Let's do that.

You can also see in this brief example that the partner is holding my feet to the fire—not letting me off the hook too easily. Such an accountability conversation might go on for some time and may involve multiple partners (as in a team member being held accountable by the rest of the team.) The partner(s) help the giver of the promise create a structure that supports not only the fulfillment of the promise, but the developmental possibility that that promise might afford.

This is what *holding another accountable* looks like—a combination of tough love and tender compassion. Such a holding of another is itself developmentally catalyzing: it grows the holder of accountability as much—though perhaps in different ways—as it grows the one making the promise.

A Rigorous Focus on Developmental Growth

The focus of *Evolvagility*, and of the deliberately development ecosystem it supports, is on *developmental* growth—not on simply getting better behaviorally. This requires a special kind of *rigor* because the tendency is to fall away from aspects of the practice that are either intellectually challenging or emotionally confronting.

The first aspect of this kind of rigor is **intellectual**. Developmental growth has an *intellectual* aspect in that it requires us to think through and understand certain models and theories. These models and theories, and the kind of thinking their comprehension forces us to process, are important agents in psycho-activating inner growth in that they stimulate different ways of *thinking* and hence of *making meaning*. Along these lines, it's helpful to remember, while in the midst of our developmental growth, that our meaning-making processes have three aspects: affective (emotional), relational (social), and cognitive (mental). We want to have a good part of our focus in whatever development work we do, on the cognitive aspect by maintaining a high degree of intellectual rigor. This means that we want to understand the models and the theory, and allow that understanding to infuse our very thinking, how we speak, and how we relate with others and to our world.

Something to beware of is the all-too-common impulse for those whose predominant meaning-making falls within the *Individualist* Action Logic sphere to reject anything that smacks of intellectualism. Under the spell of the *Individualist* Action Logic, we tend to grant greater privilege to the affective and relational aspects of development, while devaluing the cognitive aspect. While this embrace of a more heart-centered focus can be liberating for those emerging from the heavily intellectual and cognitive orientation of the *Expert* and *Achiever*, we want to avoid throwing out the baby with the bathwater. In general, giving false preference to one aspect of psychological functioning over another—for instance, to privilege the cognitive over the relational, or the relational over the cognitive—stunts genuine developmental growth. What we want to do instead is to consider them all as relevant and perhaps valuable depending on the circumstances.

Another aspect of all of this, which is important to maintaining a developmental focus, is **emotional** rigor. Developmental growth is not all roses and sunshine—it calls forth, and requires, a range of emotional experiences—from joy to anger to boredom to anxiety—and everything and anything in between. Feeling good is not the point of developmental growth (as one teacher I once had might say, feeing good is the *booby prize* of developmental growth). Nor is feeling bad. The hallmarks of emotional development are to be able to be present with whatever we are feeling, in the moment; to develop the capacity to name it and talk about; and to not have our behavior and reactions be wholly taken over by whatever feeling we may have at a given moment.

A common obstacle to maintaining a rigorously developmental focus on an emotional level is to imagine that inner development *feels* a certain way. We may believe that when we are developmentally growing, we feel inspired, excited, or happy. Or, conversely, we may believe that developmental growth necessarily entails feeling anxious, down, or unhappy. In conflating inner development with a specific feeling, we end up missing an entire range of experiences that could be pivotal to our unique and particular developmental journey.

Still another aspect related to maintaining a rigorous focus on the developmental dimension of this work calls for **relational** rigor. There is tendency for those who collectively join together within a deliberately developmental ecosystem to anchor themselves in the positive feelings of togetherness, relatedness, and solidarity. Such feelings are particularly pronounced for people who have shared a deep and developmentally enriching experience, such as can happen in a workshop or cohort environment.

While those feelings of mutual positivity and loving regard are an important part of the development of any group undergoing any kind of developmental journey, to become overly identified with those feelings can end up becoming an impediment to real collective growth and development. Part of the unique developmental opportunity afforded by the coming together of a group of people arises from the relational and interpersonal dynamics that naturally emerge when people come together. Within the context of an intention for shared developmental growth, these dynamics tend to get amplified. Consequently, surprising and inexplicable events and situations happen, which can be quite challenging for groups. Sudden conflicts flare up. Certain moods descend upon a group. Individuals suddenly drop out or are habitually late.

These are examples of signs that (as yet unacknowledged) relationship forces are at play. This is when the power of *shared sensemaking conversations* can come into play. Though they can be challenging, these moments and situations can become occasions for growth when groups are able—and are willing—to stay present; when they can name what's happening; and when they can lay bare the underlying dynamics that might be at work in those moments—all while avoiding the temptation to judge them, to avoid them, or to somehow sweep them under the rug.

Escaping into the feel-good tendency of developmentally engaged groups is a common obstacle to doing this kind of work. But then again, so too can *over*-analyzing situations impede such work when we take ourselves away from our emotional presence in the moment.

In light of all of these considerations regarding *intellectual, emotional,* and *relationship* rigor, it can be helpful to have a kind of reminder—particularly when pairs or groups start to veer off in some way—of the developmental focus of the work of *Evolvagility*. Here's what such a reminder, or developmental cheat sheet might look like.

QUESTIONS FOR DEVELOPMENTAL GROWTH

<u>Cognitive (Intellectual Rigor)</u>

- What is the nature of meaning-making? Of the theory of development?

- What is the nature of Action Logic?

- What other ideas and theories might inform our development?

- Where might we need to bring more *intellectual* rigor here?

Affective (Emotional Rigor)

- What do I (or we) believe developmental growth to feel like?

- In what ways might I (or we) be trying to produce (or reproduce) in us a certain feeling?

- Where might we need to bring more emotional rigor here?

Social (Relational Rigor)

- What kinds of (potentially challenging) situations or conversations might we be avoiding?

- Are we more interested in feeling good (validated, happy, "in love") together than we are in challenging ourselves and each other?

- Conversely, have we fallen into a pattern of "challenging" each other all the time, and failing to bring more compassion in?

- What are the relational patterns and dynamics we are seeing here?

- Where might we need to bring more relational rigor here?

You may have more of your own questions—this is not meant to be exhaustive, but only suggestive of the kinds of things you might want to be asking yourselves and each other as you continue your developmental work together.

Evolvagility:
A Deliberately Developmental Take on
Organizational Development

Putting the practices and conditions together yields for us the full deliber-ately developmental design model of *Evolvagility*, as shown in Figure 24.

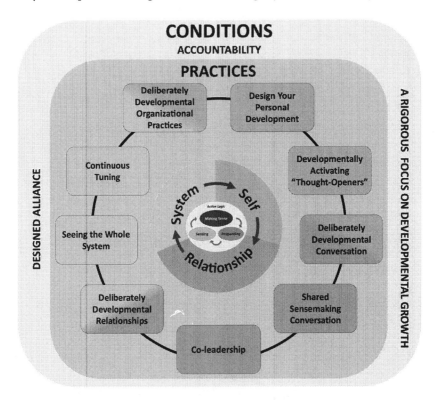

Figure 24: Evolvagility Model

Together, the *practices* and *conditions* of *Evolvagility* engender a deliberately developmental approach to organization development. The decades-old field of organization development endeavors to leverage research in human and organizational systems and in behavioral science to help organizations get better. By "better" I mean essentially that the structures and behaviors that define how an organization performs are more congruent with its mis-sion, purpose, and goals. Traditionally, the responsibilities and tasks associated with the practice of organization development tend to fall to management and to HR professionals. And the means by which it is applied tend to take the form of professional training programs and, for top leaders, one-on-one coaching.

While honoring the spirit of, and the deep wisdom provided by, the tradition of organization development, *Evolvagility* conceives of its practice from a slightly different angle. Rather than relying on professional training and mentoring programs in order to develop people, *Evolvagility* offers practices and conditions that people everywhere can take up and use to develop *themselves*. And, rather than falling to management and HR professionals, *Evolvagility* imagines organization development as that which is owned by people at all levels, and from all walks of life, within an organization, regardless of position, title, or role. In this sense, the practices of *Evolvagility* —and the conditions within the context of which people engage in those practices—enact a form of organization development that is explicitly activated from the *inside out*.

Another way in which *Evolvagility* takes a different angle on organization development is in its differentiation between developmental growth (*vertical* growth) and learning (*horizontal* growth) and in its foregrounding of the developmental dimension of growth. This is key, since an underlying assertion on which this book is founded is that the kind of organization that is required for a VUCA world—a *Sense-and-Respond* organization—requires a different kind of mind, one that is able to take on the characteristics of an *Individualist* Action Logic and beyond—a *Sense-and-Respond* **mind**. The practices and conditions of *Evolvagility* are intended to grow just such a quality of mind, as reflected within the individuals, relationships, and systems that constitute an organizational whole.

In Part V, we will dive into the role of organizational leadership and management in a VUCA world and investigate the nature of the paradigm shift required for management and leadership in such a world—a notion of leadership and management often identified with the hashtags #agileleadership and #agilemanagement. Here we will find a new paradigm of leadership and management made possible when small-l leaders throughout the organization—in partnership and collaboration with others—engage in the practices and conditions of *Evolvagility*, and by that engagement, work to grow their own capacity for *Sense-and-Respond* leadership.

PART V

The Role of Organizational Leadership and Management

As a way for people to developmentally grow themselves and others, the tools and practices of *Evolvagility* create the foundation for a self-managing organization. In a self-managing organization much of what traditionally constitutes "management" is carried out by people throughout the organization. What then becomes of the role of organizational management and leadership? In the context of *Evolvagility* and the distinctions and practices it provides for growing the developmental capacity of an organization's people, organizational management, and leadership now has the critical role of catalyzing and sustaining the conditions necessary to support that growth at an organizational level.

In Part V, we examine the nature of this new role of organizational leadership and management and the kinds of perspectives and orientations such a role calls for—a kind of management I will be calling *management by indirection*. The term "indirection" refers to a form of management in which the manager "manages" by effectively taking him or herself out of the middle of things, and steps back in order to be better able to pay attention to the greater unfolding of things, and to "manage" the situations and circumstances which condition that greater unfolding.

In this part, we will examine the specific *conditions and agreements* whose existence serves to support the growing of the inner capacity of an organization's people. We will also uncover specific *practices* that are intended to catalyze that inner growth and the emergence of behaviors and actions that are reflective of that growth. Finally, we will look at the perspectives and tools that make it possible to manage *the larger system*, not from the perspective of its constituent parts and components (as is the case with a traditional Predict-and-Plan management approach) but from the standpoint of the organizational ecosystem.

In managing from the standpoint of the greater systemic whole, by establishing an environment of developmentally catalyzing conditions and agreements, and by engaging in management and leadership practices that catalyze the inner growth of your organization's people, you go a long way toward enhancing the self-managing capacity of the organizations you lead and manage.

Management Agility

Evolvagility provides a set of tools and practices that support the emergence of an everywhere capacity for *Sense-and-Respond* leadership—a form of inner agility that creates a foundation for deep and sustainable organizational agility.

As individuals and collectives across the organization grow in their capacity for both inner and outer agility, they quite naturally gain an increased ability to address more of the kinds of tasks and responsibilities previously held by management and leadership: holding deadlines, interacting (and collaborating) with business stakeholders, resolving interpersonal issues and conflicts on their teams, planning their work, and so on. And, as individuals and teams continue to grow the complexity of their Action Logic—at both the individual and collective level—and become more skillful in the spheres of relationship and organizational systems, the range of tasks and responsibilities they are able to take on only grows.

This shift in role capability fostered through the growth of both outer and inner agility follows a key adaptive organizational principle: The people closest to the work are in the best position to make decisions, and coordinate and organize the activities related to that work. And as people take on more management responsibility related directly to their work, they become better able to assess, think through, and intelligently resolve larger institutional impediments that impact that work, but which ordinarily fall upon management to resolve. And just as the tasks and activities directly related to their work fall naturally within the purview of those closest to that work, so too do ways of assessing, understanding, and resolving the larger institutional impediments which impact that work.

As individuals increase their leadership capacity in this way, it makes sense for management and leadership to step back and loosen the reins in order to make room for individuals and teams throughout the organization to step in. As individuals and teams throughout the organization take on more of the tasks, responsibilities, and activities traditionally held by management and leadership, the job of management and leadership changes dramatically.

For many leaders and managers, this can be a daunting prospect. Among the many questions which they now face, their most pressing question is probably this: If so much of what I've been doing will be done by others—those closest to the work being done and the outcomes being generated—what is *my* job? What is the nature of *my* role?

The answers to these questions are to be found when we shift the context—the very meaning—of what it is to be an organizational leader or manager. The context of this newly constituted role has two, interrelated parts.

At the heart of it all is **growing inner agility in *you*,** which has been the primary focus of this book; it is the inner foundation on which everything else sits and is the source of inner capabilities needed for all that you do. It is here where each of us grows our capacity for *Sense-and-Respond* leadership, as I've been describing it in this book: as that which is an *everywhere* phenomenon, which one grows from *inside out*, and which arises in *relationships*—and as that which is defined as "showing the way," not by *doing* or *telling*, but through the complexity and quality of one's *sensemaking*. In this regard, *Sense-and-Respond* leadership distinguishes a leadership that is, for the most part, *role agnostic*. One could be a Scrum Master and **be** a leader; one could be a QA engineer and **be** a leader; one could be a product manager and **be** a leader.

Role plays a part in the growth of Agile leadership within an organization when we come to the position of organizational leader—whether a development manager, a middle-level director, or a top-level executive leader. What is different for the organization leader or manager has to do with their *role*, and the job associated with that role.

This brings us to the second part of the new context for the role of the organizational leader and managers, which is **growing inner agility across the *organization*.**

The philosophical grounding for this part of the new role of organizational leadership is that to the degree people—both as individuals and as collectives—throughout the organization grow the complexity of the ways in which they make sense of their world—their *Action Logics*—they will increase their ability to deal with, and solve, the complex organizational challenges that ordinarily fall into the lap of organizational management. Your role as an organizational leader therefore shifts from managing for the things people *do* (and need to do) in order to realize key organizational initiatives—to growing capability in people so that they find *themselves* managing

203

themselves to do the things that need to be done in order to realize key organizational initiatives.

Management by Indirection

This new management imperative calls for a shift in focus: from managing through directing, coordinating, and motivating people to do this or that—to creating conditions that empower and enable ways of thinking that make it possible for people to do their own directing, coordinating, and motivating. From the perspective of *Evolvagility*, and the practices through which it promotes the growth of people's *inner* agility capabilities, the job of organizational leadership is to bring about the emergence of environmental conditions and structures that enable the growth and mastery of those practices and the growth of those capabilities.

The nature of this new kind of leadership and management calls for several mindset shifts:

- *From* posing and pushing (and in some cases *enforcing*) specific processes and practices needed to realize key initiatives—*to* creating the conditions necessary for individuals and teams, throughout the organization, *themselves* to grow the processes and practices best suited to the work needed to realize those initiatives.

- *From* trying to get others to exhibit certain kinds of behaviors and to execute particular kinds of actions—*to* creating the conditions necessary for those others to cultivate those behaviors and that capacity for action *in themselves*—by deliberately growing themselves, and those around them, *developmentally*; that is, from the *inside out*.

- *From* establishing institutional structures, procedures, rules, and systems that support the day-to-day operations of an organization—*to* creating conditions necessary for individuals and teams, throughout the organization, to develop the wherewithal *in themselves* to grow those structures, procedures, rules, and systems in ways that *organically* support those operations.

Organizational and management theorist Robert Chia calls such a management approach *management by indirection*.[77] The term "indirection" refers to a form of management in which the manager "manages" by effectively taking him or herself out of the middle of things, and steps back in order to be better able to pay attention to the greater unfolding of things. From this place of remove from the hurly-burly of organizational goings-on, management happens, not through *direct* control, but through the *indirect* introduction of small adjustments, catalyzing ideas, vocabularies, or through the design of organizational structures—all of which have the effect of altering some aspect of the organizational environment in which people are working. As such, the manager manages by *catalyzing* rather than through *directing*.

I want to be very clear that I am not advocating a complete abandonment of management by direction. Moving toward a deliberately developmental organization takes time. Things evolve and emerge as the organization grows the leadership capacity of all of its members. In a VUCA world there is much we need to retain in terms of the skills, competencies, roles, and structures that are offered by a management by direction—and we need the stability and predictability that such a stance affords. So rather than throwing out the baby with the bathwater (in this case, throwing out the stabilizing and structuring qualities that management by direction brings), we want to include that which management by direction *can* bring, even as we move toward an increasing embrace of all that management by *indirection* can bring.

Shifting from Management by Direction to Management by Indirection

Management by Direction

Two pictures can help us compare management by direction, and management by indirection.

---

[77] See Robert Chia, "In praise of strategic indirection: An essay on the efficacy of oblique ways of responding," *M@n@gement* 16, no. 5 (2013).

The first picture depicts the management flow as it occurs more tradition-ally—that is, as a form of management by *direction*.

Figure 25: Management by Direction

This management approach seeks to *direct*, in some way, the *behaviors* and *actions* of others to get them to produce some particular result or outcome in service of this or that institutional aim. Such an approach can take a variety of forms: accountability structures, performance management systems, training and development programs, development goals, and professional mentoring to name a few.

Let's take one specific example: the practice of setting professional development goals in which a direct report sets personal performance goals for the next year. Such goals are typically related to specific behavioral improvements (though we may not call them "improvements"), or to more effective actions they could take, which both you, as their manager, and the other person envision *for that person*. Those goals, and the specific behavioral and action-taking improvements they entail, are among the criteria that management and HR use during a person's annual performance review to assess overall progress.

Another example: Many organizational training programs aim to help people improve on a behavior or develop a new skill (or set of skills). Consider, for instance, a workshop on interpersonal communication. A person's manager might suggest such a workshop; or perhaps that person herself sees ways in which she could improve her communication skills. Typically, in such a workshop, one learns practices or skills that are intended to improve specific skills in communicating and relating with others. Such skills might range from that of active listening—which is the saying back to another person what you just heard them say—to the practice of body language mirroring—a neuro-linguistic programming trick to establish a more direct emotional connection with another person when they are upset.

Interventions like these are entirely are valid—and in fact *necessary*—ways to invoke change and improvement in others. However, they are limited in the depth to which they can stimulate a deep, organic, and sustainably growing *Sense-and-Respond* leadership capability for two main reasons. First, the source of the impetus for an individual's personal growth points, in subtle ways, to *you*, the manager. When push comes to shove, the direct report will do this or that thing in order to please the manager in some way (with or without conscious awareness), or to fulfill some important emotional expectation in that relationship—or simply to follow what feels like a subtle institutional expectation or directive. The arrangement has the effect of playing to the power dynamic in which one person holds a subservient position in relation to another. In such a relationship dynamic—reminiscent of the parent-child relationship—individuals relinquish, in subtle ways, their own power, including their power to think outside the box, to offer solutions which may go against the grain of cultural habit, and to effect change, whether in themselves, in others, or in the organization. That quality of individual *power* is a key asset within any organization living in a VUCA world—it is the very atomic energy on which an organization depends if it is to become a sustainably *Sense-and-Respond* organization; its loss or diminishment destroys your chances of moving toward deep and sustainable agility.

Second, the nature of personal growth that these forms of intervention stimulate focuses almost entirely on *behavioral* growth, not on *developmental* growth. Such behavioral growth—along the horizontal axis of learning we discussed in Part II—while important, fails to generate longer term, more sustainable, more broadly enabling *capability*, unless developing that deeper capability is an explicitly and deliberately held aim. Such a deeper, enabling capability applies pointedly not just to this or that particular skill or competency; rather, it informs and enables an entire range of skills and competencies—it defines the deeper *operating system* capacity on which all of those applications will now run.

When we focus on behavioral growth and improvement, one might learn, for instance, the technique of active listening—along the horizontal axis of learning and behavioral change discussed earlier—and might even come to be able to practice that technique effectively in one's conversations. But, unless such a skill comes along with a deeper capacity for authentic relationship with others, a deeper capacity to hold perspectives different from one's own, and a deeper capacity for genuine curiosity, that practice will have a wooden, brittle quality, coming across as staged and vaguely inauthentic.

Management by Indirection

The following picture depicts a management by indirection, one that is better suited to catalyzing the emergence of deep *Sense-and-Respond* leadership.

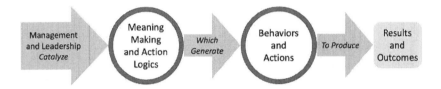

Figure 26: Management by Indirection

As shown in Figure 26, rather than trying to elicit some desired set of behaviors and actions through managing, management by **indirection** focuses on catalyzing the emergence of the inner meaning-making and Action Logics by which those behaviors and actions are informed and determined. Rather than instituting rules, policies, processes, and structures intended to change how people behave and act—as the more traditional, directive approach to management would do—a management by indirection instead endeavors to establish the conditions, expectations, ideas, and vocabularies necessary to support the growing of people's inner meaning-making and Action Logic schemas. Similarly, rather than outsourcing the development of people to behaviorally-oriented and competency-based training events, a management by indirection conceives of employee development as integral to people's day-to-day work and is deliberate about establishing conditions by which that development happens. Rather than putting in place rules and policies to try to get people to change, a management by indirection would create the kind of broader, organizational **holding environment** that would empower and enable people to *change themselves*.

The body of tools and practices of *Evolvagility* defines locally activated *holding environments* (teams, working groups, partnerships, etc.) in which people engage, together, in order to uncover and enhance the quality and complexity of their inner meaning-making and to grow the kinds of skills—

emerging directly from that enhanced meaning-making—needed to work effectively in a VUCA world.

> *Evolvagility provides many of the elements for just such a broadly applied organizational **holding environment** and becomes a key ally to management by indirection by supplying tools and practices that people throughout the organization can use to develop the deep capacity to change themselves.*

The adoption of *Evolvagility*, with the goal of creating a deliberately developmental organization and ecosystem, creates and manifests a *holding environment* in several ways.

First, it establishes a **developmental vocabulary** that helps people clearly see and, perhaps more importantly, *name* the meaning-making that underlies and determines how they perceive and understand the world around them. Vocabularies are among the most important leverage points managers have in catalyzing the emergence of organizational transformation. Language acts as doorways to ways of thinking; words determine what we can see around us (Sensing), what kinds of actions we can imagine taking (Responding), and the manner in which we come to understand things around us (Making Sense). By introducing a research-based vocabulary that points directly to people's inner meaning-making strategies—as does the Action Logic vocabulary described in Part III, and the *Thought-Openers* and *Deliberate Sensemaking* practices in Part IV—*Evolvagility* makes it possible for people to deeply examine the nature of their own thinking, and the impact that their thinking has on their actions in the world.

Second, *Evolvagility* provides a body of **practices** that, when practiced, has the effect of ***psycho-activating* inner growth and development**. As was explained in Part III ("Deliberately Facilitating Inner Development: Foundational Principles"), "psycho-activating" refers to changing something in one's mind through the introduction of something from *outside* the mind. For instance, when you teach people new skills and practices—such as the professional coaching skills of focused listening and asking powerful questions—you *psycho-activate* their inner growth, and this activates a new way of thinking or being.

A third quality that *Evolvagility* brings to bear is that its practices foreground the **social context** of inner development. Inner development is an individual phenomenon, and yet in the workplace setting, it necessarily happens in relationship with others. Specific practices such as *deliberately developmental conversations*—a form of peer coaching that helps an individual see how the way in which they make meaning of a situation may be helping or hampering their ability to deal with a specific challenge they are having—and *shared sensemaking conversations*—a specific conversational format that helps people be deliberate about the deeper meaning-making that shapes how they collectively view, and respond to, particular workplace situations—are inherently and necessarily *social practices.*

Meanwhile, as individuals grow their inner capacity for more complex meaning-making—and specifically as they do so within the social and organizational environments in which *Evolvagility* practices are cultivated—a new capacity for **skillful relating and communication** emerges. Though such skillfulness certainly is one that individuals come to hold, that skillfulness also becomes a capability trait of those very relationship systems themselves. That is, as individuals develop themselves within the environment of a deliberately developmental relationship system, the relationship systems themselves evolve and develop.

As a *human technology* designed to facilitate the inner growth of both individuals and the relationship systems in which they are engaged, the distinctions and practices of *Evolvagility* make it possible to grow a deep and abiding sensemaking capability on the basis of which a new level of behavioral competence arises. This deep capability—and the new competencies it gives rise to—forms the very DNA necessary for establishing a sustainable organizational agility. Such a deep and sustaining capability is an organization's most precious internal capital—from such a capability grows everything that defines what an organization *is* and what it can *do.*

In this regard, *Evolvagility* itself is a key tool—in that it contributes to the shaping of the larger organizational *holding environment* that supports and enables people's developmental growth—for a management by indirection.

A New Organizational Bargain: The Yin and Yang of The Self-Managing Organization

As a way of developmentally growing people, the tools and practices of *Evolvagility* create the foundation for a *self-managing organization*. In a self-managing organization much of what traditionally constitutes "management" is carried out by people throughout the organization,[78] and the people whose role is that of manager or executive leader need to shift their focus. Their focus now needs to be on creating the conditions necessary for others to grow their own inner capacity. In the context of *Evolvagility* and the distinctions and practices it provides for growing the developmental capacity of an organization's people, organizational management has the critical role of *catalyzing and sustaining* the conditions necessary to support that growth at an organizational level.

The notion of self-management points to the context for *Sense-and-Respond* leadership. At the heart of *Sense-and-Respond* leadership is the idea that people manage themselves, not just in terms of what they **do**, but by managing how they **make meaning** in the face of the complex and challenging organizational situations that define their day-to-day work life.

> *It is precisely in this way that Evolvagility becomes a key lever to management by indirection.*

What do I mean by lever? In the third century BC, in reference to designing war machines for the Greeks, Archimedes said, "Give me a lever long enough and a place to stand, and I can move the world." In his book *The Fifth Discipline*,[79] Peter Senge envisioned managers using such levers; that is, managers can take small actions within their organizations that have an outsized effect.

---

[78] For more thoughts on the notion of the self-managing organization, see Ronald Purser and Steven Cabana, *The Self-Managing Organization: How Leading Companies Are Transforming the Work of Teams for Real Impact* (The Free Press, 1998).

[79] Senge, *The Fifth Discipline*.

Evolvagility provides a human technology by which individuals and collectives can manage themselves by managing how they make meaning. To the degree that they are successful in doing so—and to the degree they are able to bring the fruits of a more complex, adaptive, and nuanced meaning-making into skillful practice and action within the organization—they provide key **leverage** for organizational management and leadership.

> In precisely this way, Evolvagility acts as a management lever that helps to bring about a **new bargain** between management and those whom they manage.

In light of this *new bargain*, the job of individuals throughout the organization, besides carrying out the tasks related directly to their specific roles, is to grow the complexity of their meaning-making and Action Logics—to be self-managing by managing the quality and complexity of their own meaning-making.

Meanwhile, the job of organizational management as it relates to the growing of *inner* agility across an organization—besides of course growing the quality and complexity of their own meaning-making, just like everyone else—is to bring about more broadly institutional conditions in which the capacity for people to so grow their inner complexity is empowered and enabled.

These two parts—the *everywhere* activity of growing inner complexity and agility that happens across the organization, and the establishing of institutional conditions that empower and enable that activity—form the *Yin and Yang* of a deep and sustainable organizational agility:

Figure 27: Yin and Yang of organizational agility

The principles and practices of *Evolvagility* create a *holding environment* for the individuals and relationship systems who engage in those practices and learn to embody those principles. In this regard, *Evolvagility* provides one part of the infrastructure needed to support the emergence of a deep inner agility. Management provides the other part by establishing the conditions, vocabularies, agreements, and catalyzing practices that contribute—in their own way—to the growth of inner agility. The two together form a necessary symbiosis out of which the possibility for an inner agility emerges, gains force, and eventually becomes the basis for a new organizational culture.

Figure 28: Grow and Catalyze Inner Agility

213

Management Through the Design of Environments

By providing a human technology that supports people throughout the organization in holding their part of this new organizational bargain, *Evolvagility* makes it possible for organizational managers and leaders to assume their part of that bargain by moving from a position of coordinating, telling, and directing to a position of *designing environments* that bring about conditions favorable to the emergence of *Sense-and-Respond* leadership capabilities *everywhere*.

Let's take a moment to unpack this notion of *designing environments*. First, we want to recognize that organizational management is concerned, at least in part, with how to effect change in people's behaviors. How does this change happen?

Research in the psychology of behavioral change[80] identifies two different kinds of behaviors: those that are infrequent and episodic—for instance, donating blood—and those that are habitual and repetitive—for instance, the daily ritual of simply walking into the office at work. Changes in behaviors that are new and as yet untried—such as giving blood or planning a yearly work event—can be effected through the adoption of specific intentions and goals. For instance, giving blood is a behavior that can be encouraged through social campaigns—as often happens, for instance, within companies—and gentle peer pressure. It is a relatively one-off kind of behavior that is not likely to fall into a kind of mindless habit. Somewhat similarly, the design and facilitation of a yearly work event is one that can be informed and guided by specific intentions and goals. However, changes in behaviors that are old and habitual—the kinds of behaviors that can be

---

[80] Hear Alix Spiegel, "What Vietnam Taught Us About Breaking Bad Habits," *Morning Edition*, NPR, January 2, 2012, audio, https://www.npr.org/sections/health-shots/2012/01/02/144431794/what-vietnam-taught-us-about-breaking-bad-habits. See also Mindy Ji and Wendy Hood, "Purchase and Consumption Habits: Not Necessarily What You Intend," *Journal of Consumer Psychology* 17, no. 4 (2007).

most deeply entrenched within an organizational setting—are less strongly affected by the espoused intentions or goals. For these more habitual and repetitive behaviors, it is the *environment* in which those behaviors are happening that provides the catalyzing forces for change.

This principle is well understood in the world of design. The design of everyday things[81]—from doors to stovetops to automobile interiors to software—orients particular patterns of habitual and repetitive behavior. The most effective way to effect change in such behaviors is through a change in the design of the immediate environments in which those behaviors happen. To get people to buckle up in their automobiles, for instance, public information campaigns or even cajoling by friends rarely works. What works is to build something directly into the driving (or riding) environment itself; specifically, to have the car produce a repeating—and, after a while, increasingly irritating—noise which reminds the person to buckle up. Similarly, in order to reduce potentially catastrophic fire hazards, many apartment management companies install gas stovetops in their apartments that deliberately limit the maximum intensity of the flame in order to prevent people from overheating cooking utensils, which can lead potentially to very damaging fires.

> *Many of the fundamental principles of the design of everyday things are about orienting habitual, repetitive behaviors. Designing organizational environments to orient changes in habitual, repetitive organizational behaviors relies on similar principles.*

These habitual, repetitive, and largely unconscious behaviors constitute the bulk of behavioral activity in organizations. As psychologist and researcher Wendy Wood notes, "About 45% of what people do every day is in the same environment and is repeated."[82] Those repeated actions and behaviors

---

[81] For more on the principle of design I am referring to here, see Donald Norman, *The Design of Everyday Things: Revised and Expanded* (Basic Books, 2013).

[82] Wendy Hood, "What Vietnam Taught Us About Breaking Bad Habits," interviewed by Alix Spiegel.

tend to be impervious to external motivation, planning, or goal setting. Moreover, their repetitious nature is strongly reinforced by the environment in which those actions and behaviors arise. The every-day environments in which we live and work become key stimulators of our habitual behaviors, acting as agents that unconsciously direct that behavior. If we wish to effect change in those habitual actions and behaviors, we need to create changes in the environment itself.[83]

Managing through the *design of environments* is about creating conditions within the organizational environment that stimulate, enable, and encourage a shift in those actions and behaviors that are habitual and entrenched. Suppose, for example, that as an executive or manager you want to see people be more self-directing, to take greater authority, to be bolder in their actions and decisions. A traditional approach would guide you to try to encourage and motivate them to do so. However, as we have seen, this approach is more helpful for behaviors that are episodic, new, or infrequent. Shifting people to behave in more self-directed ways requires a shift in behaviors that are habitual, patterned, and entrenched. Changing something in the environment in which those people are habitually acting and deciding will have greater impact.

In the remainder of Part V, we will investigate what it means for organizational leadership and management to *design environments* that bring about conditions favorable to the emergence of *Sense-and-Respond* leadership capability. We will explore leadership and management in terms of the nature of the **conditions and agreements** necessary for that emergence, the **catalyzing practices** by which that emergence is catalyzed, and the role of leadership and management as it relates to **the larger system.**

The following graphic outlines each of these practice fields and the specific elements within each.

---

[83] A point which Dave Snowden has made rather elegantly in a number of his articles on knowledge management. See David Snowden, "Just-in-Time Knowledge Management: Part 1," *Knowledge Management Review* 5, no. 5 (November/December 2002).

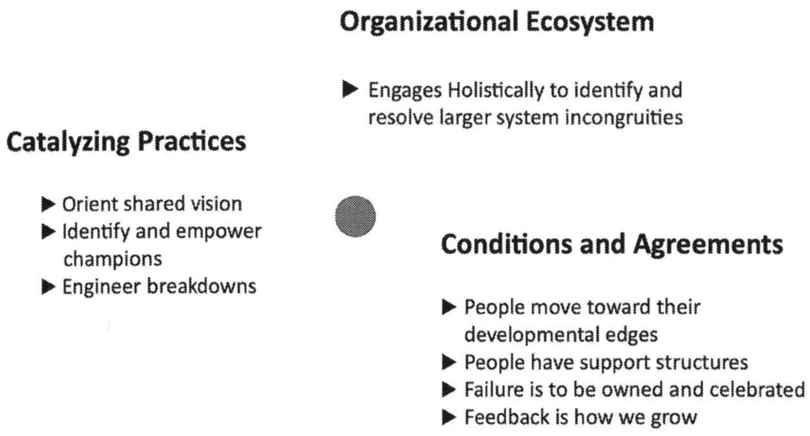

Organizational Ecosystem

▶ Engages Holistically to identify and resolve larger system incongruities

Catalyzing Practices

▶ Orient shared vision
▶ Identify and empower champions
▶ Engineer breakdowns

Conditions and Agreements

▶ People move toward their developmental edges
▶ People have support structures
▶ Failure is to be owned and celebrated
▶ Feedback is how we grow

Figure 29: The Elements of Organizational Environment Design

As we walk through each element, I will offer examples of how each one might be realized in the spirit of helping you to understand them enough so that you can begin to think about how you might apply them within your own organizational setting. I invite you to think of the following descriptions and explanations as a guide to help you think through what a management by indirection might look like for *you*, in *your* particular organizational setting—as opposed to an explicit set of instructions to follow and adhere to.

Conditions and Agreements

Conditions and Agreements constitute an aspect of the environment that refers to the circumstances that are deliberately set in order to stipulate how people will work together and what is to be expected of them, regardless of their specific role. These conditions and agreements are intended to support the growth of *Sense-and-Respond* leadership within the organization.

People Move Toward Their Developmental Edges

The first thing to say about the Conditions and Agreements we want to create—as a way of constituting an organizational environment that is deliberately designed to foster inner growth and development—is that they are all oriented around creating a *holding environment* as described in Part III in the section on *developmental holding environments*.

You, as organizational leader or manager, need to function as a *facilitative agent* to enable this growth—to provide some degree of **psychological challenge** in the form of situations or circumstances that present problems whose solutions require inner capabilities that are *just slightly* beyond a person's current developmental center of gravity. That is, you need to create an environment that enables people to move just beyond their developmental edge, to move from the *familiar* to the *unfamiliar* aspects of themselves.[84]

While they can be uncomfortable, edges are where we need to go if we are to grow ourselves—if we are to find a fuller, more complex expression of our small-l leadership in the world. Bringing in developmental distinctions and vocabularies can help people as they move toward their edges, because it provides a conceptual understanding that gives clarity and direction, which can have the effect of blunting the discomfort, at least somewhat.

There are several ways in which you, as a leader or manager, can provoke a developmentally catalyzing psychological challenge for people through the kinds of situations you pose for them. Some examples are:

- A promotion that brings on new role-related challenges, as for instance a promotion from a software developer to a software development technical lead

- Assignment to a project whose complexity forces the person to "think outside the box" in some genuinely new and developmentally challenging manner. An example could be someone moving from a project team focused on single customer to one that serves multiple customers; or movement from a small five-person team to a larger four-team program.

- Movement to a completely new role—as for instance moving from a software developer role to a scrum master role—in which the new role puts the person in a completely different social environment and task domain.

---

[84] For more on the psychological nature of "edges" and the important part they play in people's inner development, see Arnold Mindell, *Quantum Mind: The Edge Between Physics and Psychology* (Deep Democracy Exchange, 2013).

There are a couple of things to note here. First, in any such challenge, you and that person are explicit about the *developmental* nature of the challenge; the attention of any shift in situation is to help the person grow, not to achieve some organizational need. For example, you may have an occasion in which a specific promotion for someone could provide just the developmental kick-in-the-pants they need, but there is no existing slot available at the moment. It is worth overcoming this institutional barrier—and to do whatever it takes to create the slot—for the sake of this person's development, and for the sake of the more broadly shared uptick that that person's development could bring to the organization. By contrast, a specific position might become available that would be a promotion for a given person; but since you and that person agree that this particular move may not be best for them *developmentally*, you both decide that he or she should pass on that promotion.

Similarly, it is often developmentally beneficial for a person to move to a new role when their current role is no longer *growing* them. This notion flies in the face of a more traditional management thinking (management through *direction*), which sees subject-matter expertise as a key organizational asset. The logic behind this thinking is based on the idea that it can take someone years to reach a certain level of expertise within a given role and work domain (for instance, a software architect), and that it therefore makes sense for them to remain in that given role for a long time in order to fully leverage that hard-won, and greatly valued, expertise.

I don't mean to suggest that subject-matter expertise is not important, but if what you are trying to do is to catalyze the emergence of a deep, sustained, and ever-evolving organizational agility, giving preference to inner growth and development over subject-matter expertise is a better long-term strategy.[85]

---

[85] In *An Everyone Culture* Kegan and Lahey write that within a *deliberately developmental organization* (such as the investment company Bridgewater), "If you can perform all your responsibilities to a high level, you're no longer in the right job" (pp. 98–99). In such an organization, it is expected that once a person masters a

Another thing to note here is the notion of developmental fit. On the one hand, you need to be careful that the psychological challenge being posed for another person does not present too large a stretch for them. Problems whose solutions require inner capabilities that are too far beyond one's current center of gravity, too far beyond their edge, are both needlessly stressful and developmentally ineffective. By the same token, however, you need to ensure that the psychological challenge you pose is not too small a stretch. Here, you particularly want to guard against your taking an overly cautious—perhaps even overly protective—posture in relation to another person's growth.

People Have Support Structures

This brings us to the second criterion that a *holding environment* must provide, which is a high degree of **psychological support**. As I briefly explained in Part III, when one embarks on a developmentally challenging path, there can be some degree of psychological strain—one is not merely intellectually challenged, but psychologically stretched. One finds oneself—and, more often, *puts* oneself—in situations in which one's current beliefs and assumptions no longer seem to hold. Competencies and skills—formerly solid and reliably felt—begin to come into question. A sense of disequilibrium descends; one's sense of reality becomes somewhat blurry.

In the context of such a challenge, part of what constitutes *psychological support* is the encouragement and empathy we experience from others around us. As we move along our developmental path it is important to experience feeling validated about where we are at currently—to not feel ashamed of our current developmental juncture. Moreover, it is helpful to receive encouragement as we take what at times can be somewhat tentative steps on that developmental journey, and to be reassured that whatever mistakes we make along the way will be dealt with gracefully and respectfully. When you are assisting other people in their developmental journey, these are the

---

particular role, it is time to move on: At one company Kegan and Lahey documented—a company called *Decurion*—for instance, a commonly articulated phrase is "As soon as something is working perfectly, it's time to blow it up and move to the next level" (p. 99).

kinds of qualities of *support* that you can bring into your interactions with them.

These kinds of emotional supports are not the only forms of psychological support. Another kind of support is embedded in the very tools and practices by which developmental challenge is activated. Deliberately developmental conversations, shared sensemaking conversations, co-leadership practices, and the very context of deliberately developmental relationships themselves are specific examples of *Evolvagility* practices that activate an overtly social context. Such social contexts are characterized by the shared experience in which people at once *challenge* one another and *support* one another to grow, develop, and improve.

When engaging in these strong social practices, people naturally form support systems with a new level of intimacy, which in turn enables development of a deeply supportive environment of mutual support and encouragement. The close relationships and alliances that grow in such an environment—based, I would stress, on *both* challenge *and* support—form the deep social foundation essential to any kind of sustainable organizational transformation. It is for this reason that organizational leaders and managers need to foreground and emphasize the *relationship* dimension of *Evolvagility* tools and practices. It can be all too easy to miss this, given our culture's tendency to emphasize individual growth and individual development.

The mix of *psychological challenge* and *psychological support* forms a necessary compound in the *holding environment.* Too much *challenge* without enough support, and the person will end up overly stressed; they will withdraw from the challenge, and become discouraged over the frequent failures that too extreme a challenge presents. Too much *support* and not enough *challenge* create a dynamic in which the manager ends up as an *enabler* of that other person's developmental weaknesses, yielding no developmental at all—or worse, facilitating a developmental regression. The other thing that can happen with too much support and not enough challenge is that people effectively hold one another prisoner within what can become a socially stifling straightjacket. In such an environment—perhaps ironically—people reinforce one another's developmental weaknesses and hesitancies; people become even more reluctant to grow due to the silently held desire to not break out of whatever socially conservative mold that has been set.

Failure is to Be Owned and Even Celebrated

A third condition that supports the growth and emergence of *Sense-and-Respond* leadership is related to how people relate to failure. As I explained in Part IV, the problem with failure is not so much the mistake or the error itself, but what the covering up and the avoiding of failure does to an organizational culture. I talked about what Chris Argyris referred to as "organizational defense routines"—which arise around the covering up of errors—and the effect they have on individuals and relationships.

Here, I want to point out and emphasize the corrosive effects these routines have on organizational performance, and on the broader organizational culture. When the covering up of errors—and the covering up of that covering up—becomes routine in an organization, serious errors, sometimes with catastrophic outcomes, often result. These get covered up first through blaming and scapegoating; and then—in an effort to avoid having the difficult conversations that would otherwise arise—through the introduction of organizational policies and rules that only serve to further disable people from getting to the real source of those errors. The resulting organizational dance comes to be the basis for how we interact, and becomes the reigning model against which organizational and management competence is measured and assessed.[86] Chris Argyris documents numerous calamitous organizational and institutional breakdowns—from Enron to the Vietnam War to the disaster of the Columbia space shuttle—and attributes them to the organization defensive routines—the covering up of errors and the covering up of that cover-up—which became an endemic part of the culture of those organizations and institutions.[87]

In Part IV, I revealed two *Evolvagility* practices—the *failure bow* and *my biggest mistake*—which teach us to own and even *celebrate* our mistakes. These practices help us to relate to mistakes both as things that naturally

---

[86] For an incisive discussion of this particular dynamic—which Chris Argyris calls "skilled incompetence"—see his article "Skilled Incompetence," *Harvard Business Review*, September 1986.

[87] For a discussion on Argyris's analysis of the ways in which organizational defense routines have affected cataclysmic errors within large institutions, see Chris Argyris, *Organizational Traps: Leadership, Culture, Organization Design* (Oxford University Press, 2010).

happen in the course of our day-to-day lives and as possible signals of movement beyond our edges. However, it is not enough for management to simply say something like "Hey, mistakes are OK" or to trumpet phrases such as "Mistakes are how we learn." While such sloganeering has its place, the recognizing and celebrating of our mistakes, and the learning we take from them, needs to be embedded in the very structures, policies, and practices of every-day organizational life.

Practices like the *failure bow* and *my biggest mistake* teach us—individually and culturally—the benefit and the spirit of full disclosure and openness. Through the exercise of these practices, mistakes get revealed so that whatever needs to be done to remedy them is openly addressed and, therefore, quickly remedied. Moreover, the person who made the mistake is empowered toward responsible action, both in declaring the mistake and in committing to whatever action he or she needs to take in order to clean it up. But perhaps more importantly, mistakes are no longer viewed as something to be avoided at all costs. That reduction in the aversion to making mistakes makes it possible for people to be bolder and more confident—a quality of being that is a critical foundation for the growing of any kind of organizational agility.

One way in which organizational leaders empower and enable these practices—and in the process create conditions in which people take responsibility for their errors rather than trying to cover them up—is by making them an explicit part of routine daily habit. This can happen in one-on-one meetings, in departmental meetings, and even in casual chats in which the public declaration of failure and learning becomes as much a part of any relevant discussion as status reports and check-ins. Another way in which organizational leaders can help shift the culture is to resist their own inclination, and the tendency of other managers around them, to impose new policies upon everyone in response to the mistake of one individual. Instead, organizational leaders can have those difficult conversations with the individual in such a way that supports the person's ability to reveal the failure fully, learn from it, and take full responsibility for cleaning it up.

Turning something that is new into routine practice often starts with you, as manager or leader. For those practices to begin to stick and to become routine, you yourself need to model these tools and practices. Modeling in this way sets the tone organizationally and signals to others what constitutes good and acceptable behavior. When organizational leaders and managers are openly transparent about their errors and failures, a certain kind of openness and vulnerability can start to become more of the norm, and resets the parameters for what constitutes leadership.

One executive leader I worked with regularly used these tools to great effect. For example, she once gave an end-of-the-year retrospective presentation entitled "My Ten Greatest Errors This Last Year," in which she talked through a number of mistakes she made, a couple of which were quite revealing of her own weaknesses and limitations. The effect was powerful and, combined with other messages and practices, helped to convey to people the message that it is not only okay to admit to their mistakes, but that it is actually a *leaderful* thing to do—so long as one is willing to own those mistakes, to clean up whatever needs to get cleaned up in the aftermath, and, perhaps most importantly, to declare what was learned, particularly in public.

Feedback is How We Grow

In Part IV we examined the practice of feedback as a way to sustain individual developmental growth. Feedback acts as an institutionally sanctioned *uber*-practice—a forcing function for growing people's small-l leadership capability. And, to the degree it assists in growing people's small-l leadership capability, it elevates broader, organizational capability.

In Part IV, you learned two protocols for giving and receiving developmentally oriented feedback: *impact feedback* and *what I make up*. Both of these feedback protocols are oriented around principles that I want to bring to the foreground here in order to create a deeper understanding of how feedback works, and how it can become a key driver of individual growth and of cultural evolution across your organization, as seen from the perspective of organizational leadership and management.

Feedback is a way to help another grow their leadership capability by helping them have a better sense about their impact on others. Such glimpses into our impact on others help us assess whether how we are showing up in the world reflects and projects our *intention*. It helps us find the gap between how we intend to be in the world and how others are actually seeing us.

The practice of *impact feedback*, described in the section "Developmental Feedback," is a practical application of this principle. It is markedly different from the more commonly practiced form of feedback that is often referred to as *performance* feedback. Performance feedback happens when one person—usually a manager—tells another person about something they did well or poorly. For instance, you might tell someone how well they did in an important presentation to senior leadership; or you might share with another some thoughts as to what they could have done better in a presentation they gave to a product management team. In either case, the force of the communication presumes—in subtle and not-so-subtle ways—that the feedback *giver* knows more, has more insight, or simply has the authority to assess and judge the performance of the feedback *receiver*.

The effect is to put the feedback receiver into an inferior position, leaving them feeling at least mildly defensive and less-than-ready to truly receive the full benefit of the feedback. But, perhaps more significantly, the suggestions and the abstractions in which performance feedback tend to be framed provide relatively little concrete information that the feedback receiver can actually use to assess and potentially improve their behavior. There is a difference, for instance, between me telling someone what a great job they did in the presentation they just gave (*performance* feedback—relatively little concrete information) and me telling them that when they told a personal story—around slide #4—about how their life was changed, I found myself really drawn into the remainder of the presentation (*impact* feedback—more concrete information). Or between my telling someone that they were dominating the conversation in this morning's team meeting (*performance* feedback—relatively little concrete information), versus my telling them that when on three different occasions they talked for a minute straight I found myself getting annoyed and disengaged (*impact* feedback—more concrete information).

Impact feedback is one of the most effective ways for growing leadership agility because people tend to be less defensive when receiving impact feedback than when receiving performance feedback, partly because it focuses so naturally on concrete examples. Impact feedback helps people clearly see—sometimes to a shocking degree—the gap between who they aspire to be in their leadership—their *intention*—and how they actually show up to others—their *impact*. And if people cannot see that gap, they cannot close it. Closing the gap between our *intention* and our actual *impact* provides a key aid to our inner development and to the growing of our leadership.

Feedback is as much about the *giver* as it is about the *receiver*. Feedback is as much about the way in which the giver *senses* and *makes sense* of their world as it is about the way in which the *receiver* acts and behaves in the world. Healthy feedback conversations are not unidirectional—they are, effectively, *shared sensemaking conversations* in which the feedback becomes a context for people in the conversation to understand themselves (and each other) more deeply. In the context of the growth of a deliberately developmental organization, feedback conversations are bidirectional. In this way, feedback becomes a conversational form that transcends the Newtonian notion of linear cause-and-effect and instead embraces the Postmodern, *quantum* notion of the co-emergence of cause-and-effect.

This emergent, bi-directional, and co-creative quality of feedback has several beneficial effects. First, it permits a person to regard the feedback they receive in a highly neutral manner. In a more unidirectional mode of feedback—epitomized by the practice of *performance* feedback—one tends to feel somehow obliged to change one's behavior in very specific ways. In the bidirectional mode of feedback, by contrast, one regards feedback as simply *information*; one is in no way obliged to do anything at all, or change anything at all, with the feedback they receive. They can simply receive it, store it away, and then—perhaps at some later moment—assess that information, discern its meaning for them, and, on the basis of that discernment, decide what **they** want to do about it—decide what, if anything, **they** might want to change in *themselves* in response to that information. From such a perspective, one neither has to agree or disagree with the feedback they receive—it is all simply *information* that they can use to help them more accurately see themselves and their impact in the world.

Another beneficial effect of this emergent, bi-directional, and co-creative quality of feedback is that it becomes a context in which relationships themselves can grow. Seeing feedback as bi-directional, revealing as much about the giver as the receiver, creates a context for deeper mutual revelations. The giving (and receiving) of both *impact feedback* and *what I make up* require considerable intimacy and vulnerability, which, in turn, generate conditions for deeper, more profound, and more resilient and sustainable relationships.

Finally—and this applies directly to organizational leadership—it removes the barriers that exist within the traditional unidirectional approach to feedback in which people are hesitant to give feedback to their managerial superiors. In a *Sense-and-Respond* organization, we as organizational managers and leaders need feedback ourselves. As such, it is customary within a truly *Sense-and-Respond* organization for organizational leaders and managers to receive as much feedback as they give.

When feedback reflects the kinds of qualities I'm describing here—through the practice methodology outlined earlier in the book—and it becomes an institutionally sanctioned and a widely practiced convention, feedback provides a key foundation for the emergence of a deep, sustainable, and systemically engaged leadership agility. When manifested both individually and collectively, healthy feedback can have a tremendous impact across organizations and raise organizational agility capability to a higher level.

The feedback loop needs to be as short as possible. All-too-often, something happens that causes a problem or upset, but we don't find out about it until much later. Often by the time we hear about something, our own recollection of the event is foggy, which makes it harder to discern what actually happened—as opposed to one person's recollection of the incident, which may or may not be colored by that person's own emotional reaction to it. By tightening the feedback loop—by minimizing the duration of time between incident and feedback—we create conditions in which (a) both the giver and receiver of the feedback can corroborate concrete information; (b) the receiver can immediately discern and put into place any necessary corrections, rather than waiting until "next time" it happens—which might never occur; and (c) the receiver can make whatever amends or cleanup necessary right away with the people involved.

Creating a culture in which feedback is commonly and readily given and received makes possible the tightening of feedback loops. Some practices for creating such a culture include (though are not limited to) the following:

Personally mastering feedback practices and consistently modeling their use

Not including feedback as part of the yearly performance review

Setting aside in your weekly meetings with direct reports, and in your "skip level" meetings (meetings in which one meets with one's manager's manager), time for mutual feedback. The *observation-story-assumption* ("what I make up") feedback protocol can be very effective here since it may actually be a somewhat longer period of time between incident and feedback

If you manage a department, hosting a monthly departmental retrospective in which part of the time is allotted for an exchange of feedback between management and performers

Catalyzing Practices

While conditions and agreements form an environmental background for the broader, systemic practice of *Evolvagility*, catalyzing practices refer to the specific things that you as an organizational leader or manager can do that are deliberately intended to bring about or enhance a particular circumstance—whether operational or cultural—that empowers and enables people's inner growth. These acts include orienting a shared vision for the organization, identifying and empowering *Evolvagility* champions, and engineering breakdowns in order to help people think in new and more complex ways.

Orienting Shared Vision

A key catalyzing force for any self-organizing or self-managing social system—whether it is a team, a start-up, a department, or a company—is the orientation toward a shared vision and purpose. The verb "orient" means to "align or position (something) relative to the points of a compass or other specified positions," while the noun "orientation" means the "relative position or direction of something."[88] The key role of the organizational leader is to continually orient people toward this shared vision.

As a management activity of *environment design*, the orienting of shared vision means that people throughout the organization are "positioned to the points of a compass"—in this case a vision for a desired future. I would emphasize here that this is *not* the same notion of corporate vision provided

---

[88] From the definition of "orient" and "orientation" given on my MacBook Dictionary.

by management and appearing on placards, posters, and corporate advertising. This type of corporate vision serves only to create a collective of followers, not of leaders. Engaging and aligning others around shared vision in the way I am advocating here moves from vision as that which is *inert* and *non-inclusive* to that which is *active* and *inclusive*; from that which is created by management, and then passed down, to one whose qualities everyone has a part in creating; from that which is fixed and immutable to one that is ever-emergent and ever-responding to the plurality of perspectives, identities, and interpretations that constitute complex organizational life; from that which is a solely cognitive *abstraction* to that which engages a mix of emotions and aspirations—including desire, curiosity, pride, competition, and excitement.[89]

> The phrase "orienting shared vision" reminds us that vision is not just something that is, but something people do—together. It is one of the ways in which people come together to create a desired future, even as that future is unfolding.

In this sense, the orienting of shared vision acts as that which complexity scientists call an "attractor." An attractor is a set of points toward which a complex system tends to move—and it is a point of stability around which its otherwise complex behaviors revolve. Rushing water going into a basin will eventually stabilize around a swirling pattern as it goes down the drain; flying geese eventually fall into formation; otherwise scattered and chaotic family systems stabilize around particular rituals, such as the Christmas gathering.

Similar attractors exist for teams and organizations. Scrum teams, for instance, stabilize around a sprint goal, which acts as a kind of compass that orients where they are headed for any given two-week iteration. A similar phenomenon arises in a larger collective, whether a unit, a department, or an organization. One of the ways for those with an organizational leadership role to orient behavior within the larger collective is to create conditions in

---

[89] Richard Pascale, Mark Milemann, and Linda Gioja, *Surfing the Edge of Chaos: The Laws of Nature and the New Laws of Business* (Three Rivers Press, 2000), 72.

which people orient themselves around a future that they themselves can envision and commit to creating. Behavior that emerges from the envisioning of a desired future, which people themselves have a hand in co-creating, tends to be more powerful, more effective, and more impactful than behavior that is directed, coordinated, or otherwise managed from above.

Engaging and aligning others around a shared common purpose involves a give-and-take process: It begins with leadership initiating a conversation in which business imperatives are revealed and aspirations shared, and continues when others are explicitly encouraged to find meaning for themselves and to reveal their own aspirations and "business" imperatives. Through such a process, vision, meaning, and direction emerge from the co-creative conversations and activities of all. There exist a variety of forums for doing this—from those that are large in scale, formal, and planned, to those that are small in scale, informal, and spontaneous.

One such forum involves bringing together large groups of people for the purpose of creating common purpose and direction. Two of the most common well-established and facilitated methods[90] for doing this are *Future Search*[91] and *Appreciative Inquiry.*[92] One approach I've seen work on a number of occasions is patterned after the organizational "town hall" and combines elements of both *Future Search, Appreciative Inquiry* as well as others.

To describe this process very briefly: A top-level leader brings an entire unit, department, or organization together and begins with sharing his or her own aspirations for the organization. People are then invited to work in small groups in which they define for themselves personal aspirations that resonate with what the leader shared with them. Samples from these resonances are shared out to the whole group in order to spark further

---

[90] See Barbara Benedict Bunker and Billie Alban, *The Handbook of Large Group Methods: Creating Systemic Change in Organizations and Communities* (John Wiley & Sons, 2006). See also Holman, *The Change Handbook.*

[91] Marvin Weisbord and Sandra Janoff, *Future Search: An Action Guide to Finding Common Ground in Organizations and Communities* (Berrett-Koehler Publishers, 2010).

[92] Diana Whitney, David Cooperrider and Jacqueline Stavros, *Appreciative Inquiry Handbook: For Leaders of Change* (Crown Custom Publishing, 2008).

discussion. From here, both personal and shared aspirations serve as a platform from which people—still working in their groups—generate for themselves, both individually and collectively, commitments that they will take forward. As with personal aspirations, samples are once again shared with the whole group. From here, individuals, armed with a shared sense of purpose, go back to their work worlds better able to invent and innovate for improvement and performance, both locally and organization-wide.

Such large scale, formal events are most effective when supported by periodic informal events. For example, a vice president I worked with hosted sumptuously catered monthly breakfasts. During this hour-long event the vice president sat amidst everyone else and simply asked questions that were designed to get people talking frankly and in ways that elicited connection for people to their work-life aspirations. It was also an opportunity for him to share and elaborate upon his own vision for the organization and even, on occasion, share his own failures and mistakes along the way.

Another way to co-create meaning and direction, on a smaller scale and with less formality, is similar to what Jack Welch did back in the early '90s, which is for leaders to meet with groups of people throughout the company and engage in direct dialog. During these conversations, people are encouraged to speak their minds, helping to uncover assumptions and discover their differences. This method recognizes, first, the substantive value of the perspectives of employees and, second, creates a forum in which shared meaning emerges from the dialog itself.

One-on-one conversations, whether they happen during scheduled meetings or arise impromptu while waiting in line for coffee, are also occasions to connect around shared vision and aspirations.

Organizational leaders and managers need to remain almost fixated on organizational vision, and the ideas and vocabularies that that vision elicits. Every moment is an occasion to engage people in conversations that in some way make that vision immediately present and palpable. One executive leader I worked with, who was fixated in just such a manner on a vision for what a truly lean value stream could look like, purposely carried a different book around with him to meetings. These books typically sported evocative titles that invariably prompted questions and comments, inevitably spawning conversations that somehow connected back to that vision.

Relate-Repeat-Reframe

There are three specific behaviors and practices that organizational leaders and managers carry out in support of *orienting a shared vision* that, besides providing support, have their own benefits as well. These specific practices and behaviors reflect three key principles related human systems change, which Alan Deutschman, in his book *Change or Die*, cleverly calls "Relate-Repeat-Reframe."[93]

The "Relate" part refers to Deutschman's assertion that in order for change to occur, there needs to be a relationship between leaders and others, a sense of personal connection. This relationship piece—already so central to the practice of *Evolvagility* more generally—is key to *orienting a shared vision* because it is the psychological arena in which depth of vision and purpose can be most deeply felt. It is in our relationships with others that our vision becomes an emotional and psychological reality because it is there that it becomes a social and, ultimately, cultural reality.

The second part of Deutschman's template—Repeat—is also key. Shared vision and purpose activate—and are activated *by*—particular themes, concepts, words, and distinctions that are not only *technologically* relevant—for example, the specific business you are in, the particular business processes and technologies you are leveraging—but are *psychologically* relevant in that they reflect deeper feelings and emotions that make shared vision and purpose emotionally *salient*. Repeatedly articulating, and engaging others in thinking through these themes, concepts, words, and distinctions helps people to assimilate this new vocabulary in ways that subtly influence how they think and act.

The third part of Deutschman's template—Reframe—reminds us that leaders will often want to help people see their day-to-day activities, behaviors, and interactions in new ways. We talked about the *Evolvagility* practice of reframing in Part IV, which is to help another have a new way of thinking about something in order to have access to a new, and potentially more effective, avenue of action. Departmental retrospectives serve this purpose

---

[93] Alan Deutschman, *Change or Die: The Three Keys to Change at Work and in Life* (HarperBusiness, 2007).

very well, since they provide an opportunity for people not only to examine what has and hasn't worked, but perhaps more importantly, to understand how new ways of thinking and working are reframing the general orientation of the department or company.

In all these approaches, the result is an emerging culture in which employees internalize organizational vision precisely because they contribute, regularly and personally, through actions and words, to its creation and, from that internalized vision, are prepared to act in ways that are congruent with that vision, without necessarily having to be told what to do.

Identify and Empower Informal "Champions"

Returning for a moment to the language of complexity science, the practice of *orienting a shared vision* is about establishing an "attractor" that acts as a point of stability around which the otherwise complex behaviors of an organizational collective revolve. In a somewhat similar manner, you can think of the practice of identifying and empowering informal champions as a way to activate *catalyzing agents* within an organizational system. These catalyzing agents act like "sleeper cells" in which people who have internalized the deep meanings related to the cause of the organization know what they need to do when the moment arises for them to "wake up."

Informal champions are self-selected catalyzing agents in your organization. They have a deep sense of alignment with, and emotional connection to, the emerging future you envision; they see your vision and their own as deeply intertwined. They are deeply knowledgeable and skillful in their area of expertise, have a desire and an ability to relate well with others, and are respected and looked up to by their co-workers. Informal champions are natural innovators—they love new ideas and want to spread them. This synthesis of qualities makes these people uniquely qualified to act as informal organizational champions.

It's usually easy to find these people because they stick out in any crowd and in any meeting due to the high quality of the questions they ask, the insights they share, and the energy with which the engage. They're the ones who want to initiate this or that community of practice; they're the ones who pose evocative (and provocative) questions; they're the ones who you notice because of their energy and vitality. As informal champions they are ready, at the drop of a hat, to promulgate the ideas, concepts, and distinctions associated with the new future you (and they) are envisioning.

> These people are your partners. They stand shoulder-to-shoulder with you to catalyze new ways of thinking and acting in others, usually well out of earshot of your direct influence and sometimes even of your knowledge.

Find out who these people are and schedule one-on-one meetings with them. Engage their managers in joining you in empowering and enabling them to create small projects (or other forms of meaningful engagement) that will help them find ways to realize their part of your shared vision. All the while, know that it is important that their actions come from *them* and not from *you*; this will deepen their ownership and better engage their imagination.

The special projects of these informal champions can take any number of forms, from establishing an effective community of practice meetings such as brown-bags and pizza parties (which you will want to happily fund where appropriate) to convening internal special interest groups, or organizing deep-dive 1/2-day practice sessions in which they and other passionately interested people gather to learn new cutting-edge practices. They organize and host book clubs and discussion groups. They are the ones leading the charge in growing and cultivating local *deliberately developmental ecosystems*. They are the ones who speak up at vendor-procurement meetings in order to see to it that the decisions that are made reflect priorities and criteria that align with the principles, ideas, and distinctions that are at the heart of the future they, and you, and others aspire to create together.

Keep in mind that these passionate, effective, and influential people are the eyes, ears, and voices for change, distributed throughout your organization. In the various roles they play, informal champions help realize Geoffrey

Moore's innovation curve in that, as innovators, they powerfully influence early adopters, who in turn influence early majorities.[94]

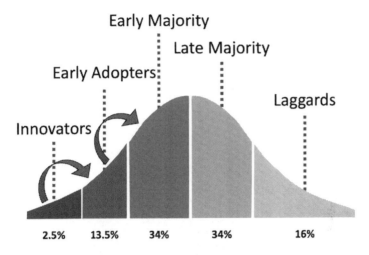

Figure 30: The Nature of Large Systems Change

This enacts a powerful and critically important dimension of managing through the design of environments by leveraging the power of informal networks in activating broad organizational change.[95]

---

[94] Geoffrey Moore, *Crossing the Chasm, 3rd Edition: Marketing and Selling Disruptive Products to Mainstream Customers* (Harper Collins Publishers, 2014); Seth Godin, *Free Prize Inside: How to Make a Purple Cow* (Portfolio, 2007).

[95] I have been especially influenced in this aspect of our work with managers by Jeffrey Goldstein, James Hazy, and Benyamin Lichtenstein, *Complexity and the Nexus of Leadership: Leveraging Nonlinear Science to Create Ecologies of Innovation* (Palgrave Macmillan, 2010); Mike Thompson, *The Organizational Champion: How to Develop Passionate Change Agents at Every Level* (McGraw Hill, 2009); and by Margaret Wheatley, *Leadership and the New Science: Discovering Order in a Chaotic World* (Berrett-Koehler Publishers, 2006).

Engineer Breakdowns

The management practice of *engineering breakdowns* is closely aligned with organizational management's role in bringing about conditions and agreements that support people in *moving toward their developmental edges* and in *owning and even celebrating their mistakes.* The engineering of breakdowns is a key practice for a developmentally oriented management by indirection.

A breakdown occurs when something unexpected happens—when a previously predictable and unambiguous flow of events is rendered, perhaps suddenly, *unpredictable* and *ambiguous.* Your computer suddenly crashes, your car suddenly dies, or you have a terrible fight with your significant other. What a breakdown does is that it throws you—unexpectedly—into a "situation of non-obviousness."[96] You have a brief moment when you quite literally don't know what to do—you can no longer depend on the normal, predictable, flow of events and cues to remind you what to do and even who you are. You find yourself—even if only for a brief moment— existentially on your own.

Typically, we regard breakdowns as undesirable interruptions to the flow of what we're doing. However, within the developmental context, sometimes having something interrupt the flow of ordinary occurrences is a good thing. Breakdowns can serve as developmental accelerators, both at the individual level and at the level of the organization. To the degree that a breakdown presents a break with business as usual, it can afford an opportunity to move us into a new way of making meaning with respect to those occurrences. At such moments, we are forced to engage with the situation newly, perhaps with a fresh sensemaking lens through which we might look at it.

Many of us have had an experience in life when an unexpected event—the loss of a job, a serious illness, a divorce, the estrangement of a close relative, the death of a loved one—precipitated a shift in the way in which we view

---

[96] Terry Winograd and Fernando Flores, *Understanding Computers and Cognition: A New Foundation for Design* (Addison-Wesley Professional, 1987).

our lives. Those events change us by changing how we see the world, how we think, how we *are*—that is, they change us *developmentally*.

We can leverage this positive, developmental characteristic of breakdowns to facilitate another person's development, without having to introduce the kinds of extreme events I just mentioned. This is a bit like the principle behind weight-lifting, which is to produce small micro-tears in muscles in order to stimulate new growth; you don't want to completely rip the muscles—in fact doing so would defeat the purpose entirely. In a similar fashion, as managers we can stimulate *inner* growth within others by introducing relatively small breakdowns and supporting people through the consequent new meaning-making that those small breakdowns might engender.

From the perspective of organizational management and leadership, deliberately engineered breakdowns can take many forms. The fundamental principle is that a breakdown introduces some new challenge that helps people move toward a new *developmental edge*. Some examples include a promotion that provides a developmental challenge; an assignment to a new project that forces a person to think in new and complex ways; a shift to a new role that places the person in a new task domain or social environment, thus stretching that person developmentally.

In all such cases, you are deliberately placing a person in a situation in which, at first, they will have lots of *breakdowns*: They'll make mistakes, they'll feel anxious, they'll feel unsure of themselves, and so on. Such conditions are the very nature of breakdowns felt experientially, and they are—like muscle tearing when weight-lifting—necessary contributors to inner, developmental growth. As such, having conversations in which you and the other are both open and transparent—and in which you have the developmental *vocabulary* to lean on—about the developmental dimension of the breakdowns they are facing helps the other person weather those breakdowns and enables them to leverage them in aid of their inner development. Meanwhile, creating conditions and structures that provide the element of *psychological support* will serve to further strengthen the developmental container so necessary when those breakdowns occur.

Engineering breakdowns works at the larger scale of teams and organizational collectives. One senior vice president I worked with decided to reduce the number of product delivery teams serving a particular product stream from nine down to seven. At first, this created a great deal of consternation among product managers who now found themselves with an apparently smaller pipeline through which to move projects. The move was highly unpopular; employees accused the senior vice president of needless cost cutting and of reducing staff in order to save money. In point of fact, however, his intention was to engineer a breakdown—to create a condition that forced people to confront certain assumptions that he thought deserved more scrutiny, the primary assumption being that throughput was determined solely by capacity. In reducing capacity (by reducing the number of product delivery teams) he forced the whole system to find other ways to realize the goals around which they were oriented.

The product management team realized that by breaking projects into small chunks, they could still thread the different projects through the delivery pipeline. More significantly, however, they realized that in breaking those large projects into small chunks (what in later years came to be called "features" in the Scaled Agile Framework (SAFe)), they found they could achieve more coarse-grained prioritization of product features. This allowed them to not have to make so many difficult business decisions at the beginning of the project; those decisions could be delayed until later, at a point in time when they usually had more information—specifically as it related to what customers would actually want, which features they would actually use, and what they would ultimately pay for—on which to base those decisions.

Engineering this breakdown caused many other effects that contributed to the overall learning across the organization. The bottom line, however, was that the kind of learning that happened could not have happened in a workshop or training; it was a learning that had to be spawned through the introduction of a new *condition in the environment*—in this case, a condition that forced people to question their assumptions and re-categorize their thinking.

This brings me to a rather delicate matter in relation to the use of positional power. Sometimes an individual or a group of people simply can't see the developmental angle you, as manager or leader, might see. That was certainly the case in the scenario above; few of the other stakeholders could see the organizational learning benefit that could be gained by deliberately reducing delivery capacity. This senior vice president was left with a choice: Either wait until people could see the benefit (which might never happen), or simply exercise unilateral power to push the change through—to engineer a breakdown—in order to bring about the conditions in which that learning could happen. This is similar for you in those cases when, as someone's manager, you can see the developmental possibility for that person in switching to a new role—a possibility that they can't yet see.

The question for the manager or leader at such moments is whether or not to exercise unilateral power for the sake of the learning and growth of others, or for the organization more broadly. Some managers—especially those who have embraced the more facilitative management style promulgated in much of the recent thinking on Agile leadership—are instinctively reluctant to exercise unilateral power. Others are willing to wield it all too willingly. Such a question—and the dilemmas it gives rise to—point to your own inner development; there are no easy answers or resolutions. Rather, these questions and dilemmas give rise to developmental challenges that, in the end, have the effect of growing *you* in your role as organizational manager and as organizational leader.

The Larger System

In this section, I will introduce some perspectives and thinking tools for working with and tuning the larger organizational system. Describing them all would require a book-length treatment in itself. In lieu of that my primary aim in this section is to introduce a thinking orientation centered on enhancing deep learning, both at the individual and at the organizational level. In doing so, I will leverage all that we have learned in the earlier parts of this book, while laying doing a new track directed toward the role of the organizational leadership or manager working with the larger organizational system.

> The primary management outcome we seek is to enhance and support the role of organizational leadership and management in **engaging holistically to identify and resolve larger systemic incongruities.**

What do I mean by *systemic incongruity*? In terms of *Evolvagility*, an incongruity is any situation or condition in which the outcomes being generated are out of alignment with the organization's intention, vision, or aspiration. For example, if our intention is to increase the agility capability of our company or organization—and we understand that the growing of inner agility, or *Sense-and-Respond* leadership, is a key part of that—then any behaviors, processes, structures, or systems that are not in alignment with that intention and that understanding are *incongruent*.

Incongruities are not dysfunctions. The word dysfunction suggests there is something *wrong*—when all that could be happening is that our behaviors and actions, and the structures and systems we create, are not aligned with our intention. Similarly, incongruities are not impediments. Impediments are what prevent us from achieving a goal and are therefore viewed as things that need to be removed. Goals are important and key to achieving any kind of vision, but I have seen managers become fixated on organizational goals and lose sight of the connection with the greater organizational vision. *Evolvagility* encourages organizational leaders to manage in a way that helps people orient themselves around a shared vision, as opposed to only working toward specific goals. Helping people remain congruent with the organization's vision—through the design of organizational environments—is the essential task for organizational leaders and managers.

What do I mean by *engage holistically?* When organizational leadership engages this way, they see the whole system, and are capable of identifying and resolving larger systemic incongruities in the organization. The organizational thinker Russel Ackoff has spent a lifetime arguing that you can't improve an organization's performance (however you define that) by trying to improve its parts.[97] I have certainly found this to be true during my years engaging in the process of large-system change.

You can find plenty of tools, backed by decades-long management traditions, to solve problems in the *parts* of organizations. There are relatively few (though still a good many) tools and traditions that engage the *whole* organization.[98] What *Evolvagility* offers is a set of practices and tools that engage the whole organization, and which work from the inside out—that is, from the level of individual consciousness and relationship and from there out into the broader organizational context.

If we, as organizational leaders or managers, are to bring about a culture of everywhere-leadership aligned with our organization's deepest purpose, we need to engage in the process of identifying and resolving larger system incongruities in ways that promote and invite people, from all walks of life within the larger system, into that very process—that is, we need to engage holistically. In order to be able to engage holistically to identify and resolve larger system incongruities, we're going to need to tune the way we think about organizational systems in general—to move from a *parts* orientation

---

[97] For a concise summary of his thinking on systems thinking, see Russell Ackoff, "A Lifetime of Systems Thinking," retrieved on October 21, 2018 at https://thesystemsthinker.com/a-lifetime-of-systems-thinking/.

[98] Some examples of these include Otto Scharmer, *Theory U: Leading from the Future as it Emerges* (Berrett-Koehler Publishers, 2016); Barry Oshrey, *Seeing Systems: Unlocking the Mysteries of Organizational Life* (Berrett-Koehler Publishers, 2007); Cindy Adams and William Adams, *The Whole Systems Approach: Involving Everyone in the Company to Transform and Run Your Business* (Executive Excellence Publishing, 1999).

to a *whole* orientation; and to move from a *goals* orientation to an orientation around *vision*.

What might that look like? How might we go about bringing about for ourselves, and others, such an *orientation*?

Looking at Organizational Complexity Through Multiple-Lenses

As I've been saying throughout this book, organizations are inherently *complex*, and I'm not convinced that we can ever see any complex system in its entirety. What we *can* do, however, is adopt models to help us open up new perspectives that help us see more deeply into that complexity.

Here I will introduce three such models. As you learn about each of these, I invite you to think of each as a very fine-tuned **lens** that reveals some important aspect or dimension of an organizational setting or situation. Taken together, these *lenses* provide a richer, more multi-layered, view of the complexity of organizational conditions and situations, and helps us see the kinds of things we need to see if we, as organizational leaders and managers, are to create organizational *environments* that naturally and organically grow deep and sustainable organizational agility, from the *inside out*. Relying solely on any single lens will almost always leave something out. Hence the value of having a small collection of different lenses, with each of them revealing a particular aspect of an organizational situation.

In the following pages, I will reveal such a set of *lenses*. Each lens brings into focus one particular aspect, or one dimension, of the more complex whole.

- **Integral Four-Quadrant Lens**: A manner of looking at organizations that recognizes the different ways we might talk about any given organizational phenomenon—from the perspective of individual consciousness, individual behavior, relationship and culture, and organizational systems and structures.

- **Dynamic Systems Lens**: A way of looking at organizations that sees the dynamic interplay of systemic forces as distinct from looking at organizations from the perspective of their static parts.

- **Cultural Value Meme Lens:** A manner of looking at organizations that recognizes and seeks to *harmonize* (not homogenize) the different values and cultural perspectives that exist in organizations, while at the same time helping each of them evolve toward greater maturity and complexity.

An Integral Four-Quadrant Lens

Based on the substantial work of Integral philosopher, Ken Wilber, the Integral Four-Quadrant Lens recognizes that organizational reality is multidimensional and that in order to account for its complexity, we need to be able to look at it from the view of at least three perspectives.

First-Person Perspective sees the world from in terms of subjective experience—from the perspective of our sensations, feelings, and thoughts; and of our awareness, impulses, desires. It is primarily from this perspective that I have been talking about one's inner meaning-making and Action Logic.

Second-Person Perspective sees the world from the perspective of *relationships* and *mutuality*. Second-person perspective is emergent: it arises when two or more individuals come together, whether in a conversation, in working on a task together, or in an activity or gathering, such as a meeting or conference. This is the perspective of shared identity, shared meaning, and shared commitment. It is the perspective from which *culture* arises and which gives a specific definition or quality to this or that relationship system or group.

You could say that First-Person Perspective is *subjective*, and that Second-Person Perspective is *inter-subjective*—both have the quality of seeing the world from the *inside*. By contrast, **Third-Person Perspective** gives the view of reality as seen from the *outside*. It is what allows us to see the organization as a whole, and to observe and measure things *objectively*—that is in terms of observable objects and movements.

These three perspectives map to four different *quadrants* through which a manager or leader might view organizational situations and conditions:[99]

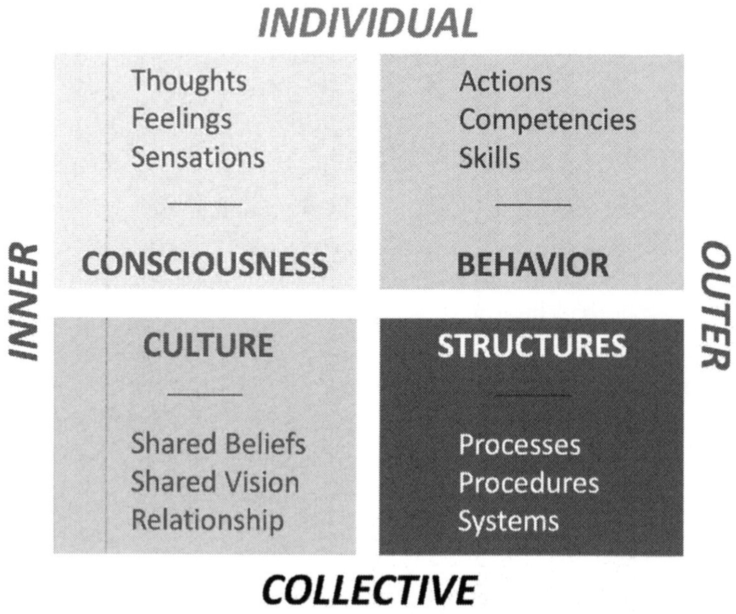
INDIVIDUAL
Thoughts
Feelings
Sensations
CONSCIOUSNESS
Actions
Competencies
Skills
BEHAVIOR
INNER
OUTER
CULTURE
Shared Beliefs
Shared Vision
Relationship
STRUCTURES
Processes
Procedures
Systems
COLLECTIVE

Figure 31: A Four-Quadrant Perspective

You can think of each of the four quadrants as panes of a window, each pane providing a different perspective on whatever organizational phenomenon or situation you, as a leader or manager, might be looking at—whether that be a raft of defects on a recent product release, low morale on several teams, or an unexpected uptick in sales.

Let's look at the particular perspective that each quadrant reveals and at some of the kinds of things you might think about, and be on the watch for, from that perspective.

Quadrant 1: Individual Consciousness: This quadrant maps directly to first-person perspective; it is the domain of *inner* subjective experience.

[99] See the work of Integral theorist and philosopher, Ken Wilber, for more on first-, second-, and third-person perspective and on the four quadrants. One place to start is Ken Wilber, *Integral Psychology: Consciousness, Spirit, Psychology, Therapy* (Shambhala Publications, 2000).

From the perspective given by this quadrant, or "pane," leaders and managers pay attention to the inner growth of individuals, recognizing that an individual's *outer* performance is determined by the complexity of that individual's *inner* meaning-making capability. Many of the practices of *Evolvagility* speak directly to this quadrant as they seek to raise an individual's inner complexity of meaning-making and of mind.

Quadrant 2: Organizational Culture: This quadrant maps directly to second-person perspective. Within the organizational context, this quadrant points to the domain of shared values, beliefs, and to culture more generally. It also speaks to the quality of relationships, and to the capacity for genuine and fruitful collaboration throughout the organization. From the perspective of this quadrant, leaders and managers pay attention to the nature of shared values and beliefs and how those may limit or enhance both individual and organizational performance. It is also from the perspective of this quadrant that the *orienting of shared of shared vision* has its basis. Many of the practices of *Evolvagility*—such as *deliberately developmental conversations, shared sensemaking*, and *co-leading* as well as the *deliberately developmental relationship*—are immediately germane to this quadrant since they seek to raise the capacity for relationship intelligence between and among individuals and, consequentially, across the organization more broadly.

Quadrant 3: Individual Behavior: This quadrant maps to third-person perspective, looking from the angle of individual behavior. Unlike individual consciousness, which we can't observe from the outside, individual behavior refers to those actions and behaviors—and any related competencies and skills—that we can readily observe, assess, and even measure from the outside. From the perspective of this quadrant, leaders and managers pay attention to what individuals are able to *do* and how they are able to *behave*. Many *Evolvagility* practices, in providing means for individuals to grow themselves *developmentally*, cultivate the grounds for the growing of the kinds of skills and competencies that can be readily observed from the perspective of this quadrant.

Quadrant 4: Organizational Structure: This quadrant also maps to *Third-Person Perspective*, but in this case, looking from the perspective of the observable rules, procedures, processes, and structures that determine how people in an organizational setting work together. From the perspective of this quadrant, leaders and managers pay attention to the rules, systems, processes and structures that govern how people work, and to the ways in which those rules, systems, processes and structures help or hinder the capacity of the organization to meet the challenges it faces.

Any situation, challenge, or condition can be viewed through any single quadrant or window "pane," or it can be viewed from the vantage point of several at the same time. Each one gives us a different way of looking at the situation, challenge, or condition, helping us to see aspects we may not otherwise be able to see as clearly. In this sense, we can say that each quadrant provides a perspective that helps us see a different dimension of the organizational environment.

Leveraging an Integral Four-Quadrant Lens: Action Learning Revisited

One way in which one might leverage the Integral Four-Quadrant Lens in an organizational setting is in the practice of Action Learning as described in Part IV. The process begins in much the same way described earlier: We start with a statement that describes the situation or challenge, and we ask some general questions to help us dig deeper—this constitutes the **Sensing** phase.

From here, we begin to move to the **Making Sense** phase. It is when we come to this phase that we explicitly leverage the *integral four-quadrant lens* we've been talking about. Here we engage in a *shared sensemaking conversation* in which we explicitly look at the situation or challenge from each of the four perspectives:

From the perspective of the **Consciousness**, we ask the question: In what ways might individual meaning-making and Action Logics account for what we're seeing—including our own?

From the perspective of the **Behavior**, we ask the question: In what ways might the level of skill and competence (or lack thereof) account for what we're seeing—including our own?

From the perspective of the **Culture**, we ask the question: In what ways might collectively held assumptions and beliefs account for what we're seeing?

From the perspective of the **Structure**, we ask the question: In what ways might current structures, processes, and procedures account for what we're seeing?

The shared sensemaking conversation that these questions—and the multiple perspectives by which they are informed—elicit can generate vivid impressions of the deep nature of the situation, leading to the formulation of an experiment we might try: the **Respond** phase of the process. This is where we formulate a hypothesis as to what might be happening, and an action or experiment we might try next that will help us get more information, gain greater insight, or affect some (perhaps small) move toward resolution in the system.

Once the experiment or action for a given iteration has been completed, we **Observe the Impact and Effect** of the action or experiment. At this point we ask ourselves: Shall we continue on with this Action Learning? Do we feel that we have learned what we would have wanted to learn? Did we generate an outcome that satisfies the question that got us started in the first place (with respect to the situation or the challenge with which we kicked off this Action Learning process)? Have we identified and/or resolved an important system incongruity?

From here we choose whether to initiate a next iteration, or to complete the Action Learning for this particular situation/challenge. If we choose to continue, we start again, as before, with the **Sensing** phase, and continue the next iteration from there.

A Dynamic Systems Lens

The *Dynamic Systems Lens* brings us into an entirely new territory. It recognizes that organizations have a great variety of dynamically unfolding interactions between and among organizational agents (individuals, groups, behaviors, and structures) and that it is those interactions—and the dynamic patterns they yield—that constitute the behavior of organizations. And, it is those interactions and the unpredictable and often surprising behaviors they generate that make organizational situations complex.

Consider this scenario. You have an important milestone looming in three months for the company's customer website, and the software development team you manage is falling behind. You decide to put gentle pressure on the team to work later and on weekends, and to incentivize them with free meals and with the promise of the high visibility that the successful addition of these services will bring to the company. The team members love and admire you and want to do everything they can to create a big win for you.

The team works evenings and many weekends to crank out the code as fast as they can. At first it seems to be working; their velocity is increasing to a surprising degree. Then, at some point their progress begins to slow. Meanwhile, defect reports are suddenly starting to come in, and online customers are getting annoyed. You talk with the team, and they are certainly concerned too, so they push all the harder. But now they don't only have new code to write, they also have defects they need to track and fix. Things are not looking all that great.

This situation has an underlying dynamic structure that is being repeated—perhaps in a dozen places, on a variety of different levels of scale—even as we speak. The *Dynamic Systems Lens* holds that there are particular patterns to the way in which systems behave, and that when we understand the nature of these patterns, not only are we better equipped to deal holistically with situations as they arise—but, armed with a systems view, we can also anticipate certain kinds of situations before they even occur, because we have a vocabulary for understanding the dynamic systems behavior which underlie them.

This common scenario is happening right now, in companies large and small, and it has an underlying dynamic structure that experienced managers of software teams surely can discern. By enjoining the developers to work overtime, the managers have created conditions likely to introduce bugs into production, because when people are under pressure and not well rested, they make more errors. A typical response is to work *more* hours, thus introducing more bugs, resulting in more stress, and a vicious cycle has begun.

A manager in the scenario above, armed with the tools and distinctions given by a Dynamic Systems Lens, might have been able to foresee trouble with asking his team to work overtime, and might have instead presented a clear vision for the team, complete with due dates, and asked them to self-organize a way to align their work with this vision, thus tapping into their creativity and drive without risking burnout.

Causal Loop Diagrams:
Tools for Revealing Dynamic Systems Behaviors

Causal loop diagrams (CLDs) are a classic tool for understanding and assessing the behavior of dynamic systems, because they vividly portray the dynamic interplay of agents in a system, showing how the behavior of one part of the system effects that of another, and how the feedback of those local behaviors produces behaviors at the system level in ways that can be truly confounding and vexing.

Over the decades of their use, and of a rich and deep research that informs their construction and application, common behavioral patterns have been documented, forming what Peter Senge termed dynamic systems *archetypes*.[100] Each archetype can be rendered as a CLD depicting a specific systemic behavior, with a brief title that says something about that behavior.

There are small handful of archetypes that are commonly found within the organizational setting. A full set of these is well documented in a number of places online.[101] Here, I will walk through two of the most commonly found of these: *Fixes That Fail* and *Limits to Success*.

The *Fixes That Fail* archetype describes the dynamic behavior of the situation I just described. The following is a CLD depicting this particular pattern:[102]

---

[100] Senge, *The Fifth Discipline*.

[101] For an excellent introduction to systems thinking archetypes and the tools to use in working with them, see Daniel Kim, *Systems Archetypes I: Diagnosing Systemic Issues and Designing High-Leverage Interventions*, (Pegasus Communications, 2000). A brief description of some of the most commonly found archetypes starts on page 6. If you are at all interested in this, I highly recommend spending 30 minutes with this document.

[102] For a short introduction on how to read a Causal Loop Diagram, here's a very simple 4-minute YouTube video: https://www.youtube.com/watch?v=da5ZNPBhHwU.

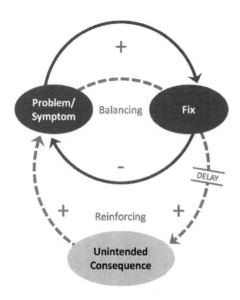

Figure 32: Fixes That Fail

The pattern has two feedback loops—shown here in blue and red—with the red one counteracting the blue. Here's what's happening: You start with a problem (which is really a symptom) that prompts in you the need to take some kind of action in order to fix the problem. The blue plus sign in Figure 32 represents this action. To the degree the fix works, it reduces the problem, or at least it dials down the symptoms, represented by the blue minus sign. That's the first loop: a balancing loop in which more of one thing produces less of another thing.

Meanwhile, however, whatever action it is that you have taken to fix the problem generates an unintended consequence or side effect, represented by the red plus sign after the "Fix" in the diagram. The problem is exacerbated by the existence of a delay in the appearance of the unintended consequence; it may be days or even weeks before we see evidence of its existence. That unintended consequence has the effect of causing the problem to reappear or its symptoms to get worse, as shown by the second red plus sign on the left. This, in turn, drives a need in you to take that same action that seemed to fix the problem before. This, of course may reduce the problem or symptoms, but it will also, at the same time, amplify that unintended consequence. And on it goes.

Think back to the earlier scenario above with the software development team, and consider it in terms of systemic dynamic structure. We could draw a CLD like this to portray what is happening:

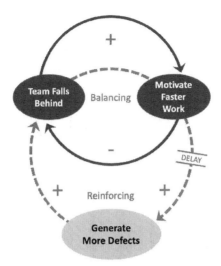

Figure 33: Example of Fixes That Fail

Though all we have is a hypothesis (in working faster, the team is taking short cuts in the coding, which has the effect of generating more defects), diagraming it in this way helps us see things more clearly and suggests any number of possible experiments we might try next.

If you were to graph the behavior of this pattern over time, here's how it might appear:

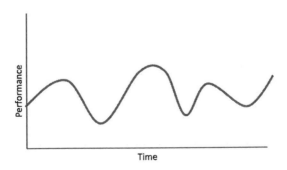

Figure 34: Performance over Time

In examining this graph, you can see evidence that we just can't get any traction—performance (however you are measuring it relative to the particular situation and context you are observing) goes up for a while, and suddenly plunges. To break such a cycle, you need to recognize that the short-term fix might be helping in the near-term, but in the long run, it is preventing you from really solving the problem. Perhaps a short-term fix is all you want right now. Or perhaps you and others need to buckle down and work to solve the deeper issue. Either way, visualizing the pattern makes it possible to more clearly see what's going on, systemically, and to make the decision that is best for the situation and for the larger whole.

Another, somewhat similar pattern (in that it combines a single *reinforcing* loop with a single *balancing* loop)—also commonly found in organizational settings—is referred to as *Limits to Success*:

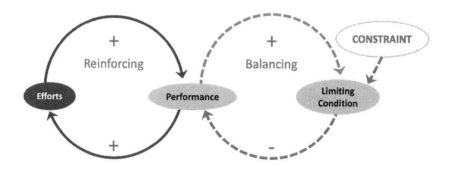

Figure 35: Limits to Success

This pattern describes the dynamics of a situation in which a growing effort leads to increased performance, which in turn inspires and emboldens greater efforts—resulting in a reinforcing loop. However, as performance increases it puts increasing pressure on a limiting condition whose limit is determined by a constraint in the system—a constraint of which we may or may not be aware—resulting in a balancing loop. Once the limit defined by the constraint is reached, negative pressure is exerted upon performance, offsetting the positive pressure that comes from the efforts.

Examples of this pattern abound: A popular product generates a growing customer base, which in turns puts pressure on the order department, whose size is constrained due to budget. When orders cannot be fulfilled fast enough, customers get unhappy, putting a drag on sales performance.

A classic example of this dynamic, within the context of organizational change, happens with the introduction of any new practice or technology into an organizational setting. At first, the enthusiasm of the innovators and early adopters drives an initial cycle of increasing successes and optimism. Meanwhile, however, the attitudes and actions of the late majority and of the *laggards*—those who are resistant to the change—put an increasing opposing pressure on that cycle of success. The increasing pressure put on by the innovators and early adopters in pushing for the change builds until it pushes up against a hidden constraint, which in this case is a kind of tipping point in which silent non-agreement and non-alignment turns into outright resistance.

Here's the telltale signal of the occurrence of this dynamic, seen as a trending pattern in time:

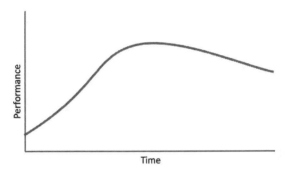

Figure 36: Performance Over Time

As shown, there is an initial rise in performance, followed by a tapering off and flatlining—and then, by a gradual decline.

One of the most common ways in which organizational managers and leaders react to such behavior is to ramp up the efforts and to treat any countervailing force as

simply acts of resistance that somehow need to be countered. However, those countervailing forces may pose legitimate and deeply layered needs of the organizational system to which we should pay attention, rather than thinking of them as small acts and attitudes of resistance. When it comes to long-term organizational change in particular, sometimes we need to slow down to speed up. The way to work with a situation that exhibits this deeper systemic behavior is to locate the constraint—there may be more than one—and work with that. As an organizational leader, this can mean finding the so-called resisters, getting into relationship with them, finding out what needs we might be violating, or what deeply held values we might be challenging.

The key to the use of a CLD is not so much to "solve" this or that problem, though that is important. Rather, the real benefit in practicing and using CLDs is to help you to more clearly see the *dynamic behavioral patterns* that underlie problems in order to come up with hypotheses for experiments you might try to solve them. Another benefit is that the practice and use of CLDs helps you and others to learn *to think systemically*—to *see* the dynamic causes and patterns that are at the heart of many of your greatest organizational challenges.

> *This ability to think systemically—especially as it becomes prevalent throughout an organization—is a key organizational skill in a VUCA world. It is just as important as any other analytical or root-cause skill you expect professional organizational players to have.*[103]

CLDs are so very useful that people have created dozens of common organizational dynamic behavior *archetypes*, each of which portray some common dynamic organizational patterns.

A Cultural Value Meme Lens

A *Cultural Value Meme Lens* looks at the differing values and cultural perspectives that coexist and, to varying degrees, harmonize (or don't) within an organizational setting. The word "meme" comes from the Greek noun *mimema*, or that which is imitated. In this case, what is imitated is an idea (such as "success" or "personal freedom") or a catchphrase (such as "it is what it is") that takes hold across a particular social sphere. It is something that gets lodged in our psyche, becoming part of the psychological

---

[103] In fact, in some ways one could make the case that CLDs and the systems thinking that their use elicits are the opposite of root-cause analysis.

atmosphere from which our thoughts and feelings—both individual and collective—materialize.

Within the context of the Cultural Value Meme Lens, a meme refers to a value system, to a set of social standards or ideas around which people tend to coalesce. A *value meme* emphasizes a set of values, patterns of behavior, or mindsets that inform that which is being imitated. The concept of a *cultural value meme* is based on the research of Clare W. Graves and in the subsequent applied work of Don Beck and Chris Cowan—a field of study and application called "Spiral Dynamics"—which examines how value memes come to be propagated within a broader culture, and within the minds of the individuals that form from that culture.[104]

As informed by the ideas and insights of Spiral Dynamics, the Cultural Value Meme Lens has important aspects that I want to highlight. First, it recognizes that every organization is defined by a predominant set of cultural values and motivating ideas, and that those cultural values and motivating ideas form the social and psychological landscape in which people live and work within that organization—what some people refer to as an organization's cultural center of gravity.

A Cultural Value Meme Lens recognizes, however, that even though any given organization has a cultural center of gravity, there exist numerous pockets within any organization—individual departments or functional groups such as Accounting and HR, and differing areas of subject matter expertise such as software development and finance—in which the predominant set of cultural values and motivating ideas differ from those which characterize the broader cultural landscape, even as they are to some degree modulated by that broader set of values and ideas.

Finally, a Cultural Value Meme Lens posits that human systems—whether individuals or social collectives—can, and often do, evolve their capacity to

---

[104] Graves, ed. Cowan and Todorovic, *The Never Ending Quest*; Beck and Cowan, *Spiral Dynamics*. Key aspects of this work have recently been popularized within the business press, due to its overt application to organizations and organizational leadership; see Laloux, *Reinventing Organizations*.

embrace ever-greater complexity, as the life conditions in which they find themselves requires it and as their own internal capabilities allows it.

Let's step through each of these aspects, starting with the main foundational research findings and ideas that inform them.

Main Foundational Research Ideas

Spiral Dynamics describes a developmental model of human maturity that is very similar to that which we've been examining in this book: The *inner process* of increasing mental complexity that defines human mental development. But there are some important ways in which Spiral Dynamics differs from the developmental model I've described in this book. One is that it tends to bring more overt focus to social collectives, such as those found in organizations, townships, and even entire nations, moving beyond the purely individual sphere.[105] Another is that it tends to focus on the *values* that people hold—what they think of as most important in their lives, how they think people should behave, what they believe it means to belong socially—and on the ideas, or *memes*, that motivate people and inform how they think.

Each and every social system—whether a team, a department, an enterprise, or even a country—revolves around a particular set of values, beliefs, and motivating ideas; that is, each has a cultural *center of gravity*. Within each such social system, people identify with, and understand themselves in terms of, those values, beliefs, and motivating ideas.

Despite the apparent cultural variety that differentiates social groups, there exist enough similarities among them to strongly suggest a kind of cultural

---

[105] Indeed, much of Don Beck's work and the work of his many colleagues with Spiral Dynamics is in bringing its thinking and insights onto the global stage into overtly social contexts, most notably in places like South Africa and the Middle East. For specific applications in South Africa, see Beck and Cowan, *Spiral Dynamics*. For applications in economics, see Said Elias Dawlabani, *MEMEnomics: The Next-Generation Economic System* (SelectBooks, 2013). For applications in democracy in the Middle East, see Elza Maalouf, *Emerge!: The Rise of Functional Democracy and the Future of the Middle East* (SelectBooks, 2014). There is also Frederic Laloux's application to organizations and organizational leadership in Laloux, *Reinventing Organizations*.

typology—a grouping of value memes according to common themes and patterns. Moreover, across the entire set of these cultural value meme typologies there is a developmental progression from less complex to more complex. By "complex," I mean that each successive typology—or *stage* in the developmental progression—is able to deal with greater environmental, situational, social, and political nuance and complexity than the previous one. In this regard, the developmental model that underlies Spiral Dynamics is very similar to that which we've been talking about in this book.

What drives the evolutionary movement from one value meme to the next in the developmental sequence is the life conditions in which a given human system finds itself, and the inner capacity for change within that human system. This is a key finding in the research on which Spiral Dynamics is based. Just because the life circumstances of a given human system demands a more evolved value meme complex doesn't mean that human systems will adopt such a value meme complex. In fact, most of the time, this does not happen. Much depends on the internal capacity of that system to change and its readiness to embrace the behaviors and ways of thinking that the new conditions call for. This is the nature of the reality of human systems change, whether it's a seven-person software delivery team or an entire organization.

Four Stages of Cultural Evolution Found in Modern Organizations

Let's come back to the developmental aspect of sequential value meme stages. The Spiral Dynamics model describes eight value meme stages. Each stage—or "altitude" as it is often referred to in the Spiral Dynamics literature—has particular and unique qualities that Clare Graves (and others) documented very thoroughly. Four of these stages are commonly found within the modern organizational setting. In the descriptions of these below I combine elements from both Clare Graves's and Frederic Laloux's explication of these stages. And again, bear in mind that while any given human system may have a center of gravity in one of these value meme stages (or across two immediately adjacent ones), each such human system is made up of a unique mix of several.

Conformist Blue. The most abiding quality of Conformist Blue is its value for stability and predictability. When Julius Caesar conquered lands across Europe, he did so primarily through force and violence. The result of this strategy was that he periodically had to go back to re-conquer lands previously conquered. His successor, Augustus Caesar, did things differently; he conquered lands first by subduing them through force, as did his predecessor. However, what he did subsequently was different—after conquering a given land, he set about establishing laws, infrastructure, and civic roles—a strategy by which, through the creation of stable and predictable systems and structures, conquered lands *stayed* conquered.

This is the nature of Conformist Blue—to create social stability through the establishment of laws, procedures, processes and rules that transcend, and live beyond the lifetimes, of those who established them. It is this powerfully stabilizing and sustaining quality that made the nation state possible; and, while perhaps not ideal by today's standards, it was a significant advance over the social chaos that tended to precede it.

Within the organizational context, Conformist Blue is reflected in the stable processes and structures exemplified in the factories of Henry Ford about 100 years ago. In its value for stability, Conformist Blue tends to gravitate to the notion of one truth, of the centrality of a single authority, of the idea that there is really only one right way of doing things. In modern organizations, Conformist Blue finds its home in accounting and governance and in strict organizational hierarchies—anywhere reliable processes and stable authorities are required. In its organizational heyday (around the '50s and early '60s) it was what gave lifetime employment and the stability of marital and societal roles.

The unhealthy underbelly of Conformist Blue is its rigidity, its adherence to a single authority and the one right way, and its extreme ethnocentricity. It's what justifies slavery, inequality, and underlies the authoritarian impulse that has driven—and continues to drive—many of the worst atrocities in human history.

Achievement Orange. While Conformist Blue is driven by its value for stability and predictability, Achievement Orange is driven by its desire to win, to achieve results, and to have autonomy and personal freedom. Achievement Orange has its historical basis in the Enlightenment, where commerce, freedom, and the scientific method took ascendency over static rules, authority, and doctrine.

Within the organizational context, Achievement Orange heralded an era—beginning in the 1950s—of innovation, risk, accomplishment, and great wealth. Unlike Conformist Blue, where change is anathema, Achievement Orange welcomes and embraces change—but only so long as *it* can control what that change will look like and who it will benefit. Orange is the impulse for competition, in both its healthy and unhealthy expression, and for pragmatism, new ideas, and for the urge to better ourselves in the workplace.

In its unhealthy expression, Achievement Orange informs the cutthroat nature of hard-core business decisions, the increasing concentration of wealth, and the drive toward profit, no matter what the cost to our communities and to the world at large. It is the impulse to drive out Conformist Blue, both its unhealthy tendency toward bureaucracy as well as the often-necessary regulating and stabilizing forces its healthier aspects bring.

Pluralist Green. The most abiding quality of Pluralist Green is its embrace of diversity, personal fulfillment, and the empowerment of all. Pluralist Green steps away from the cold scientism and achievement orientation of Achievement Orange in order to be able to embrace the bigger picture. In this way, Pluralist Green opens out beyond the one-dimensional world of Conformist Blue and the two-dimensional world of Orange, into the three-dimensional world that includes relationships, feelings, and social equality (in contrast to individual liberty, the brand of freedom favored by Orange).

Pluralist Green has its historical basis in the flowering of liberation philosophy of the late 18th and 19th centuries when it fought—oftentimes very successfully—against slavery, for religious freedom, for equality for women, and for greater emphasis on the inherently democratic principles that emerged out of the Enlightenment. Another zenith of the Green impulse occurred during the 1960s with its push for the establishment of equal rights for minorities, women, and gays; in its push the environment; and in its opposition to the colonial tendencies still very much alive at the time (as for instance the Vietnam War).

Within the organizational environment, Pluralist Green reflects an increasing orientation toward collaboration, participative management, and anything that emphasizes workplace equality and the embrace of diversity. Pluralist Green has the capacity to see multiple sides of a situation—one of the qualities we see reflected in the Postmodern mind we investigated earlier. As such, Green recognizes that the best business decisions are those that benefit from a plurality of perspectives, and the bigger picture it makes

259

possible. In many ways Green is the philosophical birthplace of the Agile movement, in its valuing of bottom-up decision-making, of collaboration, and of the rejection of traditional management structures.

Evolutionary Yellow.[106] As we move into the value meme of Evolutionary Yellow, a key shift happens. People become able to move beyond their fixed view of things; they develop an inner flexibility and an ability to truly see the necessity for the existence of *all* perspectives. By contrast, Pluralist Green values only those perspectives with which it agrees—which stands in ironic and paradoxical contradiction to its espoused value for diversity and minority voices. Evolutionary Yellow is motivated not by the one right truth (as is the case with Conformist Blue), nor by achieving results (as is true with Achievement Orange), nor by equality and relationship (a key value of Pluralist Green), but by a deep sense of inner purpose and the sense that we, as individual human beings and social systems, are ever-unfolding and ever-evolving. *Individualist* and *Strategist* action logics shine brightly in an Evolutionary Yellow social environment.

Within the organizational environment, Evolutionary Yellow recognizes the necessary layered dynamics of human systems that reflect the healthy aspects of all value memes that may be present within any given social system. It has the capacity, along with a matching curiosity, to see the larger system in all of its complexity.[107]

Organizational Managers and Leaders as "Spiral Wizards"

Informed by the insights given us when looked at through a Cultural Value Meme Lens, we want to come back to the role of organizational leader and manager as a *designer* of organizational environments. From the perspective of the Cultural Value Meme Lens, Don Beck and Chris Cowan have a

---

[106] Frederic Laloux adopted the term "Teal" to describe what Spiral Dynamics calls "Yellow" (and beyond). Laloux's use of the color "teal" derives from a different, though parallel color-coding and naming convention which Ken Wilber and others in the Integral community adopted in their interpretation and systematization of the work of Clare Graves, Don Beck, and Chris Cowan.

[107] Frederic Laloux documented more than a dozen companies worldwide that were found to be operating at Yellow—what he called "Teal" organizations. See Laloux, *Reinventing Organizations.*

260

name for this role: *spiral wizard*. A spiral wizard is someone who pays attention to the entire organizational "spiral"—which is the composition of value memes that define a particular human social system or organization (see Figure 37 below)—and ensures the overall health of that spiral.

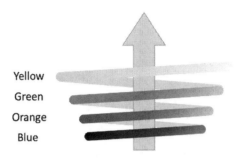

Figure 37: The 'Spiral'

Let's consider what such a role would entail.

As was the case when we were looking at Action Logics, we want to consider the value meme "stages" we've been discussing from two vantage points. The *developmental* perspective points to the fact that human systems evolve through a set of value meme stages of ever greater complexity, where each stage is able to deal with increasing levels of complexity in its environment. From this perspective, we can say that every human system—from a two-person partnership, to a team, to a program, department or entire organization—has a "center of gravity" in which one value meme is predominant.

At the same time, a second vantage point recognizes that any given human system consists of a blend of all of the value memes. What characterizes each human system and differentiates one from another is the particular nature and composition of that blend.

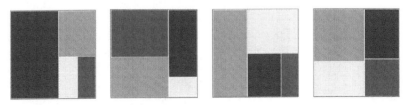

Figure 38: Different Human Systems Constitute Different Value Meme Configurations

From this perspective—which is sometimes referred to as a human systems value meme "stack"—we are looking at an organization as a whole and noting the relative strength of the various value memes. Different human systems—and even the same human system at different points in time—are constituted by a different meme stack constitution.

In addition, these different meme stack compositions are rendered differently within different parts of a given human system, especially those that are greater in size. Some parts of a given human will *light up* more of a given value meme than others. For instance, your accounting department will surely—and appropriately—light up more Conformist Blue than will your HR department; the very nature of accounting requires predictability, stability, reliable processes, and a reliance on a single right way to do things, whereas the nature of the work of a human resources department is such that it must be able to recognize and deal with ambiguity, non-linearity, unpredictability, and the valuing of relationship—all qualities of a strongly Pluralistic Green value meme.

All of this points to a key aspect of the role of organizational management and leadership when looked at from a Cultural Value Meme Lens. Your job is to ensure the healthy expression of all value memes that need to exist in a given human system—to use the language of Spiral Dynamics, to ensure that the organizational "spiral" is *healthy*. This means that the different value memes, wherever in the system they exist, have a healthy expression and that they balance and harmonize with one another.

All too often what happens in any organizational setting, however, is that one or another value meme dominates the spiral by forcing its values and perspectives on others. For example, you may work within a company that lives within a highly regulated industry (such as banking), and which has recently failed a major audit. This emboldens the regulatory parts of the company to overextend and try to impose their Conformist Blue value for stability and predictability—so appropriate for regulatory and accounting—on other parts of the company—for instance product delivery or even marketing—where such an ideology has the effect of stifling innovation and speed-to-market.

Part of your role as an organizational leader is to see to it that in the almost continuous shuffling of priorities in response to surprising events, both internal and external, the overall spiral remains balanced and healthy.

Sometimes you need to strengthen Conformist Blue (as might be the case in the above example); however, in strengthening Blue you want to be sure that the unhealthy aspects of Blue don't affect those parts of the organization whose natural coloration is that of Orange, Green, or Yellow.

Similarly, sometimes you need to strengthen Pluralist Green, as might be the case when the vision and direction of the organization calls for a culture of greater collaboration and cross-functionality (for example when companies move toward the implementation of Agile processes and practices). However, what you, as an organizational leader or manager, need to beware of in this case is Pluralist Green's tendency to want to unduly impose its value—for relationship, openness, equality, and diversity—on other parts of the organization where there is neither the real need, nor the cultural and psychological *readiness*, for such a way of working. This particular issue with Pluralist Green is a fairly common and significant problem in organizations that are attempting to adopt Agile delivery practices; the desire for Green to proselytize its message to the entire organization—where it might be neither wanted nor needed, and where it could in fact be harmful—can lead to an us-versus-them organizational dynamic that will eventually bring an otherwise well-intentioned Agile transition to a screeching halt.

This brings us to the notion of organizational transformation, more generally. Coming from a Cultural Value Meme Lens—and allowing ourselves to be influenced by the research in Spiral Dynamics on which it is based— we will begin to see that organizational transformation is as much about helping a human system become more of what *it already is*—though in a much healthier and balanced version—than it is about getting it to become something different. The notion that transformation automatically means dramatic and whole-scale change can, in some instances, simply be an expression of Achievement Orange's zeal for change for the sake of change.

Becoming more true to what it already is doesn't mean that an organization remains static and immutable. Human systems, when healthy and balanced, have their own natural impetus for change when the life conditions in which they operate trigger in them an urge to do so, and when their own internal capacity enables them to follow that urge. The role of organizational leadership and management—seen from the perspective of a Cultural Value Meme Lens—is to help those systems face these conditions head on, to help them uncover and/or manifest whatever that urge might be for themselves, and to help them develop within themselves the capacity needed to navigate that change—all in order to increase the health of that spiral.

The lenses we have just considered—the Integral Four-Quadrant Lens, the Dynamic Systems Lens, and the Cultural Value Meme Lens—can help organizational leaders and managers have different ways to take in the greater complexity of organizational wholes and be able to lead and manage with respect to those greater wholes and to that greater complexity. Each lens carries with it a great body of research on which its unique distinctions and practices are founded. And, just as highly competent managers and leaders maintain a solid footing in the various engineering disciplines on which traditional management is founded—and which serve most usefully in the Predict-and-Plan organization—so too do they need to ground themselves within the distinctions and disciplines offered by the lenses (or any others like them which embrace a holistic and complex systems perspective) just presented.

Bringing it All Together: Embracing the Strategist Action Logic in Yourself

We have just explored three fields—**conditions and agreements, catalyzing practices, and the larger system**—across which a management by *indirection,* through the design of environments, might be practiced. What is common across all three fields is a certain *attitude* regarding leadership, supported by an Action Logic that takes a multiple-paradigm approach to management. This means that at times you necessarily occupy the role of *enforcer*—telling and dictating. At other times you take the role of the *mentor/coach* as you help others learn and grow through giving advice, offering perspectives, and asking questions. At other times, you occupy the role of *facilitator*—designing and creating conditions that make it possible for others to navigate the territory of their own situations and challenges, while giving them the tools they need to do so successfully.[108] Finally, there are still other times when you are the *witness*—standing back and letting things play out in order for the people to learn for themselves from whatever breakdowns happen, and stepping in—in whichever other kind of role seems right—only when you deem it as absolutely necessary.

You can think of these different management positions as falling across a continuum of management approaches and attitudes:

Figure 39: A Continuum of Management Approaches

---

[108] For a wonderful description of the organizational leader as facilitator, see Rod Collins, *Leadership in a Wiki World: Leveraging Collective Knowledge to Make the Leap to Extraordinary Performance* (Dog Ear Publishing, 2010).

This continuum traces a range of leadership and management approaches or attitudes one might take at any moment, moving smoothly from one to another depending on what the moment or occasion might call for.

In the position of **Enforcer**, you are the "boss" in the traditional sense of the word. From this position, you might be *commanding*, which means that you are making pronouncements as to how things are going to be, usually in the form of a policy or rule that is announced through a variety of management channels. From a slightly different position, you might also be *telling*, which happens when you personally state what will happen or how people are to behave relative to a specific situation or issue, usually in a meeting with your leadership team or in a department-wide meeting. Somewhat differently still, you are *directing* when you are pointing to a goal you are asking people to move toward, or to a route along which you expect them to travel. This could be a strategic goal around which others are expected to rally, a new policy that people must adhere to, or a set of behavioral standards you are setting.

In the position of **Mentor/Coach**, you are no longer the "boss" in the traditional sense. Here you exercise your management authority not by commanding, telling, or directing, but through conversation and dialog. In this capacity you are helping others to adjust their own thinking in ways that are in alignment with the initiatives you want to see realized, or the kind of organizational culture you wish to foster; or you are helping another realize a more fully developed version of themselves, whether within the domain of inner development or with respect to a new range of behaviors or actions.

From the position of Mentor/Coach, you might find yourself *persuading* another person to adopt a point of view that you feel is important to a specific goal, or in order to foster a particular kind of cultural environment. You might take a slightly different tack by *advising* others—advising them as to their career path, the kinds of actions they might take in a given situation, and so on. In advising others, you're explicitly integrating the offering of your opinions and perspectives while eliciting of their own ideas and aspirations. As a Mentor/Coach, you are no longer trying to get them to think a specific way or do a specific thing. In this way, the conversation becomes more *other* focused than is the case when you are in a persuading mode of conversation.

As you move from mentoring to *coaching*, that *other* focus is magnified significantly. Here you find yourself in the realm of conversation where your aim is to help another person increase their self-awareness, their connection to purpose, their capacity for effective action, their clarity around goals and direction. A primary conversational vehicle when coaching is the asking of powerful questions, as are any of the other conversation moves associated with the *deliberately developmental conversation* described in Part IV.

In the stance of **Facilitator**, you move away from the more direct one-on-one kind of interaction you find in the position of Mentor/Coach into a position of greater remove from the people you may be managing. From this position you are more like a musical orchestrator and conductor than you are a counselor or a coach. From this position, you might overtly *facilitate* events or situations, which means that you are creating conditions in real time that support a group of people to realize a goal or a purpose that is important to them. Your sole mode of intervention from this position is limited to whatever is needed to help this group work productively, including making sure that all voices that need to be heard are heard, that the group is not veering too far off topic, that their conversations are production, and so on. This could occur during a leadership team or a department meeting, when you stand back and help the system find its way—whether that is your role for the entire meeting or for this or that moment only.

From a position of slightly less involvement as a Facilitator, you might move toward *designing* in which you create conditions—whether in a meeting or within an institutional setting—that promote and favor particular kinds of behaviors and activities over others. An example of designing might be a thoughtful physical reorganization of the workspace.

From a place of even greater remove as a Facilitator, you may create conditions that catalyze a *holding environment*—one in which people are both challenged and supported developmentally and in which you see to it that people have tools to support their development and learning, as well as the *facilitative agents* necessary to its success.

In the stance of **Witness**, you stand back even further, moving away from influencer or even designer or holder, to one in which you act as the person who is seeing and watching what is going on. As Witness, you watch the goings on around you with an intent and steady eye, capturing patterns of events and interactions among parts and players that others may not be seeing. And yet, as Witness, you withhold any offer of intervention, whether it's the simple offering of feedback or a more direct offer of a suggestion or correction. From the position of Witness, you might simply *observe* what is going on, reading the body language, noticing who speaks and who doesn't, taking in the emotional tone of what is going on. Or, you might more simply *stand back*, checking in on things only periodically and ready to offer assistance, but only very sparingly. Finally, you might *stand away* completely, leaving the system to look after itself without any intervention at all from you.

Such a multi-paradigm approach to leadership calls forth—while, at the same time, its very practice *psycho-activates*—the meaning-making of a *Strategist* Action Logic. (See the Action Logic section in Part II.)

As you step into such a relationship to your role as organizational leader or manager, you realize that your capacity to lead and act within the complex milieu in which we all find ourselves in today's organizational environment is **tied directly to your own inner development**, and vice versa. As you step into the modes of action—and the variety of perspectives that those modes of action build upon—you find your inner, developmental capacity for leaderful engagement in your role as manager or leader growing and evolving.

As is the case for anyone else on such a developmental journey, this is not yours alone: Everyone who seeks to grow a capacity for a deep and sustainable *Sense-and-Respond* leadership needs support. The practices and distinctions of *Evolvagility* are there for you, just as they are for everyone else. And yet, the uniquely complex nature of your role as organizational manager or leader can itself be a developmentally psycho-activating force—but only to the degree that you are willing to expand your emotional and intellectual horizons by embracing the heterogenous disciplines that informed management in a VUCA world calls for. And only so long as you take seriously the perspective of the Postmodernist worldview—especially as it resides within the *Strategist* Action Logic—which understands that organizational transformation is always a product of the inner development of those who lead it.

PART VI

Concluding Thoughts

There is a tale of the 4th century Greek philosopher Aristotle who proclaimed that women have fewer teeth than men—a notion that was taken as fact for nearly one thousand years. This tale points to two things. First, the tendency of early science to rely unquestioningly on authoritative proclamation passed down through time. Second, the supremacy of "enumerative induction"—a form of inductive reasoning whereby one can prove the truth of a claim once a threshold number of instances can be counted—was an article of faith in the scientific community reigning from Aristotle all the way to the early 17th century. An example of enumerative induction might be:

All of the swans I have seen are white. Therefore, we know that all swans are white.

Of course, we now know that this form of logic is wrong—not because the statements themselves are wrong, necessarily, but because the method of induction—of *thinking*—is wrong.

By the mid 17th century that had changed radically, and a completely different way of thinking emerged—a way of thinking that no longer relied blindly on the word of authority, nor on enumerative induction—but that sought to know reality for itself. It was the beginning of the notion of a world that can only be known by being *discovered*—a world with deeper, unseen forces to be studied and dissected by the exploratory power of the human mind. Commerce, treaties, advances in medicine, the explosion of art and music, unprecedented wealth, an economic middle class, a Bill of Rights—all were made possible by this new way of thinking. The way we make sense of the world, and the ways of thinking that we now take completely for granted, were made possible by that signal shift in 17th century thought.

This is the power of a new way of thinking: It generates entirely new horizons for what's possible—whether at the level of an individual person's life, at the level of an organization, or at the level of an entire civilization. Each new age is brought about by a new way of thinking, a new way of seeing things. The big changes in the world have always been cast from big changes in how people think about their world.

> What might be the new catalyzing thought for the world that is emerging now—a world in which the speed of change and the complexity of the challenges we face seem to be far ahead of our ability to keep up or even to comprehend?

I'd like to suggest that this question itself—that is, the nature of the thought with which we might come to know a world that is increasingly volatile, complex, and unpredictable—is indeed *a question*, a question that, however, points to the nature of the mind that is doing the questioning—and a question that points to the very activity of that questioning. To understand our minds in this manner—not as an object, but as a process that is ever-unfolding and evolving—is to equip ourselves with the *inner* technology needed to think the thought that the ever-changing, the ever-uncertain, the evermore complex world in which we live and work requires of us.

And then—from this place of questioning—to *lead*. Not from what we already *know* but from a place of *not* knowing. And standing in that not-knowing, to lead from a willingness to create that which does not yet exist. To lead in the face of the anxiety—both our own and that of others around us—of not knowing precisely what we are facing, where we are going, or where we *should* go; and to step forward anyway, regardless of the anxiety, with the realization that who we are is not defined by our fears or anxieties but by that which we envision, that which we long for in the world. Such a manner of leading is one that can move beyond its reliance on certainty and predictability and out into the crucible of the complex and unpredictable world in which it finds itself. Its only mooring being that of its vision and purpose; its only certainty and confidence being in its capacity to create that which does not and could not exist without the thought it creates. It is a leadership that honors *thinking*, which gives the world at least as much as it honors the world itself; and, from this place of honoring, prepares itself to generate the thought most congruent with the world it wants to create.

Such an attitude and approach to the growing of leadership constitutes a form of *building*. In this case, what we're building is the inner capacity of the individuals within an organization to operate in the face of the volatility, uncertainty, complexity, and ambiguity that characterize the world we now find ourselves in. And, in the very process of that *inner* building, elevate their capacity to generate outcomes that most matter, not by trying to *overcome* the forces of VUCA through brute force, but by joining with its natural unfolding and embracing the very volatility and uncertainty that characterizes that unfolding. And then *creating*—at each and every moment—in a way that builds off that natural unfolding;which leverages that very volatility, that very uncertainty, that very complexity. It is precisely in this way that we come to be able to create that which does not yet exist, at the very moment that it is arising, while building from the unpredictability and complexity that defines the environment for which, and in which, we are creating.

Such a capacity for *creation* in the face of VUCA is as key to today's businesses as it is to institutional governance as it is to managing the world's resources—as important to businesses as it is to non-profits, hospitals, NGOs, and universities. We are confronted by serious challenges, not just in our organizations and businesses but also in the world at large. Challenges that call for not just a new way of acting, but for a new way of thinking—and for a new way of leading. In order to meet these challenges, we need to be far more deliberate about the manner of our thinking, the quality of our relating, and the capacity of our sensemaking.

In this book I have attempted to lay out a philosophical orientation around—and a methodological framework for the growing of—just such a manner of leadership. Not leadership as a collection of behaviors to adopt or attitudes to adjust to. But rather leadership as a path along which we might traverse as we endeavor to grow ourselves—from the *inside out.* To grow within ourselves the complexity of mind congruent with that of the world in which we find ourselves—the ability to generate the thought that the volatility and complexity of that world calls for. And to bring that thought into our relationships and into the organizational and social systems in which we live and work.

Evolvagility provides a philosophical perspective and an organizational setting in which such a Sense-and-Respond leadership can be deliberately and manifestly cultivated.

The growing of such a manner of leadership—what I have been calling a *Sense-and-Respond* leadership—is necessarily an *ecosystemic* pursuit as much as it is a strategic one. It must come to be a part of the day-to-day life that constitutes the activity by which organizations operate and function—as key to that functioning as is the expertise and related technical competence called for by all of that which defines the business of that organization.

Evolvagility delivers on what I see as the fundamental charter of the 21st century organization, which is to become an *incubator* for the growing of human consciousness—for elevating the complexity with which people are able to make sense of their world. To the degree to which organizations see as their fundamental charter the growing of the sensemaking capacity of their people, those people become not only better, more capable organizational players—they become better, more capable social citizens.

It is this capacity for growing the complexity of our sensemaking—both as individuals and in our relationships with others—that I believe to be the germinating idea of today. It is this germinating idea that gives me a profound sense of hope for the future of humanity. Hope in our ability to create our world, from nothing and without evidence. A hope that is not about what we, as human beings, might, or can, *do*. Nor is it even about that we might, or can, *think*. Rather, it is a hope that is grounded in the realization—one that has sharpened over the last decades—that we as human beings are no longer bound to the thinking we inherit. That it is, in fact, possible for us, as human beings, to deliberately change the very constitution of our thinking—that we can *change our minds*. And, perhaps more significantly, that we can build technologies—*human* technologies as opposed to engineering technologies—that can help us be deliberate in the nature of that change, and of that constitution.

During the Scientific Revolution of the 17th century we discovered an *outer* world that is malleable—bendable to our intentions, our vision, our longing—and we created, in our thinking and actions, a technology for leveraging that very malleability. Today we are discovering an *inner* world that is malleable—bendable to our intention, our vision, our longing. And, in a similar fashion, we are creating, within ourselves, a technology—a *human* technology—for leveraging that very malleability. *Evolvagility* provides a human technology that helps us leverage this newly discovered *inner* malleability in order not just to create a world *out there*, but to create the world *in here* from which a world out there, newly envisioned and newly created, might emerge. We no longer need to master the world by conquering it. Rather, we might now master it by mastering the very process of thinking that creates it, and by mastering our capacity for the kind of relationships in which, together, we might cultivate the new world's emergence.

Selected Reading

In the following pages you will find a selection of resources for readers who wish to follow up and take a deeper dive into the research and thinking which underlie the ideas, concepts, and practices discussed in this book. They are organized very roughly according to the main themes covered in the book. Note that while any single resource could be listed under more than one category, each resource appears only once, within a single category. This is not intended to be an exhaustive list; rather, these are resources that have most significantly influenced the concepts and ideas that are at the heart of this book.

Adult Human Development

Basseches, Michael. *Dialectical Thinking and Adult Development*. Norwood, New Jersey: Ablex Publishing, 1984.

Beck, Don, and Chris Cowan. *Spiral Dynamics*. Oxford: Blackwell, 2006.

Cook-Greuter, Susanne. "Nine Levels of Increasing Embrace in Ego Development: A Full-Spectrum Theory of Vertical Growth and Meaning-Making." Accessed on March 26, 2018. http://www.cook-greuter.com/Cook-Greuter%209%20levels%20paper%20new%201.1'14%2097p%5B1%5D.pdf

Graves, Clare, and Chris Cowan, Natasha Todorovic, eds. *The Never Ending Quest*. Santa Barbara: ECLET Publishing, 2005.

Hy, Le Xuan, and Jane Loevinger. *Technical Foundations for Measuring Ego Development*. Mahwah, New Jersey: Lawrence Erlbaum Associates, 1998.

Joiner, Bill, and Stephen Josephs. *Leadership Agility*. San Francisco: Jossey-Bass, 2007.

Kegan, Robert. *The Evolving Self*. Cambridge, Massachusetts: President and Fellows of Harvard College, 1982.

Kegan, Robert. *In Over Our Heads*. Cambridge, Massachusetts: Harvard University Press, 1994.

Lahey, Lisa, Emily Souvaine, Robert Kegan, Robert Goodman, and Sally Felix. *A Guide to the Subject-Object Interview.* Cambridge, Massachusetts: Minds At Work, 2011.

Laloux, Frederic. *Reinventing Organizations.* Brussels: Nelson Parker, 2014.

Laske, Otto. *Measuring Hidden Dimensions of Human Systems.* Cambridge: Laske and Associates, 2009.

Laske, Otto. *Dialectical Thinking for Integral Leaders.* Tucson: Integral Publishers, 2015.

Lewis, Phillip M. *The Discerning Heart.* Amazon Digital Services, LLC, 2011.

Merron, Keith, Dalmar Fischer, and William Torbert. "Meaning-Making and Management Action." *Group and Organization Studies* 12, no. 3 (September, 1987): 274-286.

Mezirow, Jack and Associates. *Learning as Transformation.* San Francisco: Jossey-Bass, 2000.

Perry, William. *Forms of Intellectual and Ethical Development in the College Years.* San Francisco: Jossey-Bass, 1999.

Rooke, David. "Organizational transformation requires the presence of leaders who are Strategists and Magicians." *Organizations and People* 4, no. 3 (Fall 1997): 16-23.

Rooke David, and William Torbert. "Organizational Transformation as a Function of CEO's Developmental Stage." *Organization Development Journal* 16, no. 1 (Spring, 1998): 11-28.

Torbert, William. *Managing the Corporate Dream.* Homewood, Illinois: Dow Jones-Irwin, 1987.

Torbert, William. *The Power of Balance.* Newbury Park, California: Sage Publications, 1991.

Torbert, William. "The Pragmatic Impact on Leaders & Organizations of Interventions Based in the Collaborative Developmental Action Inquiry Approach." *Integral Leadership Review* 17, no. 2 (August-November 2017).

Torbert, Bill, Dalmar Fisher, and David Rooke. *Action Inquiry.* San Francisco: Berrett-Koehler Publishers, 2004.

Wade, Jenny. *Changes of Mind*. Albany, New York: State University of New York Press, 1996.

Business and Organizational Agility

Appelo, Jurgen. *Management 3.0*. Boston: Pearson Education, 2011.

Blank, Steve. *The Four Steps to the Epiphany*. Palo Alto: K & S Ranch, 2013.

Cagan, Marty. *Inspired*. Hoboken: John Wiley & Sons, 2018.

Denning, Stephen. *The Age of Agile*. New York: AMACOM, 2018.

Denning, Stephen. *The Leader's Guide to Radical Management*. San Francisco: Jossey-Bass, 2010.

Gothelf, Jeff, and Josh Seiden. *Sense & Respond*. Boston: Harvard Business Review Press, 2017.

Goldratt, Eliyahu M. *The Goal*. London: Routledge, 2016.

Haeckel, Stephan. *Adaptive Enterprise*. Boston: Harvard Business School Press, 1999.

Liker, Jeffrey. *The Toyota Way*. New York: McGraw-Hill, 2004.

Little, Jason. *Lean Change Management*. [no location provided by publisher]: Happy Melly Express, 2014.

Reinertsen, Donald G. *The Principles of Product Development Flow*. Redondo Beach: Celeritas Publishing, 2009.

Ries, Eric. *The Lean Startup*. New York: New York: Crown Business, 2011.

Sull, Donald. *The Upside of Turbulence*. New York: Harper Collins, 2009.

Womack, James P., and Daniel Jones. *Lean Thinking*. New York: Free Press, 2003.

Complexity and Neuroscience

Axelrod, Robert, and Michael Cohen. *Harnessing Complexity*. New York: Basic Books, 2000.

Costandi, Mohab. *Neuroplasticity*. Cambridge, Massachusetts: Massachusetts Institute of Technology, 2016.

Doidge, Norman. *The Brain That Changes Itself.* New York: Penguin Books, 2007.

Newberg MD, Andrew, and Mark Robert Waldman. *How Enlightenment Changes Your Brain.* New York: Avery, 2017.

Snowden, David, and Mary Boone. "A Leader's Framework for Decision-making." *Harvard Business Review,* November, 2007.

Stacey, Ralph, Douglas Griffen, and Patricia Shaw, *Complexity and Management.* London: Routledge, 2000.

Deliberately Catalyzing Developmental Growth

Allen, Jane, and Heidi Gutekunst, with William Torbert. *Street Smart Awareness and Inquiry-in-Action.* Helsinki: Amara Collaboration, 2018.

Johnson, Barry. *Polarity Management.* Amherst, Massachusetts: HRD Press, 2014.

Kegan, Robert, and Lisa Lahey. *How the Way We Talk Can Change the Way We Work.* San Francisco: Jossey-Bass, 2001.

Kegan, Robert, and Lisa Lahey. *Immunity to Change.* Boston: Harvard Business Press, 2009.

Kegan, Robert, and Lisa Lahey. *An Everyone Culture.* Boston: Harvard Business Review Press, 2016.

Manners, John, Kevin Durkin, and Andrew Nesdale. "Promoting Advanced Ego Development Among Adults." *Journal of Adult Development* 11, no. 1 (January 2004): 19-27.

Marko, Paul W. "Exploring Facilitative Agents that Allow Ego Development to Occur." In *The Postconventional Personality: Assessing, Researching, and Theorizing Higher Development,* edited by Angela Pfaffenberger, Paul Marko, and Allan Combs, 87-100. Albany: State University of New York Press, 2011.

McNamara, Robert. *The Elegant Self.* Boulder: Performance Integral, 2013.

McNamara, Robert. *Elegant Leadership.* Audio program available from Ten Directions at https://tendirections.com/elegant-leadership/commanding-influence/.

Integral Theory and Applications

Dawlabani, Said. *MEMEnomics*. New York: SelectBooks, 2013.

Maalouf, Elza. *Emerge!*. New York: SelectBooks, 2014.

McIntosh, Steve. *Integral Consciousness and the Future of Evolution*. St. Paul: Paragon House, 2007.

Wilber, Ken. *Sex, Ecology, Spirituality*. Boston: Shambhala, 2000.

Wilber, Ken. *Integral Psychology*. Boston: Shambhala Publications, 2000.

Wilber, Ken. *Integral Spirituality*. Boston: Integral Books, 2007.

Language, Conversation and Discourse

Anderson, Harlene. *Conversation, Language, and Possibilities*. New York: Basic Books, 1997.

Clark, Sue, and Mel Myers. *Managing Difficult Conversations at Work*. Gloucestershire, England: Management Books, 2007.

Flores, Fernando. *Conversations for Action and Collected Essays*. North Charleston, South Carolina: CreateSpace Independent Publishing Platform, 2012.

Gottman, John M. *The Relationship Cure*. New York: Three Rivers Press, 2001.

Isaacs, William. *Dialog*. New York: Doubleday, 1999.

Kahane, Adam. *Collaborating with the Enemy*. Oakland: Berrett-Koehler Publishers, 2017.

Kantor, David. *Reading the Room*. San Francisco: Jossey-Bass, 2012.

Rosenberg, Marshall B. *Nonviolent Communication*. Encinitas, California: PuddleDancer Press, 2003.

Winograd, Terry, and Fernando Flores. *Understanding Computers and Cognition*. New York: Addison-Wesley Professional, 1987.

Leadership

Anderson, Robert, and William Adams. *Mastering Leadership*. Hoboken: John Wiley & Sons, 2016.

Arbinger Institute. *Leadership and Self-Deception*. Oakland: Berrett-Koehler Publishers, 2002.

Barrett, Frank J. *Yes to the Mess*. Boston: Harvard Business Review Press, 2012.

Block, Peter. *The Answer to How is Yes*. Oakland: Berrett-Koehler Publishers, 2003.

Calarco, Allan, and Joan Gurvis. *Adaptability*. Colorado Springs: Center for Creative Leadership, 2011.

Cashman, Kevin. *Leadership from the Inside Out*. Oakland: Berrett-Koehler Publishers, 2017.

Collins, Rod. *Leadership in a Wiki World*. Indianapolis: Dog Ear Publishing, 2010.

Conner, Daryl R. *Leading at the Edge of Chaos*. New York: John Wiley & Sons, 1998.

Day, David V., Michelle M. Harrison, and Stanley M. Halpin. *An Integrative Approach to Leader Development*. New York: Psychology Press, 2009.

Heifetz, Ronald A. *Leadership Without Easy Answers*. Cambridge, Massachusetts: Harvard University Press, 1994.

Heifetz, Ronald A., Alexander Grashow, and Marty Linsky. *The Practice of Adaptive Leadership*. Boston: Harvard Business Press, 2009.

Jaworski, Joseph. *Synchronicity*. Oakland: Berrett-Koehler Publishers, 2011.

Kimsey-House, Karen, and Henry Kimsey-House. *Co-Active Leadership*. Oakland: Berrett-Koehler Publishers, 2015.

Martin, Roger. *The Opposable Mind*. Boston: Harvard Business School Press, 2007.

Raelin, Joseph. *Creating Leaderful Organizations*. Oakland: Berrett-Koehler Publishers, 2003.

Silsbee, Doug. *Presence-Based Leadership*. Ashville, North Carolina: Yes! Global, 2018.

Snook, Scott A., Nitin N. Nohria, and Rakesh Khurana, eds. *The Handbook for Teaching Leadership*. Thousand Oaks, California: Sage Publications, 2011.

Organizational and Management Theory

Argyris, Chris. "Skilled Incompetence," *Harvard Business Review*, September 1986.

Argyris, Chris. *Overcoming Organizational Defenses*. Upper Saddle River, New Jersey: Prentice Hall, 1990.

Argyris, Chris, and Donald A. Schoen. *Organizational Learning II*. New York: Addison-Wesley, 1995.

Boland, Richard J., and Fred Collopy, eds. *Managing as Designing*. Palo Alto: Stanford University Press, 2004.

Chia, Robert. "In praise of strategic indirection: An essay on the efficacy of oblique ways of responding." *M@n@gement* 16, no. 5 (January 2013): 667-675.

Czarniawska, Barbara. *A Theory of Organizing*. Cheltenham, England: Edward Elgar Publishing, 2014.

Giddens, Anthony. *The Constitution of Society*. Berkeley: University of California Press, 1984.

Hamel, Gary. *The Future of Management*. Boston: Harvard Business Review Press, 2007.

Morgan, Gareth. *Images of Organization*. Oakland: Berrett-Koehler Publishers, 1998.

Pascale, Richard, Mark Milemann, and Linda Gioja. *Surfing the Edge of Chaos*. New York: Three Rivers Press, 2000.

Poole, Marshall Scott, and Andrew H. Van de Ven. *Handbook of Organizational Change and Innovation*. Oxford: Oxford University Press, 2004.

Purser, Ronald, and Steven Cabana. *The Self-Managing Organization*. New York: The Free Press, 1998.

Taleb, Nassim Nicholas. *Antifragile: Things that Gain from Disorder.* New York: Random House, 2012.

Thompson, Michael. *Organising and Disorganising.* Devon, United Kingdom: Triarchy Press, 2008.

Organizational Change

Bunker, Barbara B., and Billie T. Alban. *The Handbook of Large Group Methods.* Hoboken: Jossey-Bass, 2006.

Peter Block, *The Right Use of Power,* Audio Program. Boulder: Sounds True, 2002.

Deutschman, Alan. *Change or Die.* New York: HarperCollins, 2007.

Everette Rogers, *Diffusion of Innovations.* New York: Free Press, 2003.

Godin, Seth. *Free Prize Inside.* London: Penguin, 2005.

Goldstein, Jeffrey, James Hazy, and Benyamin Lichtenstein. *Complexity and the Nexus of Leadership.* New York: Palgrave Macmillan, 2010.

Holman, Peggy, Tom Devane and Steven Cady eds. *The Change Handbook.* Oakland: Berrett-Koehler Publishers, 2007.

Ji, Mindy, and Wendy Hood. "Purchase and Consumption Habits: Not Necessarily What You Intend." *Journal of Consumer Psychology* 17, no. 4 (October 2007): 261-276.

Mindell, Arnold. *Quantum Mind.* Portland, Oregon: Deep Democracy Exchange, 2012.

Moore, Geoffrey. *Crossing the Chasm.* New York: HarperCollins, 2014.

Norman, Donald. *The Design of Everyday Things.* New York: Basic Books, 2013.

Olson, Edwin E., and Glenda H. Eoyang. *Facilitating Organization Change.* San Francisco: Jossey-Bass, 2001.

Rowland, Deborah, and Malcolm Higgs. *Sustaining Change.* San Francisco: Jossey-Bass, 2008.

Snowden, David. "Just-in-Time Knowledge Management: Part 1." *Knowledge Management Review* 5, no. 5 (November/December 2002): 14-17.

Thompson, Mike. *The Organizational Champion.* New York: McGraw Hill, 2009.

Weisbord, Marvin, and Sandra Janoff. *Future Search.* San Francisco: Berrett-Koehler Publishers, 2010.

Weisbord, Marvin, and Sandra Janoff. *Don't Just Do Something, Stand There!.* San Francisco: Berrett-Koehler Publishers, 2007.

Wheatley, Margaret. *Leadership and the New Science.* San Francisco: Berrett-Koehler Publishers, 2006.

Whitney, Diana, David Cooperrider and Jacqueline Stavros. *Appreciative Inquiry Handbook.* Brunswick:, Ohio: Crown Custom Publishing, 2008.

Organizational Culture

Argyris, Chris. *Organizational Traps.* New York: Oxford University Press, 2010.

Cameron, Kim, and Robert E. Quinn. *Diagnosing and Changing Organizational Culture.* San Francisco: Jossey-Bass, 2011.

Mezick, Daniel. *The Culture Game.* United States: FreeStanding Press, 2012.

Pixton, Pollyanna, Paul Gibson, and Niel Nicholaisen. *The Agile Culture.* Upper Saddle River, New Jersey: Addison-Wesley, 2014.

Schein, Edgar H. *Organizational Culture and Leadership.* Hoboken: John Wiley & Sons, 2017.

Schneider, William. *The Reengineering Alternative.* Burr Ridge, Illlinois: Irwin Professional Pub, 1994.

Relationship and Relationship Systems

Albere, Patricia. *Evolutionary Relationships.* Independence, Virginia: Oracle Institute Press, 2017.

De Quincey, Christian. *Radical Knowing*. Rochester, Vermont: Park Street Press, 2005.

Gunnlaugson, Olen, and Michael Brabant, eds. *Cohering the Integral We Space*. United States: Integral Publishing House, 2017.

Hirschhorn, Larry. *The Workplace Within*. Cambridge, Massachusetts: The MIT Press, 1988.

Rød, Anne, and Marita Fridjon. *Creating Intelligent Teams*. Randburg, South Africa: KR Publishing, 2016.

Siegel, Daniel J. *The Developing Mind*. New York: The Guilford Press, 2012.

Shapiro, Edward R., and A. Wesley Carr. *Lost in Familiar Places*. New Haven: Yale University Press, 1991.

Whittington, John. *Systemic Coaching and Constellations*. London: Kogan Page, 2012.

Sensemaking

Ancona, Deborah. "Sensemaking: Framing and Acting in the Unknown," In *The Handbook for Teaching Leadership*, edited by Scott Snook, Nitin Nohria, and Rakesh Khurana. Thousand Oaks, California: Sage Publications, 2012.

Dervin, B. "An overview of sense-making research: Concepts, methods and results," Paper presented at the annual meeting of the International Communication Association, Dallas, TX, May 1983. Retrievable on September 17, 2017 at https://web.archive.org/web/19970710233153/http://communication.sbs.ohio-state.edu:80/sense-making/lit/1983_4.html

Weick, Karl. *The Social Psychology of Organizing*. New York: McGraw-Hill, 1979.

Weick, Karl. *Sensemaking in Organizations*. Thousand Oaks, California: Sage Publications, 1995.

Systems Thinking

Ackoff, Russell. "A Lifetime of Systems Thinking." Accessed October 21, 2018. https://thesystemsthinker.com/a-lifetime-of-systems-thinking/.

Adams, Cindy, and William Adams. *The Whole Systems Approach*. Provo, Utah: Executive Excellence Publishing, 1999.

Dettmer, H. William. *The Logical Thinking Process*. Milwaukee: American Society for Quality Press, 2007.

Gharajedaghi, Jamshid. *Systems Thinking*. Burlington, Massachusetts: Elsevier, 2011.

Jackson, Michael C. *Systems Thinking*. Hoboken: John Wiley & Sons, 2003.

Kim, Daniel. *Systems Archetypes I: Diagnosing Systemic Issues and Designing High-Leverage Interventions*. Cambridge, Massachusetts: Pegasus Communications, 2000.

Meadows, Donella, and Diana Wright, ed. *Thinking in Systems*. White River Junction: Chelsea Green Publishing, 2008.

Oshrey, Barry. *Seeing Systems*. Oakland: Berrett-Koehler Publishers, 2007.

Scharmer, Otto. *Theory U*. Oakland: Berrett-Koehler Publishers, 2016.

Senge, Peter. *The Fifth Discipline*. New York: Doubleday, 2006.

Index

F

Facilitative Agents, 90-93, 218
Failure bow, 181
Feedback, 56-57
 Developmental, 174-175
 Double-loop, 23
 Impact, 176-178, 225
 in organizational leadership
  context, 224-228
 What I Make Up, 178-179
Ferrari engine, 21, 24
First, second, third person
 perspective, 243
Focused listening, 144
Formal operations, 40, 46, 121
Four-quadrant lens, 242-247
Frederick Taylor, 20

G

Gothelf, Jeff, 3
Graves, Clare, 59, 61, 72, 78,
 255, 257
Growth Cycle, 96-98

H

Holding accountability, 191-194
Holding Environment, 88-90,
 100-101, 135-136, 162
 Criteria of, 217-221
 Facilitator of, 267
 Organizational, 208-213
Horizontal growth, 40-41, 55-
 58, 60, 89, 103, 105, 118,
 121-122, 199
Human systems capability, 34
Human systems operating
 system, 28-30

I

Inner agility, 1, 3, 8, 203-204,
 212-213
Inner growth
 and Deliberately
  developmental ecosystem,
  99-104, 108, 114-115, 118
 and Developmental stages,
  59, 62
 and Holding environment, 89
 as Developmental journey, 62
 Being deliberate about, 82
 Catalyzing, 115, 211-213,
  219
 Dialectic of, 55-58
 Dimension of, 39-41
 Process of, 122
Integral four-quadrant lens, 242-
 247

J

Joiner, Bill, 63, 82
Josephs, Stephan, 63, 82

K

Kegan, Robert, 36, 42, 59, 61,
 63, 85, 88-89, 99-101, 107-
 108, 116, 128, 180, 219-220

L

Lahey, Lisa, 36, 59, 85, 100,
 107-108, 128, 180, 219
Laloux, Frederic 72, 255-257,
 260
Leaderfulness, 11-12
Leadership, see Organizational
 leadership
 Small-l, 11, 81, 175, 224
Liberating structures, 93-98
Listening, levels I and II, 144

M

O

About the Author

Michael Hamman is committed to the possibility that the workplace be a site for personal, professional, and social transformation. Trained in the 1980s in coaching and large group facilitation with Werner Erhard and Associates, Michael went on to train in systems thinking (with Peter Senge), facilitation (with Marvin Weisbord), and leadership and systems coaching (at Coach U, Coaches Training Institute, CRR Global, and Interdevelopmental Institute). He was a PhD candidate for three years in Human and Organization Development at Fielding Graduate School, where he was ABD (All-But-Dissertation).

Michael's work experience began as a software developer. Combining his technical expertise with his early coaching experience, Michael made a name for himself for his ability to help start-up software teams achieve both technical and team collaboration excellence.

In the late 1990s, he began integrating Agile practices into his work with software teams. In 2004, Michael began to bring Agile coaching into the corporate environment, being among the first Agile coaches to do so. Since then, he has coached dozens of Fortune 500 companies and teams, and hundreds of leaders, toward greater holistic team and enterprise-level agility. Since 2013, as a Principal at Agile Coaching Institute and Co-Founder of the Agile Leadership Institute, he has continued to train and develop agile coaches, managers, and leaders in the art and practice of transformational leadership.

Michael lives with his wife, Susanne, and his canine friend, Duchamp, in Taos, New Mexico.

Made in the USA
Las Vegas, NV
24 March 2022

46237944R10173